23 SEp 16
#2

Four Days in September

Four Days in September

The Battle of Teutoburg
Revised Edition

Jason R. Abdale

Pen & Sword
MILITARY

First published in the United States by
Trafford Publishing (Bloomington, Indiana) in 2013

First published in Great Britain in 2016 by
Pen & Sword Military
an imprint of
Pen & Sword Books Ltd
47 Church Street
Barnsley
South Yorkshire
S70 2AS

ISBN 978 1 47386 085 8

Typeset in Ehrhardt by
Mac Style Ltd, Bridlington, East Yorkshire
Printed and bound in the UK by CPI Group (UK) Ltd,
Croydon, CRO 4YY

Pen & Sword Books Ltd incorporates the imprints of Pen & Sword
Archaeology, Atlas, Aviation, Battleground, Discovery, Family
History, History, Maritime, Military, Naval, Politics, Railways, Select,
Transport, True Crime, and Fiction, Frontline Books, Leo Cooper,
Praetorian Press, Seaforth Publishing and Wharncliffe.

For a complete list of Pen & Sword titles please contact
PEN & SWORD BOOKS LIMITED
47 Church Street, Barnsley, South Yorkshire, S70 2AS, England
E-mail: enquiries@pen-and-sword.co.uk
Website: www.pen-and-sword.co.uk

Contents

List of Plates

List of Maps

Chronology of Events

46 BC	Publius Quinctilius Varus is born.
31 BC	The Roman Republic ends and the Roman Empire begins. Gaius Octavianus becomes Rome's first emperor.
31–28 BC	German raiding parties make forays across the Rhine into Gaul.
27 BC	The last pockets of Celtic anti-Roman resistance are quelled in Gaul. Gaius Octavianus takes the title of 'Augustus'.
19–17 BC	Romans extensively fortify the Rhine border, and Roman settlers begin squatting on Germanic territory.
17 BC	Three Germanic tribes declare war on Rome.
16 BC	Arminius is born. Noricum becomes a Roman province.
15 BC	Rhaetia becomes a Roman province.
11–8 BC	General Drusus Claudius Nero commands the legions in the conquest of Germania. He dies after contracting a disease.
9 BC	Pannonia is conquered and incorporated into the province of Illyricum.
9–8 BC	Varus is Governor of Africa.

8–6 BC	After Drusus' death, his brother Tiberius commands the legions in Germania.
7–4 BC	Varus is Governor of Syria.
6 BC-1 AD	Western Germania is under Roman military occupation. Anti-Roman sentiment grows.
1–4 AD	Germanic tribes revolt, but are quelled by Roman forces.
6 AD	Judea and Moesia become Roman provinces. Revolt erupts within the province of Illyricum. Varus is made Governor of Germania Magna.
7 AD?	Arminius, after serving in the Roman army against the Illyrian rebels, returns to Germania to act as one of Varus' advisors.
9 AD	The Great Illyrian Revolt ends. The province of Illyricum is afterwards split in half into Pannonia and Dalmatia (date uncertain).
Late September, 9 AD	The Battle of Teutoburg.
10–12 AD	General Tiberius Claudius Nero leads a revenge campaign against the Germans.
13–17 AD	Tiberius is replaced by his nephew Germanicus, who now leads the revenge campaign.
14 AD	Caesar Augustus dies, and Tiberius becomes the second emperor of Rome.
18 AD	Cappadocia becomes a Roman province.
19 AD	Germanicus dies, possibly poisoned.
21 AD	Arminius is assassinated.

Introduction

In late September of 9 AD, a four-day long battle raged in what is now northwestern Germany. The military of the Roman Empire, the strongest civilization in Europe, was pitted against the native warriors of the North. After years of being defeated on the battlefield by Rome's professionals, the Germanic tribes scored their first great victory on their own soil. In the end, the 17th, 18th, and 19th Legions would be no more. This battle would become an event engraved on the German national consciousness for years to come, and its leader, the heroic Arminius, would be the personification of all that was the wild northern frontier and its spirit of freedom.

I first became aware of this battle when I saw a documentary on the History Channel many years ago called *The Lost Legions of Varus*. Ever since then, I've been interested in this battle and the various persons involved in it. Several books have been written on this subject within the past ten years, both historical and fictional, some good and others poor. One thing that is noticeably different about my book in contrast to the others is the mere title. It is sub-titled *The Battle of Teutoburg* as opposed to the more traditional *The Battle of the Teutoburg Forest*. I did this to resolve an ongoing debate regarding the correct naming of the battle, stating that I believe the entire area was known as 'Teutoburg' in ancient times, and that this name didn't specifically apply to just the forest or the mountain pass. I explain this viewpoint in more detail in the chapter on the battle itself.

I wrote this book in the summer of 2009, inspired by the fact that the year marked the 2,000th anniversary of the battle. During the course of researching this book, I discovered that the Battle of Teutoburg and the events surrounding it were not isolated. In fact, there were several examples of similar circumstances happening between Rome and the various peoples (especially the Germans) that it was in contact with during the twenty years preceding the battle's date – the Germans' destruction of a Roman military unit and the loss of its eagle, and Rome's revenge campaign afterwards; the German ambush and near massacre of a Roman column in the forest; the sudden uprising of a supposedly pacified population and the catching of the Romans completely off guard. The Romans should have anticipated something like this would happen, since it had happened several times in the recent past. Why they failed to take precautions isn't clear. As a result, the Romans lost 10,000 men in a four-day battle.

The first edition of this book was published by Trafford Publishing in May 2013 on my birthday, making it the best birthday present ever. Since then, I have received mostly favorable reviews. One professional historian said that he enjoyed my analysis of Germanic tribal culture, and was also pleased that I mentioned recent discoveries made in the area. I was also happy to see that my book was referenced in several internet articles, which made me feel like I was now a genuine historian. In late 2014, *Four Days in September* was given a positive review by The US Review of Books, which classified my book as 'recommended' reading – a rarely-applied rating, indicating the book's worth. During the same time, I was awarded Trafford Publishing's Gold Seal of Literary Excellence.

However, those who read my book did have two major criticisms. The first was the overwhelming cascade of spelling and grammar mistakes. In my eagerness to get the book published faster, I decided to forego professional editing – a very stupid decision on my part, and one which I will never repeat. The second major criticism, and one which I took more seriously than the spelling mistakes, was that some parts of the book were confusing and people had to re-read certain sections in order for everything to make sense.

To solve both of these problems, I began an extensive revision of the book in late 2014, correcting all of the mistakes that I could find and re-writing certain sections so that they were easier to read. I also included facts and analysis which were not present in the earlier edition, thereby making the book fully up to date. In late 2014, my book came to the attention of Pen & Sword Books, located in England. In March 2015, they agreed to re-publish my book through their company, but several changes had to be made to suit the publisher's style.

This book relies on ancient documents, archaeological evidence, analysis by modern historians, and my own hypotheses. I have tried to the best of my limited abilities to create an accurate portrayal of locations, persons, and events. All quotations are clearly cited as being the words of their authors. Any personal interpretations or opinions are clearly stated as such. If there are any errors in facts or translations, I truly apologize.

It is customary for the author of a book to say a few thankful lines for those who made their book possible. I would like to thank my teachers and professors for cultivating a love of history inside me, and for substantially improving my researching and writing skills. I would like to thank my family and my friends for giving me their unwavering support to me in my goal of being a recognized writer. Finally, I would like to thank both Trafford Publishing and Pen & Sword Books for believing in the worthiness of my book.

'The most common beginning to a disaster is a sense of security'

Gaius Velleius Paterculus

Chapter One

Rome

The City by the Tiber

The origin of the name *Italia*, which was later Anglicized to 'Italy', is vague. One idea states that it is a corruption of the Oscan (one of the Italic tribes) word *viteliu*, meaning 'land of young cattle'. Considering that the bull was a symbol used by the Samnites, one of the major Italic tribes, during the Social War, this hypothesis seems plausible. Another possibility is that the name originates from one of the land's tribes, the Itali. Greeks who landed in southern Italy ascribed this name to all of the natives that lived on the peninsula, and thus they were called the Italics and the land that they lived in was called Italia.[1]

In terms of geography, the Italian Peninsula has a wide variety of environments, from fertile coastal plains to dry rocky scrub-covered hillsides. In northern Italy lies the broad expanse of the Po River Valley, long reputed to be the most arable area in all of Italy. Vegetation in the Italian Peninsula consists of scrub and mixed deciduous-conifer trees. The Apennine Mountains run like a spine down the middle of the peninsula, more or less splitting it in half. On either side is a narrow plain. Italy suffers from sporadic earthquakes and volcanic eruptions, the most famous of which being the eruption of Mount Vesuvius in 79 AD, which destroyed the towns of Pompeii and Herculaneum. However, during the time period discussed in this book, the late first century BC to the early first century AD, there was no hint of danger. Most of Italy's earliest settlements occurred on the coasts, a majority of them being located on the western side of the peninsula. One of these western settlements was Rome.[2]

Rome began as a small hilltop settlement on the shores of the Tiber River in west-central Italy. The Romans lived in a region called Latium, where the various tribes spoke some dialect or another of the Latin language; the Romans were just one of these tribes. The city, according to Roman legend as reported by the historian Titus Livius, was officially founded on April 21, 753 BC by the divine twins Romulus and Remus. The two boys were the grand-nephews of Numitor, the king of the city of Alba Longa. King Numitor was a descendant of the Trojan prince Aeneas who had come to Italy centuries earlier after the end of the Trojan War. One day, Numitor was ousted from power by his brother Amulius, who then executed all of Numitor's heirs except his niece Rhea Silvia, making her a Vestal Virgin. However, she became impregnated by the god Mars. Amulius ordered Rhea to be imprisoned and the two newborns to be drowned in the Tiber River. As can be expected, the children survived, discovered by a she-wolf and cared for until they were taken away by a shepherd. Growing up as outlaws, living a life of robbery and brigandage, Remus was captured and brought before King Amulius to account for his conduct. He was then sent to the exiled Numitor for reasons that are unknown, and then it was revealed who he and his brother *really* were. Romulus and Remus organized a rebellion, executed Amulius, and re-instated Numitor as the rightful king of Alba Longa. That being done, the two brothers wanted to establish a city of their own, and decided to found a settlement where they were washed up on the shore of the Tiber River. However, the twins each wanted to name the settlement after themselves and quarreled. Romulus killed his brother, and named the city after himself – thus the city of Rome was founded.[3]

The Romans and Their Neighbours

The Romans were originally just one tribe among many that dwelt on the Italian Peninsula. In the north were the Etruscans; the region of Tuscany is named after them. Much of southern Italy was controlled by the Greeks. Between the Etruscans and the Greeks were a series of Italic tribes, such as the Sabines, Samnites, and Oscans.

When the Greeks explored the Italian Peninsula, expecting to find backwards savages, for no culture could surely be as advanced as the Greeks, they were astounded to find the complete opposite of what they anticipated – the highly advanced culture of the Etruscans. The Etruscans had their own language, but they wrote in the Greek alphabet – an example of cultural contact between the Greeks and the people of northern Italy. The Etruscans were a very wealthy people due to trade and due to the rich metal deposits in their realm. With these metals, they forged weapons and armour, cast large metal statues, or traded the raw metals for other goods. It is believed that the Romans were either subjugated by the Etruscans or were under their sphere-of-influence. Either of these scenarios is probable, since the Romans adopted many cultural aspects from their northern neighbours, including gladiatorial fights. Stories about Etruscan licentiousness are almost certainly false, but considering that the Romans adopted many Etruscan ways, and considering that we have many tales of Roman decadence and debauchery, one wonders if the tales are not as exaggerated as one many think.[4]

South of the Etruscans were various Italic tribes. Those that lived along the flat fertile coastline were predominantly farmers while those that lived in the hills and mountains were largely pastoralists raising livestock like goats and sheep. Prior to their contact with the Greeks, it's likely that they lived in a village-based tribal society, but after the Greeks' arrival, they quickly became Hellenized. Beginning in the eighth century BC, the Romans began subjugating or outright conquering the various surrounding tribes, beginning with their immediate neighbours, the Latins. In due course, the Romans continued their spread throughout the Italian Peninsula, taking several centuries to complete the task. The mountain-dwelling Samnites in particular were tough warriors, and the Romans had to fight three wars against them before they were finally conquered.[5]

Although the Italic tribes had been long subdued by Rome by 100 BC, the Romans still stood on shaky ground with many of their neighbours. Indeed, in the beginning of the first century BC, their Italic allies seceded from the Roman Republic and declared that they were now an independent country – 'Italia'. To further drive home the point that this Italic confederation had no love for their Roman overlords, some of the coins that they minted showed the Italic bull using its horns to gore the Roman wolf. Of course, the Romans would never let such an affront go unpunished, and thus the so-called 'War of the Allies' (*Bellum Socii*) commenced, a bloody and savage civil war that lasted for three years. In the end, the Italic confederation was crushed and the Romans emerged victorious.[6]

South of the Italics were the Greeks, who had become well-established in southern Italy and Sicily long before Rome emerged as a major power in Italy. Indeed, it can be argued that the most powerful of all the Greek city-states was neither Athens nor Sparta nor Corinth, but was Syracuse in Sicily. At first, Rome sought to ally with the Syracusans, but later declared war on them when the Romans felt strong enough to do so. In due time, the Romans would invade Greece itself.[7]

By 600 BC, the Celts, who inhabited much of Western Europe, began crossing the Alps into what is now northern Italy. By 500 BC, they occupied the entire Po River Valley, which led to the Romans calling all lands north of the Po River *Gallia Cisalpina*, or 'Gaul on this side of the Alps', as opposed to *Gallia Transalpina*, 'Gaul across the Alps'. In the early 300s BC, the Celts attacked the city of Rome itself, which led to a long history of antipathy towards the northern peoples. This anti-northerner attitude that the Romans bore at first towards the Celts alone was later augmented both in intensity as well as the numbers of different people that this fear targeted when the Germans attacked in the last years of the second century BC, defeating several Roman armies sent against them before they were defeated in turn.[8] By the time that Rome's first emperor Octavianus (later to be re-named Caesar Augustus) came to power in 31 BC, Rome was unquestionably the master of the Mediterranean, with the city's population numbering at around a million people. The empire now encompassed much of the Iberian Peninsula, Gaul, Italy, the Adriatic coast, Greece, almost all Asia Minor except the interior, Syria, most of the North African coast, and all of the various Mediterranean islands. The Roman Empire was still expanding, and it would not be until two hundred years later during the second century AD that it would reach its full size. Lands that would be acquired during the later stages of Augustus' reign, the time that this book takes place in, would be modern-day Austria, Hungary, Bulgaria, Israel, the Netherlands, and Germany.[9]

In terms of the empire's neighbours, Rome's holdings in North Africa were flanked on the west by the vassal state of Mauretania, which controlled modern-day Morocco and most of northern Algeria. To the south of the African provinces were the various Saharan tribes which to this day are collectively referred to by Europeans as Berbers, a corruption of the word 'barbarian', which the Romans had applied to these people. Britain was not yet a Roman province, but the Romans and the Britonic Celts were certainly aware of each other's existence. They conducted trade with each other, and

Rome typically inserted itself into Britonic politics saying who would and wouldn't be a particular tribal king. On the European continent, the empire was bordered by various tribal societies, some friendly and others not. The northernmost portion of Spain encompassing what would today be Galicia, Asturias, and Basqueland was not yet under Roman rule, but it would be soon. Almost all of Gaul was under Roman control, with the exception of the Alpine areas to the southeast which separated Italy from southern France. This area, with its difficult terrain and obdurate warriors, would take a long time to bring into subjection. East of Gaul across the Rhine were the Germanic tribes. Immediately to the north of Italy, occupying the lands between the Alps and the Danube River in what is now modern-day Austria, eastern Switzerland, and southern Germany were the Celts of central Europe and a mysterious people called the Rhaetians, reputed to be a fusion between Etruscan and Celtic cultures – even the ancient Romans were not sure how to classify them. To their east, in what roughly corresponds to modern Hungary, were the Pannonians, a cultural group of the famed Illyrians who controlled the western Balkans throughout most of classical

Map 1. The Roman Empire, 15 BC. Roman territories are shaded. Territories that are hashed indicate vassal states, also called 'client kingdoms'. (*Illustration by Jason R Abdale*)

history. North of Roman Greece in modern-day Bulgaria were the Moesians (possibly a Thracian tribe), and east of Greece was the vassal state of Thrace. In the East was the vassal state of Cappadocia. Beyond it was Rome's major enemy in the east, the Parthian Empire, who would be a thorn in Rome's side for many years.

The Roman Religion

The Romans worshipped a polytheistic religion that had many ties to their Greek, Etruscan, and Italic neighbours. The king of the gods was Jupiter, modelled on the Greek supreme god Zeus, and in more ways than his position as a heavenly monarch – Jupiter, according to proper Latin pronunciation, is actually pronounced 'Yoo-piter', not 'Joo-piter'. That being said, Jupiter may not be a name but a title, descended from *Eu Pator*, which in Greek means 'Good Father'. While on the subject of etymology and correct Latin pronunciation, I also want to add that Jove, another of Jupiter's names, is actually pronounced 'Yo-way', which is eerily similar to the Jewish god Yahweh. Coincidence?

Jupiter or Jove or whatever he was called may have been the king of the Roman pantheon, but perhaps the god most identified with Rome was the war-god Mars, since Mars was the father of Romulus, the founder and first king of Rome. Originally a god of fertility and agriculture, based upon the Etruscan god Maris, he slowly became a war god, which may be due in part to his duty as a protector of fields and pastures – in other words, he guarded the homeland. As Rome's borders expanded due to the frequent wars against its neighbours, the homeland expanded with it, and Mars' job as a guardian of Roman soil took on greater importance until he became a full-fledged god of battles.[10]

The chief priest in Rome was the *pontifex maximus*. Originally, this was a person appointed by the Senate, and he maintained this post until death. However, following the transition from Republic to Empire, the emperor himself became Rome's chief priest. Not only that, there soon grew the practice of an 'imperial cult', in which people prayed to the *genius* ('essence/soul/spirit') of the emperor. This act served multiple purposes: to demonstrate loyalty to the emperor, to allow a certain 'closeness' to an all-too-often distant or inaccessible monarch, and to offer some degree of stability in a religion were practices were continuously adopted, changed, or discarded altogether.[11]

One of the more well-known aspects of Roman religion was that of the Vestal Virgins, who were under the direct authority of the *pontifex maximus*. They were the six priestesses of Vesta, the goddess of the hearth, and they all took a vow of chastity. It was their duty to make sure that the ceremonial fire of Vesta never went out, believing that if the fire died, the Roman state might die soon afterwards.[12]

Every month in the Roman calendar had at least one religious festival. On many of these days, there was a general holiday, where all business would be closed. Other festivals or religious events would be carried out whenever special circumstances arose. As an example, the doors of the temple of Janus were open in times of war and closed in times of peace, although the reasoning behind the custom is somewhat ambiguous.[13]

Roman Social Culture in the Age of Augustus

When Octavianus came to power, the city of Rome had almost a million people.[14] His reign was known as the *principate*, from the title *Princeps*, 'First/Leading Citizen', which was the title that he took when he came to power. So, what was life in Rome like under the *principate*?

Roman society was divided into two orders of people: the patricians and the plebeians. The patricians were the original aristocratic families of the Roman people. According to Titus Livius, when Romulus founded the city of Rome, he appointed a hundred men to act as the city's council of elders, and upon them he bestowed the honorific address *pater*, or 'father' – the word *patrician* comes from this, denoting that these select men were the fathers or guardians and father-figures of the Roman people. All patricians claimed to be descended from one of these original hundred men.[15] As such, being classified as a patrician was purely a matter of birth and heredity, and was not based upon wealth, politics, or ability. These people enjoyed special privileges during the Republic and into the Empire. At first, only patricians could become priests, hold elected office, or be involved in the inner workings of government, but as the Republic continued, the non-patricians, generically referred to as plebeians, began to secure more power for themselves.

The plebeians were, quite simply, anyone regardless of status who wasn't descended from these original hundred men. Plebeians were the overwhelming majority of the Roman people; they could be either rich or poor, weak or powerful. After civil rights were secured for them, many plebeians could own property, take part in government, and become members of the aristocratic classes, although they were still not regarded as being on the same level as the more ancient patrician aristocracy.

But Roman social structure was far more complex than just being divided into two groups based upon hereditary credentials. The division between

Figure 1. Caesar Augustus. This particular bust shows him wearing a 'civic crown', an award given to someone who saved the life of a Roman citizen. Capitoline Museum. Rome, Italy. (*Wikimedia Commons, public domain image*)

patrician and plebeian was simply a matter of 'who was' and 'who wasn't'. A separate stratification also existed within Rome which divided its people into various classes based upon wealth and social position.

Naturally the emperor and the imperial family were at the top of the social hierarchy. Directly under them were the senators. The word senator comes from the Latin word *senex*, meaning 'old man' or 'elder'. These men were the cream of the Roman elite, coming from the richest and most prestigious of the Roman aristocracy, the so-called *nobiles*. The reason why I put money first and prestige second is that money was a determining factor in becoming a senator. Most of a senator's wealth was in the form of how much property he held. 'Senators had to prove that they had property worth at least 1,000,000 sesterces; there was no salary attached to service in the Senate, and senators were prohibited from engaging personally in nonagricultural business, trade or public contracts.'[16] A senator could be easily spotted in a crowd due to the clothes he wore – a white toga with a wide purple stripe.[17]

Below the senators were the *equites*, a word which literally means 'horseman', but which would be better translated as 'knight'. In the past, men had to purchase their own equipment when serving in the Roman Army, and understandably, only the rich could afford horses. Being a cavalryman, therefore, was not merely the type of soldier that you were, but it also identified you as an aristocrat. Following the reforms of Gaius Marius, who remodelled the structure of the Roman Army, it was no longer necessary to purchase your own equipment since it would be provided by the government. This meant that anyone could now be a cavalryman, not just the aristocrats who were rich enough to buy, feed, and equip their mounts. However, in terms of social rank, middle-ranking aristocrats were still referred to as *equites*, I'm assuming for purely traditional reasons. Now, instead of owning a horse, money was the determining factor. A prospective member of the Equestrian Order needed to have a minimum of 400,000 sesterces. Knights were distinguished by a toga with a narrow purple stripe.[18] Being made a knight could also be a reward for exceptional service to Rome. As an example, in reward for his courage on the battlefield fighting Rome's enemies, the Germanic prince Arminius, who would later in his life lead a few Germanic tribes against the Romans at the Battle of Teutoburg, was made a Roman citizen and was knighted into the Equestrian Order.

Directly under the knights were the citizens, arguably the lowest-ranking Roman aristocrats. By Augustan times, all free-born males living in Italy were citizens. They could marry women whose relatives were citizens, making the women members of the citizen class even though they themselves weren't citizens, and any male children they might have would automatically become citizens upon birth. The two chief benefits of being a citizen were that you had the right to vote and you could become a magistrate (a broad term used for any administrator who had subordinates working for you) in the government.[19]

Roman society can essentially be divided in half between the 'haves' and the 'have nots'. The aristocrats were the 'haves' – they had privileges and access to social positions that the non-aristocrats couldn't have. The 'have nots' were anyone who was not a senator, knight, or citizen. At the top of the list of 'have nots' were the freemen. The term 'freemen' was never used in ancient Rome, but it does get the point across; they were officially called *peregrini*, meaning 'foreigners or outsiders'. The word could have a double meaning. These were people who lived outside Italy in Rome's other territories who had some rights but didn't have the full rights of Roman citizenship – thus they were outsiders both geographically as well as politically. They were regarded as citizens *officially speaking*, but it was a second-class citizenship. They could own their own land and run businesses, but they couldn't vote, they couldn't become administrators in the government, and they couldn't marry anyone above their social position. For example, a freeman couldn't marry a woman who had connections to the citizenry; a freeman could only marry a freewoman or someone lower. It wasn't until the year 212 AD that Emperor Caracalla decreed that every man in the empire was to be granted full citizenship, which abolished the class of 'freeman' altogether. Auxiliaries, non-citizens who served in the Roman Army, were given citizenship after completing their terms of service. There were three types of freemen:[20] the *Latini*, or Latins were free-born residents of the region of Latium, Italy, except for places in Latium that were designated as 'municipalities'; the *socii*, or allies were free-born residents in the rest of Italy other than the region of Latium. In 89 BC, during the War of the Allies, all *Latini* and *socii* were granted full citizenship; the *provincales*, or provincials comprised all other free-born men and women who lived outside Italy.

Under the freemen were the 'freed-men'. Don't be confused. A 'freed-man' was a slave who had somehow obtained his freedom, but his position was little better than being a slave. They were, in essence 'half-frees', a term used more frequently when describing serfs or peasants in medieval societies. Although no longer enslaved by their masters, they were still obligated to render services to their former owners. They could not hold public offices, they could not vote, and most depressingly of all, a freed-man was always regarded as a freed-man. Being a slave at one point in your life left an inerasable stigma on you. You couldn't graduate from freed-man to freeman and then to citizen. Freed slaves were always merely freed slaves and couldn't be anything more. However, any children that freed-men may have were automatically freemen, the higher rank. If their former master was a citizen, and the freed-men had children, then their male children were automatically citizens, though they still had a social stigma attached to them since their parents were once slaves.[21]

At the bottom of the Roman social ladder were the slaves. It has been estimated that during the reign of Caesar Augustus, one-fourth of the empire's population was slaves, and with 200,000 residing just in the city of Rome. All ancient societies practised some form of slavery. Contrary to common belief, slavery didn't always mean that you were forced to work for free and didn't have a penny to your name. In fact, many slaves in Roman society were paid for their work, and it was possible for them to save up enough of their wages and be allowed to buy their freedom. Slaves in the Roman sense were, simply speaking, 'people with no rights'. Unlike in early American history, there were no racial connotations to ancient slavery – slaves could be anybody. Many times, they were criminals who had been sentenced to slavery as punishment for their offences, but most often they were prisoners captured during war.[22]

It shouldn't be surprising that a people who considered themselves to be directly descended from a war god would have a martial culture. From the beginnings of Roman civilization up until the first century BC, there was no permanent army. Military service was simply one of the duties of a Roman citizen, and in times of war, every available man, regardless of professional occupation, was expected to march off to battle. However, if you were a Roman man living during this time, you were expected to buy all of your weapons, armour, and equipment yourself. Understandably, only those who had money could afford to buy military gear, and only the richest could afford to purchase all of the required kit. Soldiers were classified based upon how heavily-armed they were. The poorest, who might have been able to afford only a few javelins, acted as skirmishers. There were also light and heavy infantry. Only the aristocrats acted as cavalry since they were the only ones who could afford to buy, equip, and feed horses.

By the end of the second century BC, a Roman senator and military commander named Gaius Marius sought to expand the Roman Army by filling its ranks with the *capiti censi*, the 'head count', the masses. He suggested drafting the poor, and keeping them in service for a continuous period. The logic behind his thinking was that these men didn't own any land or property, and therefore had no reason to always go back home during the harvest season. By recruiting and arming the poor, people who had nothing to go back home to, Rome could keep an army in the field for an indefinite period. Unlike earlier times when men had to buy all of their weaponry, armour, and equipment with their own money, these men would be provided with all of the necessary gear needed, paid for by the national treasury.

By Augustus' time, the Roman Army was the largest professional standing army in the western world. When he became Emperor in 31 BC, there were sixty legions within the Roman Empire. Sometime around 16 BC, Augustus consolidated this to a more manageable and cheaper-to-maintain twenty-eight legions. The soldiers were equipped with more-or-less standardized gear. A full kit for your basic legionary infantryman cost one-third of a year's salary, and the cost was automatically deducted from his wages. I'm assuming that, due to the cost deduction, most new recruits didn't spend much time in the markets, taverns, or brothels. I'm also assuming that all soldiers took very good care of their panoply, seeing as how the cost for their manufacture was deducted from the soldiers' wages, and they didn't want to lose what little money their wages brought them by asking for replacement pieces.[23]

Following the reforms of Gaius Marius, soldiers were expected to serve a minimum of six years of continuous military service. In 13 BC, Augustus substantially lengthened the service term from six years to twenty years: sixteen years of front-line service and four years in the reserves. In the year 5 AD, the service term was further increased to twenty-five years: twenty years of front-line service, and five in the reserves. Upon discharge, soldiers would receive a cash bonus. In order to cement the loyalty of the men that Augustus now commanded as the newly-made emperor, all soldiers in the army took an oath of loyalty not to the Roman Empire, and not to the emperor, but to Caesar Augustus personally. The oath to Augustus was established in all likelihood due to the chaotic civil wars that were waged beforehand, where armies swore their loyalties not to Rome, but to their generals. Having every soldier swear an oath of loyalty to the newly-crowned emperor diminished the likelihood of rebellion and civil war, and helped to further strengthen Augustus' own position. However, this practice would create problems when Augustus died in 14 AD and the army was no longer under anyone's legal control, not even the new emperor.[24]

Martial prowess and courage on the battlefield were highly rewarded. Victorious commanders were crowned with ceremonial wreathes and sometimes awarded a triumph – a parade in which the general was allowed to enter Rome with his victorious army (which was very serious, considering that soldiers weren't allowed anywhere near the capital city, as Gaius Julius Caesar knew very well when he crossed the Rubicon River), carrying with them all of the spoils of their conquests, including treasure and prisoners. The triumph was just as much a religious ritual as it was a social one; the heroic general was dressed like a god and played the part of 'god for a day'. Enemy prisoners were either sold off as slaves or were ritually sacrificed as thanks to the Roman gods for victory in war. One example was the fate of Vercingetorix, the leader of the Gauls against Julius Caesar – during the triumph, the Celtic warlord was executed.[25] A triumph was rarely awarded, and an even rarer honour was having an *agnomen* given to you – an honorific name signifying the land you conquered. One such agnomen was given to Drusus Claudius Nero, Caesar Augustus' stepson, following his successful campaigns in what is now the Netherlands and Germany. From henceforth, he and his male heirs would bear the name Germanicus.

War made the Romans rich. Captured plunder from enemy lands filled Rome's treasury and allowed its inhabitants to build those monumental structures that are so familiar to us today. The empire *as a whole* may have been powerful and rich, but it was an empire of immense contrasts, divided between the extremely rich and the extremely poor. In that regard, the city of Rome was the empire in miniature, and everyone living there would have seen it. It would have been noisy, dirty, and crowded, with slums and beggars, but with grandiose monumental buildings in the city's centre demonstrating the empire's power.[26]

Very few Romans lived in private houses; most lived in apartments. The Roman house was built in the form of a square around a central courtyard. No windows faced out onto the street; all windows faced towards the courtyard. This was privacy to the extreme, about as introverted as anyone could get. The apartments, by contrast, had windows which faced outwards. These apartments were all built adjacent to each other forming a 'block' of buildings in the most literal sense of the word – it looked exactly like a large concrete block with windows and doors. Imagine whole city blocks covered by these 'blocks' of apartments – drab grey-coloured buildings that stretched continuously without alleyways or any other separation all along the length of streets. And they were tall, too. In fact, constructing these multi-floor buildings was a real feat, but the construction was often poor and buildings collapsed, occasionally resulting in people being killed. To prevent structural failures such as this from happening in the future, Caesar Augustus issued an edict stating that all buildings within the city of Rome couldn't be higher than sixty feet. However, many buildings built after Augustus's reign exceeded this measurement, which isn't wise when you don't have reinforced steel beams and have to rely only on wood, wood that can bend and crack under the strain of too much weight. A notable example of an ancient construction disaster occurred during the reign of Augustus' successor Emperor Tiberius in the year 27 AD. In the town of Fidenae, located a few miles north of Rome, the town's timber-constructed amphitheatre, which held a fully-packed audience of 50,000 people, suddenly collapsed. 20,000 people were instantly crushed to death, and nearly everyone else was injured. It was later determined that the building collapsed because it was not built on a solid foundation and the wooden beams which were used to construct the arena were not thick enough to support the weight of the building.[27]

Roman Artistic Culture

The Romans based a great deal of their art on that of the Greeks. Hellenistic-style sculptures of stone and bronze as well as pottery were traded throughout the empire and beyond. Many people outside of Rome's borders viewed Roman goods as luxury and prestige goods, and to acquire them was a mark of high status. It therefore shouldn't be surprising that barbarians started dressing in clothes made from Roman fabric or even dressing in complete Roman style. Rich chieftains would decorate their houses with Mediterranean pottery and women would wear Roman jewellery. Some people think that ancient peoples were rather austere, but the Romans could be just as gaudy and flashy as many people today. Back then, just as now, fashion was important in society, and wearing the next in-thing was a high priority on many matrons' minds.

Not surprisingly, the artistic trade rarely went the other way, at least from the Germanic lands, except for perhaps amber. Germania didn't really have much in the way of mineral wealth, and so far there's no record of Romans in Italy buying barbarian textiles or other goods imported from across the Rhine.

Chapter Two

Germania

The Land beyond the Rhine

The land that the Romans called *Germania* is traditionally identified as all lands east of the Rhine, north of the Danube, and west of the Vistula. Lands west of the Rhine were of the Gauls. Lands south of the Danube were of various peoples, such as the central European Celts, the Rhaetians, and the Illyrians. Lands east of the Vistula were of the Baltic and Slavic tribes in the north and the Dacians and Sarmatians in the south.

The Roman historian Tacitus states in his grand ethnographic work *Germania*, written in the last years of the first century AD, that among the many tribes who lived in this region, one was called the Germani, and the Romans decided to use this name to refer to all tribes living in this territory – thus, they were all named Germans and the land was named Germania. Tacitus further states that the name 'German' was applied so frequently to the inhabitants of that region that, by the time Tacitus was writing this, the natives actually began to refer to themselves collectively by that name as well.[1] We'll never know if this story is true or not, but circumstances like this have certainly happened before and since. As stated in the preceding chapter, the name 'Italian' is a Greek invention, originally the name of one tribe, and afterwards applied to the entire population of that boot-shaped peninsula. What is more telling is that, after a while, the Germans themselves began to refer to themselves as Germans. This is similar to the usage of the word 'Indian' when referring to the native peoples of North and South America. The word became so prevalent that, after a while, the native tribes of the New World began to refer to themselves collectively by that name which had been applied to them by Europeans.

The Greek historian and geographer Strabo states that the word *germani* is a Latin word that means 'genuine'. I tried to see if this was true, and found that Latin words for 'genuine' were *sincerus*, *incorruptus*, and *germanus*, the latter meaning 'of one's own' in a familial sense, as in 'my own brother, sister, etc.'. The modern English word *germane*, which is descended from the ancient Latin word, means 'to be similar or related to something'. Many tribal societies have names that translate more or less as 'the people, the true people, the real people', and so forth. There is no reason, therefore, not to believe that the Germani, if such a tribe did in fact exist, called themselves 'the genuine people'. Considering that tribes often had family ties, where the tribe was more or less a group of people who were somehow albeit distantly related to each other, the idea of a tribe calling itself 'the genuine people', genuine being in a familial sense, now seems approachable. In reality, the Germanic tribes didn't call themselves Germans in terms of a broad ethnic sense, at least not at first. They originally referred to themselves and their neighbours only by their specific tribal names – the Chatti, the Cherusci, etc.[2]

A fascinating analysis of the etymology of 'German' was written by the sixteeenth century Flemish cartographer Abraham Ortelius, citing a long list of examples from various academics. Among them was Johannes Becanus, a sixteenth century Dutch humanist, who said that the Germanic *ger* may be related to the modern French *guerre*, or 'war', and therefore *Germani* would literally have meant 'war men', or 'warriors', although Ortelius commented that he wasn't sure if the word *ger* meant 'war' in ancient Germanic.[3]

What did the landscape of Germania look like? The traditional image is that Germania was, as stated by Tacitus, covered with dark forests and stinking bogs. Julius Caesar claimed that there was very little farmland, and that the native Germanic people were primarily hunter-gatherers. This image of a very primitive land has stuck throughout the centuries. Works written by Classically-educated Victorian-age historians and anthropologists have only served to further reinforce the Romans' statements. They claimed that only a small percentage of the land was cultivated and that the overwhelming majority of the landscape was covered in untamed wilderness, and that the people who lived within carried on in an almost Stone Age lifestyle. However, in recent years, our ideas of what ancient Germania actually looked like have changed. Germania was not, as was once Romantically imagined, a single continuous forest stretching from the Rhine to the Vistula, but was a patchwork of forests, marshland, farms, and livestock pastures. Despite his sweeping claim that Germania was mostly forests and bogs, Tacitus himself repeatedly makes references to fields of grain, and also talks about the dominance of livestock in Germanic societies. It therefore appears that our long-standing ideas about Germania's landscape are incorrect and have more to do with selective reading and over-emphasis of certain passages by previous historians, especially the haughty imperialistic Victorians, who wanted to further accentuate the contrast between the enlightened, civilized, and dare I say 'proper' ways of Rome (which the British Empire very obviously tried to emulate) and the ignorant, uncivilized, backwards Kipling-esque savages of the wild and wooly lands beyond the empire.[4]

In his *Germania*, Tacitus gives a short description of the attributes of the German landscape. In it, he states that the land, although somewhat varied in appearance, is mostly either forest or swamp. The landscape is good for growing grain but not fruit trees, and the land is seriously deficient in iron and precious metals. Livestock is very common and important in Germanic society, but the animals themselves are small and unappealing in appearance.[5]

In a section of his *Commentaries*, Julius Caesar describes the wildlife of Germania. He writes of a unicorn with a horn that, after extending straight up for a certain distance, branches outwards in either direction like the palms of a hand with fingers. I can't think of any living animal that might be the inspiration for this, but one creature that comes to mind is the Irish Elk (*Megaloceros giganteus*), but it is commonly believed this creature became extinct at the end of the Ice Age. Then he speaks of the *elk*, a strange creature that has legs without joints and therefore sleeps standing up. This may be a moose, because in Europe a moose is called an elk. He also talks about the *uri*, a large bull that's almost as big as an elephant. The uri is the aurochs, a species of wild European cattle that became extinct in the early 1600s, and although it was quite large, it certainly wasn't as big as an elephant.[6]

The Germanic Tribes

In order for us to begin an analysis of the various groups who lived in this land, we need to first understand how modern scholars perceive different groups of people and the various cultural forms that they exist in. Inextricably, the way that academics come to grips with determining what sort of society a certain group of people belongs to is by classifying them, judging them according to their own opinions of what does and what does not constitute 'civilization'. They then categorize peoples into various groups (although 'levels' or 'grades' would probably be more accurate, due to the inherent hierarchic nature of this judgment) based upon these judgments and opinions. I should state right away that it's a little dangerous for modern academics and especially anthropologists to do this, because what they are essentially doing is defining 'what is' and 'what isn't', using their own particular definitions of what constitutes 'culture'. Cultures and societies are then placed in categories, which are also the constructed products of outside scholars. These categories are made because these academics pick and choose criteria that are used to classify and determine where people belong, and therefore they determine which people belong in which group. In so doing, determining 'what is' and 'what isn't' morphs into defining 'who is' and 'who isn't', and that's dangerous.

Today, anthropologists divide societies into a stratified hierarchy based upon complexity – band, tribe, chiefdom, state, and civilized/urbanized state. I take issue with this long-used system because it carries the inherent accusations of certain groups being either inferior or superior to others by grading societies based upon how 'civilized' they are, with bands categorized as the most backwards and primitive and therefore occupying the absolute lowest rung of human society, and with modern urbanized societies categorized as the highest level, existing in a state of perfection in societal development. It's a very self-important and condescending and dare I say 'Roman' way of judging people, in which city-dwellers in modern societies are held in highest regard as the epitome of cultural and societal progress, and people who live in tribal societies are regarded as, literally, 'un-civilized' inferior second-rate cultures, unfinished in terms of their progress towards civilized and urbanized perfection.

For a long time, ignorant of this commonly-used anthropological system, I have used a pyramidal structure for categorizing societies in the broader scheme of human cultures, and I continue to use this system to this day – bands, clans, tribes, and ethnic groups. 'States' are considered a separate entity altogether, having emerged or evolved from one of the levels in this pyramid. Each one of these various groupings is done according to population size (and possibly family relation) and socio-economic complexity, because

as group size expanded, social complexity was needed to expand with it
– rules needed to be made, and administers needed to be chosen to keep
everything in order. Clans are understandably more complex than how
bands are organized, tribes more complex than clans, and so forth. It's a
system which places societies into a broader scheme based upon size and not
based upon any belief about being more advanced or primitive than others.

The smallest unit of social organization is the band, or camp. Usually
these consist of a small number of people who are related to each other and
whose internal social structure is highly egalitarian, led by a single person
who presides over the group and usually attains that position based upon the
will of the other band members. Several bands form a clan, and although
each band might not necessarily be directly related to each other, they do
share some thread which ties them together. Several clans make up a tribe,
and several tribes make up a greater ethnic group. One thing to take note of
is that in ancient times, the overall ethnic group rarely had a single leader.
Rarely did all of the tribes within a certain ethnic group coalesce into a
single unified 'state' or nation. Mostly, the unity stretched only as far as
the tribe, which maintained connections with other ethnically similar tribes,
forming what we would today call 'an ethnic identity'. This was the case
with the early Germans, who never united into a single nation. Although
confederacies occasionally sprung up, especially during the Late Antique
period, they encompassed few tribes, and the confederacies were small both
in population and power, and would gain power only by negotiations with
Rome and by exacting military victories upon the confederacy's enemies.

Simple small–scale tribal societies have all of the members more or
less in equal standing with each other, and their leader is chosen by the
people because of his personal qualities, including leadership abilities and
battlefield prowess. Property is often shared rather than privately owned.
More complex tribal societies are termed 'chiefdoms' by anthropologists.
These societies are marked by a distinct hierarchy within the tribe, comprised
of a ruling elite who are few in number and the commoners who make up
the bulk of the tribal population. There is a chief who acts as the overall
leader of the tribe, who can be either chosen by the people or can attain
this office through hereditary right, in which the crown is passed down
from father to son, thus creating dynasties. The chiefs often serve social,

military, and religious functions. The non-ruling population might have a system of social hierarchy in which the people are divided into classes. The tribal realm may practise economics, often based upon land ownership or livestock, and establish certain places to be central to its culture, either for political, military, or spiritual purposes.[7] The Germanic tribes appear to fall into both of these camps.

The first person to write in some measure of detail about the Germanic tribes was Julius Caesar, who called them 'wild and savage men'.[8] He was also the first person to cross the Rhine and explore Germania. After him came the Greek historian Strabo, whose most famous work, *Geography*, was written during the BC–AD transition period. In this work, Strabo briefly discusses Germania and its peoples. Interestingly, he writes about the Germans who inhabited modern-day Denmark in a separate chapter. According to *The Natural History*, written by Pliny the Elder and published around 79 AD near the time of his death, the Germanic tribes were divided into three culture groups, each composed of several tribes. These culture groups were named the Ingaevones, Istaevones, and Hermiones, and he stated that a majority of the tribes belonged to these groups, although there were a few exceptions. Tacitus, writing twenty years later, further refined Pliny's work in one of his most famous publications, *Germania*, the first truly comprehensive guide to the land beyond the Rhine and its peoples. He claimed that all of the Germanic tribes belonged to three main culture groups, whose founders were the three divine sons of Mannus, who himself was the son of the god Tuisco. The tribes along the coast of the North Sea, from what are today the Netherlands, northwestern Germany, and Denmark belonged to the Ingaevones. The tribes of the interior belonged to the Herminones. All of the other tribes belonged to the Istaevones.[9] Many tribes from all over the world trace their origins to a mythological or heroic ancestor, and dividing the Germans into three broad cultural groups based upon their supposed foundation by one of three divine sons of Man certainly fits with this common practice.

Unlike many inhabitants of Italy, the Germanic barbarians didn't live in walled towns or cities, but in isolated villages, living what we would call today a combined agricultural/hunter-gatherer lifestyle. Tacitus names over fifty different tribes that lived in Germania. The Germanic tribes were not united; each tribe was an independent polity. Certain tribes, like the Chatti and the Sueves, were very powerful and occupied large territories, whilst others, like the Dulgubini, were weak and their territories were miniscule by comparison. The German historian Hans Delbruck claims that each tribe held a territory at least 2,000 square miles in size, that each of a tribe's clans held twenty or more square miles, and that there could not have been more than eleven or twelve persons per square mile, which yields populations of 25,000 for small tribes, and as much as 40,000 for larger ones. As evidence for this claim, he states that the land between the Rhine, Elbe, and Main Rivers is roughly 50,000 square miles in size and is known to have held twenty-three tribes, producing an average of 2,000 square miles per tribe.[1] Those are a lot of statistics, but is Delbruck right?

Mixed hunter-gatherer/agricultural societies had small population densities, and for obvious reasons – you needed a population small enough for the land to support you without depleting your food supply. But what was the total population of Germania? For starters, a group of people need at least 500 persons to be reproductively viable so that there is no risk of genetic defects due to inbreeding. So, with fifty tribes and with at least 500 or more people per tribe, that comes to a bare minimum figure of 25,000 people for all of Germania. In reality, there were many more than that. The Marcomanni tribe alone had an army numbering 74,000 men, and a total population that was considerably larger. It's highly likely that population densities were higher in coastal areas and sparser in the interior. Regardless of what the actual numbers were, which are probably never going to be made known to us, it's likely that the population density of non-urbanized Germania was significantly lighter than urbanized areas, such as Roman Italy or Greece.

While Germania might not have been crowded in terms of population, it was crowded *politically*, meaning that there were many different tribes vying for power in relatively small areas of space. Six to eight tribes lived in the Netherlands alone, and three or four lived in what is now Denmark. Both of these are small countries and it's hard to imagine how different peoples could be at home in such confined surroundings. To give a complete individual analysis of all of the fifty-something different Germanic tribes that have ever existed would be both lengthy and distracting, so I'll just focus on those involved in the Battle of Teutoburg as well as a couple of the major tribes.

The most powerful tribe in southern Germania, and possibly the most powerful in all of Germania as a whole, was the Marcomanni. Their name might mean either or both of the following translations: 'the Forest Men' (Marc being *mark*, Viking for 'woods or forest'), or 'the Border Men' (Marc being *march*, a term used for a land along a country's border, in this case, the border between Germania and Rome). During the time of Caesar Augustus, they occupied the region of Bohemia, now part of the Czech Republic. The leader of the Marcomanni during the BC–AD transition period was King Maroboduus (might be a Latinized version of Maroboduwoz; his name might mean 'the Great Raven' in Bohemian Celtic).[11] According to Strabo, Maroboduus was a German who possessed Roman citizenship. In his youth, he lived in Rome and 'enjoyed the favour of Augustus'.[12] Paterculus describes him as 'a man of noble family, strong in body and courageous in mind, a barbarian by birth but not in intelligence'.[13] After he left Rome and returned to his tribal lands, likely to act as a client king for the empire, he began amassing power in the region. His tribe originally inhabited territory that lay further west, their original homeland territory bordered by the Main River to the north, the territories of the Vangiones and the Nemetes to the west, and the territory of the Hermunduri and Narisci to the south. After Maroboduus returned to his people, he ordered the entire tribe to relocate further east to Bohemia.[14]

The sudden absence of the Marcomanni left their original territory vacant and up-for-grabs. One tribe who wanted control of it was the Hermunduri, and they began to migrate into the region. Cassius Dio records that a man named Lucius Ahenobarbus (one of the Roman governor-generals of Germania Magna before Varus came in) 'had intercepted the Hermunduri, a tribe which for some reason or other had left their own land and were wandering about in quest of another, and he had settled them in a part of the Marcomannian territory'.[15]

A powerful northern tribe called the Chatti also wanted the land, resulting in the Chatti pushing southwards and the Hermunduri pushing northwards. Tensions remained high between the two until it eventually led to an epic clash reported by Tacitus. He records that in the summer of either 58 or 59 AD, when the Chatti and Hermunduri fought for control of a river (probably the Main River), each side vowed that if they were victorious, they

Map 2. Map of Germania, circa 15 BC, prior to the Roman invasion. Abbreviations: AMP = Ampsivarians; ANG = Angrivarians; CHAS = Chasuarians; DULG = Dulgubini; SIC = Sicambri; USI = Usipetes; VAN = Vangiones. The Sueves and Ligians are composed of several tribes. Tacitus states that the Gotini tribe is actually Celtic and that the Osi are Pannonian Illyrian. (*Illustration by Jason R Abdale*)

would sacrifice the entire losing army to their gods. The Hermunduri won the battle, and all of the Chatti were slain.[16] So the Hermunduri would have cemented their control over that region, possibly doubling or even tripling the size of their territory.

Once the Marcomanni had finished relocating to Bohemia, King Maroboduus expanded his authority through military conquests. He defeated and incorporated neighbouring tribes into his realm, some of which were powerful in their own right and would have been fearsome contenders in battle.[17] It is certain that it was through these conquests that the Marcomanni became the most powerful of the Germanic tribes and forged the large and impressive army which Maroboduus commanded.

The Marcomanni was the only Germanic tribe with a professional standing army, one that numbered 74,000 warriors: 70,000 infantry and 4,000 cavalry. Paterculus states that the army constantly drilled and was brought up to a Roman level of professionalism. In this manner, the Marcomanni bears resemblance to the rise of the Zulu kingdom under Shaka, in which he raised his men to a high degree of martial professionalism, and began the conquest of the neighbouring tribal peoples, bringing the Zulu nation from relative obscurity to being the most powerful nation in all of southern Africa. Rome would, in time, become uneasy and wary of the Marcomanni's growing power in the region, despite the fact that Maroboduus pledged that he would never provoke a war with Rome, but he also stated that if Rome were to initiate hostilities, he would not back down and give in, and his army gave him the power to resist defeat. Roman outlaws found political asylum within the Marcomanni kingdom. Roman envoys had to speak of him as an equal to the Roman emperor. Eventually the Romans became tired of having such a powerful neighbour on their front doorstep, and in 6 AD, the Romans were preparing to invade and conquer Bohemia, amassing a very large army to get the job done. However, only a few days before the invasion was scheduled to begin, a massive rebellion suddenly erupted in the Balkans, and Roman military efforts had to be diverted there.[18]

The Sueves, also known as the Suebi, might have been the second-most powerful Germanic tribe. Julius Caesar writes that they were the most numerous and most war-like of all of the Germans. This statement is corroborated by Strabo, who states that the Sueves were the largest of the German tribes and occupied the largest amount of territory, their lands stretching from the Rhine to the Elbe and beyond, although this is surely an exaggeration – their lands actually comprised a large section of central Germania between the Elbe and Oder Rivers.[19]

Julius Caesar states that the Sueves ruled over a hundred districts, and each district was required to annually supply a thousand men for war, and that everyone else who remained at home was to provide weaponry, equipment, and other military supplies; those who stayed at home during one year were required to perform military service the following year. The Sueves did not believe in the private ownership of land, and they did not stay in one location for more than one year. Their diet consisted of mostly meat and milk. They were very strong and hardy, and even in winter they wore little clothing. Also, the Sueves refused to drink wine, since they considered alcohol to be detrimental to one's self.[20]

In contrast with the report made by Julius Caesar, who states that the Sueves were a single large and powerful tribe, Strabo and Tacitus state that the term 'Sueve' was not the name of one specific tribe but rather a series of independent tribes which shared a similar culture and which were referred to collectively by this name: the Eudoses, Nuithones, Semnones, and Suardones are listed by Tacitus as being Suevian tribes. Strabo lists the Suevian tribes as the Sueves themselves, the Coldui, Semnones, and the Marcomanni. In addition to their main territory in north-central Germania, the Sueves also had smaller populations scattered in other areas. Strabo makes reference to a population of Sueves dwelling within the Hercynian Forest, and another population had crossed the Rhine and established a 'colony' in eastern Gaul, which would be destroyed by Julius Caesar. The Sueve tribes were known for a distinctive hairstyle which became known as the 'Suevian knot', which, according to Tacitus, distinguished them from other Germans, as well as freeborn Sueve men from their slaves, since only freemen were allowed to wear their hair in this style.[21]

The Chatti were the most powerful tribe between the Rhine and Weser Rivers, and might have been the number-three power in all of Germania behind the Marcomanni and the Sueves (if the Sueves were one tribe, and not the name of a Germanic culture group like the Ligians of eastern Germania). Their name means 'people', *chatt* being a corruption of *teut*, proto-Germanic for 'people/tribe'. According to Tacitus, they were people with strong bodies, shortened limbs, threatening expressions, and great vigour of heart, and had much intelligence and cleverness for Germans. The warriors elected their military commanders, and Tacitus, a staunch republican and a critic of the imperial government, must have found the idea of electing your generals pleasing. Like the Marcomanni, the Chatti's military was much more refined than other barbarian tribes in the region. According to Tacitus, during battle the warriors strictly obey their commanders' orders, keep their formations, exploit opportunities, maintain discipline and suppress impulse, plan out the day, build fortified camps for the night, reject the idea of fate or destiny, and have total courage in battle. All of the Chatti's military strength was infantry, and in addition to carrying an abundant supply of weaponry, they were also equipped with a large supply of iron tools and provisions. Tacitus ominously states that while other tribes only fight single battles, the Chatti wage full-scale wars. It was a custom of the Chatti's culture that a boy crossed the threshold of manhood only when he had killed an enemy. Before then, regardless of his age or physical maturity, he was regarded as a youth and must always shave. After he had killed another, he was called a man and was allowed to grow a beard. The Chatti also singled out their bravest warriors and awarded them an iron ring. Tacitus notes, however, that in other cultures being given an iron ring was a mark of disgrace, signifying that a person was a coward, and only when he had killed another in battle was he allowed to throw away the ring. Strangely, the Chatti did things the reverse way. Being given an iron ring was not a mark of shame, but of exceptional courage, like soldiers being given medals today.[22]

We know far less about other tribes involved in Arminius' rebellion. The Marsi (no relation to the Italic tribe of the same name) dwelt between the Ruhr and Lippe Rivers, occupying a rather small piece of land, and were no doubt considered a minor tribe even by their fellow Germans. According to one nineteenth century British historian, the name Marsi means 'the heroic people'. Considering the tribe's small size, one is tempted to think that their grandiose name was compensating for something. However, the Marsi may have been renowned for having a heroic fighting spirit rather than being a great and powerful state. No wonder, therefore, that of all of the tribes who fought with Arminius in late September of 9 AD, the Marsi were selected to be one of lucky ones to receive a captured legionary eagle following the battle. I should state that their name might also be a Roman invention. Translated from Latin, the name Marsi means 'the people of Mars', the Roman god of war. This could mean that these people were devoted worshipers of the Germanic god of war (probably known then as Tiwaz; Romans often substituted the names of their own gods in place of Germanic names) or claimed to be descended from him. It could also mean that the people themselves were of a very warlike nature. Whether you use one translation or the other, either way, the Marsi tribe appear to have been some very tough fighters despite their small territory and a possibly correspondingly small population. Since there is no mention of the Marsi being a cavalry-dominant culture as a few German tribes were, such as the Tencteri, we must assume that the Marsi's warriors were almost entirely infantry. Tacitus records that the chief of the Marsi tribe during the time of the Battle of Teutoburg was named Mallovendus. Although it isn't stated in the accounts, he must have fought in the battle, possibly as one of Arminius' top lieutenants, and if the claims of Marsi bravery are true, then he must have conducted himself with great courage.[23]

Another tribe that sided with Arminius, the Bructeri, was centred on what is now the city of Munster, Germany. Tacitus relates that by his time in the late first century AD, the Bructeri were extinct, having been massacred by other neighbouring tribes. According to multiple secondary sources which I have seen, the Angrivarians, who played an important part in Arminius' rebellion, lived in and around what is now the town of Minden. I have been told that the area around this town was once known as Angria, a corrupted form of the tribe's name.[24]

Finally, there were the Cherusci, the leaders of the rebellion. The Cherusci's location is a bit speculative – some sources and maps that I've seen on this subject speak of the Cherusci living between the Ems and the Weser, whilst others say that they lived between the Weser and Elbe. The map reconstruction seen in this book, based upon my own research of the Germanic tribes and their locations, depicts the Cherusci's territory as a fairly large swath of land stretching in a belt from the Ems to the Elbe Rivers, encompassing the territory from the modern German cities of Osnaburg to Magdenburg. The Harz Mountains, located in central Germany south of Brunswick, in what I believe was the southeastern part of the Cherusci's domain, might very well be named after this tribe. The Cherusci lived south of the Angrivarians, east of the Bructeri and Marsi, and north of the Chatti.[25]

The nineteenth century historian Thomas Smith, who wrote a very detailed but very suspect account of the Battle of Teutoburg and the various people involved in it, claims that the territory of the Cherusci tribe was divided up into at least three districts run by a distinct clan: Arminius' father controlled the central district, Arminius' uncle Inguiomerus controlled the eastern district, and Segestes, who may or may not have been another of Arminius' uncles, controlled the western district. However, I should state firmly that no ancient source states how many clans the Cherusci tribe was divided into, nor does any ancient source state which people presided over which areas. As to where Smith got this information, and indeed a large portion of the information used in his book, I don't know. It's likely that he just made it up, although some of it may have been based upon educated guesswork.[26]

In his *Germania*, Tacitus says this of the Cherusci: They dwelt in between the Chauci to the north and the Chatti to the south. In contrast to the warlike image associated with most barbarian groups, the Cherusci were pacifists and had for a long time lived in a state of peace with their neighbours. He further describes the Cherusci as always good and just.[27]

I'm not sure how to respond to such statements, since they seem so out of character with the Roman mindset towards the barbarians. Tacitus' description of the Cherusci as a virtuous, noble, peace-loving people strikes me as odd, since the Cherusci were the ringleaders behind the ambush of Varus and his legions. Tacitus definitely knew that. Furthermore, the size of the Cherusci's territory made it one of the larger and more powerful tribes within western Germania. In the old days, large territories were not held through pacifism. The Cherusci, therefore, must have been far more aggressive than Tacitus would have us believe. In regards to Tacitus' claim that the Cherusci were unassailed by their neighbours, this could be possible, but I think that this has more to do with geography than some sort of non-aggression pact between the Cherusci and the other Germanic tribes. The land that the Cherusci territory occupied sat astride a narrow belt of land composed of mountains, hills, and steep ravines, mostly covered with thick forests. I think that the reason why the Cherusci weren't attacked as often as their neighbours simply had to do with the fact that their territory might have been too arduous to enter, and therefore their aggressive neighbours preferred to attack softer targets. All in all, I am highly doubtful of Tacitus' statements, and I strongly caution anyone reading such things to be extremely wary about accepting such statements automatically.

Little is known about the Cherusci tribe's culture, but the Roman historian Publius Annius Florus writes that the Cherusci had a particular love for horses:

Next he [General Drusus] attacked simultaneously those powerful tribes, the Cherusci, Suebi and Sicambri, who had begun hostilities after crucifying twenty of our centurions, an act which served as an oath binding them together, and with such confidence of victory that they made an agreement in anticipation for dividing the spoils. The Cherusci had chosen the horses, the Suebi the gold and silver, the Sicambri the captives. Everything, however, turned out contrariwise; for Drusus, after defeating them, divided up their horses, their herds, their necklets and their own persons as spoil and sold them.[28]

There are two things that are interesting about this passage. Firstly, it's plainly stated that the Cherusci chose the horses over all other possessions, which must mean that they as a tribe placed special significance on horses, and by extension, horsemanship. Therefore, it isn't unreasonable to think that the Cherusci's fighting ability was based primarily on cavalry, or at least had a higher percentage of cavalry among its ranks than other Germanic tribes, which constituted mostly infantry, as recorded by Tacitus. To further drive this point home, it is commonly stated that Arminius led an auxiliary *cavalry* unit, not an *infantry* unit, when he was serving in the Roman Army under the command of General Tiberius Claudius Nero, Augustus' stepson and the most famous military commander Rome had during that time. The auxiliaries in question were almost certainly his own people, the Cherusci.[29]

Secondly, towards the end of that passage, it states that Drusus took away the Germans' horses. The confiscating of horses is an understandable action, considering that cavalry were a dominant force on the battlefield in those days, the Romans needed horses for their own cavalry, and that the Cherusci in particular were especially disposed towards the usage of cavalry. Get rid of the horses, and you get rid of the Cherusci's fighting potential, or at least severely cripple it, and cripple their morale as well.

This cultural focus on horses was not limited just to the Cherusci. A tribe called the Tencteri, located on the Rhine and whose lands lay immediately west of the Chatti, also placed a high value on horses and horsemanship. According to Tacitus, the Tencteri were famous for their cavalry and excelled all other German tribes in their use. The skills of horsemanship were passed down from father to son, and horses were considered one of a person's most valuable possessions. He further comments that horses were bestowed in inheritances, along with slaves and property, but horses were given not to the eldest son, but to the bravest.[30] In looking at the Tencteri, we might be able to extrapolate on the importance of the horse in Cherusci society.

The theme of horses appears to be a popular one in western Germany in later years. As examples, the states of Lower Saxony and Hanover had horses as their emblems. This might be a reference to the importance of the horse in some ancient Germanic societies which dwelt in this area in prior centuries, but this seems doubtful to me.

The Germanic Religion

Most of what we know about the Germanic religion comes from the Vikings, since they too were a Germanic people. Classical authors gave Greek and Roman equivalents to these gods, with Tacitus stating that they primarily worshipped Mercury.[31] Well, this can't be true since Mercury was a Roman god, not a German one. Among the gods worshiped were Wodinaz, Tiwaz, and Donar, who would become more familiar as the Viking gods Odin, Tyr, and Thor, but these were only three gods in a wider Germanic pantheon.

The Germans also adopted characters from other mythologies into their religion. Among their legends was a story that the great Greek hero Hercules travelled to their lands, and was held in high esteem by the tribes as the greatest of all heroes. They also believed that Odysseus travelled to Germania during his famous voyage. Moreover, they claimed that Odysseus established and named a town on the Rhine River which Tacitus calls Asciburgium (Asciburg in native Germanic; possibly the modern-day town of Moers-Asberg, Germany), a town which Tacitus, writing at the end of the first century AD, states was still inhabited. Within the town was an altar dedicated to Odysseus and his father Laertes. Tacitus states that these are not isolated occurrences – he has been told that there are several monuments and tombs dotted along Germania's border which, surprisingly, bear Greek inscriptions. However, Tacitus himself states that he had no hard evidence to back up this claim.[32]

In terms of the actual Germanic religion itself, it bore many features of the tribal or shamanistic beliefs of northern tribal peoples. Julius Caesar, writing about the Germans shortly after his conquest of Gaul, gave this description of their belief system.

> The Germans…have neither Druids to preside over sacred offices, nor do they pay great regard to sacrifices. They rank in the number of the gods those alone whom they behold, and by whose instrumentality they are obviously benefitted, namely, the sun, fire, and the moon; they have not heard of the other deities even by report.[33]

This passage shows how Caesar, whom Tacitus regards as an expert on such matters, can sometimes be absolutely dead wrong about something. There *were* tribal shamans, both men and women, as recorded by Strabo. Secondly, sacrifice was a core part of the Germanic religion, as I'll explain later. In terms of worshipping their own gods and not adopting others from other polytheistic societies, as polytheistic societies sometimes do (the Romans being a prime example), that part is more circumspect. It is known, however, that the Germans worshipped Julius Caesar as a god – they even had his sword, or a facsimile of it, placed in a temple in modern-day Cologne.[34]

The Germans did not build temples, with Tacitus claiming that the Germans believed it to be improper to confine gods within walls, or to have divine celestial beings represented in an all-too-mortal human form. They did, however, have locations that they believed to be sacred – lakes, certain tree groves, etc. – and conducted rituals there. The Germanic portrayals of gods consisted mostly of large wooden 'pillar idols'. Unlike the detailed marble and bronze Mediterranean sculptures common to Greece and Rome, these large column-shaped poles with roughly-carved faces on the top were very stylized and simple. It has been suspected that they may represent a fertility cult, since they could be taken to be large penises. The fact that many of these pillar idols are forked in two at the bottom could corroborate this, being perhaps stylized versions of testicles. However, I believe that the supposed connection between the pillar idols and phallic symbols may be a bit of a stretch, and they are simply overly-simplified human forms.[35]

Many of these pillar idols have been discovered in bogs, and it's thanks to the anaerobic quality of the water that these wooden sculptures have been preserved. The Germans made use of bogs and sacrificial pools, offering, among other things, weapons. These weapons, such as bog-iron swords, would be bent in order to render them unusable, either by tomb-robbers or by the newly-deceased spirits. Horses were sacrificed with considerable frequency; over a hundred horse skeletons have been discovered in the bogs so far.[36]

People were also sacrificed, with over fifty individuals being unearthed by archaeologists. The practice of human sacrifice was recorded by the Greek historian Strabo, who states that the Cimbri tribe would have priestesses clad in white cloaks accompanying the warriors when they went off to battle. The priestesses would gather together all of the prisoners of war, crown them with wreaths, and would have them bend over a large kettle. Then, they would slit the prisoners' throats with a sword, the blood pouring into the vessel. Other unfortunates would be disemboweled (whether they were still alive at the time isn't stated), and both the blood and the internal organs would be used in predicting the future. Sacrificing enemy soldiers or their possessions to your god if you emerged victorious in battle was a common practice among the Germans – the record of the clash between the Chatti and Hermunduri tribes in which the Hermunduri emerged victorious and then slaughtered all of the Chatti prisoners is a perfect example.[37] That being said, when the Germans emerged victorious after the Battle of Teutoburg, they began methodically executing their Roman captives.

However, the killing of persons among a tribe wasn't limited to religious sacrifices. The Germans had the death penalty for serious crimes. Tacitus relates that traitors and deserters were hanged, and the lazy, cowardly, and lustful were drowned in the bogs, the idea being that certain crimes should be publicly exposed, while others ought to be hidden from view.[38]

Tacitus states that the German priests were also skilled at prophecy and predictions, relating that no race practised such things with more fervour than the Germans. As an example, he describes how their priests would seek answers to important questions by cutting a branch off of a fruit-bearing tree (which in itself should merit criticism, since Tacitus states that Germania's soil was unfavourable to growing fruit trees), and cutting it into strips. The strips would then be cast onto a white garment. The god is invoked, and each piece is picked up three times, and based upon this, they find a favourable or unfavourable answer to their prayers. Augury – the practice of predicting the future by observing the behaviour of animals – was also practised among the Germans. Augury was commonly associated with birds, but Tacitus says that the Germans also predicted the future by using horses, which Tacitus says is unusual. He cites that white horses are kept at public expense, are housed in the forest, and prevented from performing any labour, and whose various noises are interpreted by the Germanic priests in terms of answering their questions. When it comes to war, however, the Germans have a much more direct method of finding out which side will be the winner. Having, by some method, captured a prisoner of the enemy tribe, they pit the prisoner against their strongest warrior – whoever wins the fight determines who is likely to win the war.[39]

Germanic Social Culture

It is not known whether or not the Germanic tribes had a written language by the time Augustus came to power. The runic alphabet which is commonly associated with the Vikings of the Dark Ages is actually a variation of a northern Italic alphabet used by people such as the Etruscans and Veneti during ancient times. The Scandinavians must have gotten hold of this alphabet somehow, although it must have taken quite some time for knowledge of this alphabet to eventually work its way up to northern Europe. The oldest-known runic inscriptions in northern Europe date to well after the events discussed in this book.

If the Germans *did* have writing at this early stage, then no examples have survived, so what we know about their society comes from the Greeks and Romans. Many of these writers wrote the clichéd anecdotes often attributed to people who had been labelled by 'civilized' cultures as barbarians or savages, claiming that they are very war-like and whenever they aren't fighting they go hunting.

From childhood they devote themselves to fatigue and hardships. Those who have remained chaste for the longest time, receive the greatest commendation among their people; they think that by this the growth is promoted, by this the physical powers are increased and the sinews are strengthened. And to have had knowledge of a woman before the twentieth year they reckon among the most disgraceful acts; of which matter there is no concealment, because they bathe promiscuously in the rivers and [only] use skins or small cloaks of deer's hides, a large portion of the body being in consequence naked.[40]

According to Caesar, the Germans moved constantly because every year a village council would meet and decide which family was given which plot of land. Families were shuffled around constantly in order to, among other things, prevent them from becoming attached to any one location, to prevent them from acquiring large estates by driving weaker land-owners away, and to provide a sense of equality.[41] One trait that Tacitus took note of was that the Germans lived in individual houses, which was in contrast to the Roman way of architecture, in which you had buildings adjoining each other. To a Roman like Tacitus, this form of construction was very peculiar, and he suspected that it was a precaution against fire – either that, or the Germans simply didn't know how to build *properly*, Tacitus flatly accuses. In addition to having space around their houses, Caesar relates that the Germans prided themselves on how big their 'no man's land' was on their tribal borders.

It is the greatest glory to the several states to have as wide deserts as possible around them, their frontiers having been laid waste. They consider this the real evidence of their prowess, that their neighbours shall be driven out of their lands and abandon them, and that no one dare settle near them; at the same time they think that they shall be on that account the more secure, because they have removed the apprehension of a sudden incursion.[42]

What was warfare like for the Germanic tribes? Tribal warfare is something that has been the subject of a great deal of study by anthropologists, and its basic formula is fairly well-known. Among small or less complex tribes, warfare is usually conducted on a small scale, in which the two warring sides fight battles, but no organized campaigns. This statement is important because Tacitus makes a reference to this very same observation, stating that in contrast to all of other Germanic tribes who only engage each other in isolated battles, the Chatti wage full-scale wars. Leadership is almost always based upon inspiration and force of personality. Strategy is limited, for the most part being confined to village raids, ambush tactics (which the Germans performed with great frequency and ability, according to several Roman authors), and feigned retreats, but largely there is no sense of strategy and tactics, with both sides simply charging at each other *en masse*. Many of the battles which are fought have ritualized or game-like qualities to them. The location and date of the battle is usually arranged beforehand by both parties. On the appointed day of the battle in question, men from both sides try to intimidate their opponents by shows of physical strength and loudly exclaiming their exploits. They might start hurling missiles at one another, but only from a distant range, so injuries were infrequent. Women and other family members would accompany the men to the site of the battle, giving encouragement to their own menfolk and often hurling insults at their opponents. The actual reasons for going off to war in the first place are mostly concerning either revenge – wrongs inflicted upon one tribe by another – or the upholding of personal honour; in many, if not all cases, the two are intertwined. Although hostilities between two sides are often marked by few battles with minimal casualties per battle, the conflicts between the two sides can encompass years and possibly decades with on-and-off fighting, and the cumulative casualties of such protracted hostility can be quite high. It isn't unusual for up to one-third or even one-half of the males within a tribe to be killed within the course of such protracted violence, but tribal populations tend to be small, and the deaths are spread out over a long period of time.[43]

But this is the lower end of tribal warfare – it could become more complex and more costly to the sides involved. Warfare among more 'advanced' tribes, for lack of a better word, is usually more complex than in primitive tribes. Advanced tribes usually have larger populations than simpler ones, and therefore can afford to suffer more casualties in battle. As a consequence, wars among advanced tribes tend to be bloodier and occur within a shorter time-span. 'Chiefdoms' tend to be highly warlike and often have a great deal of effectiveness in battle. It isn't unusual for tribal societies of this sort to contend with and even overpower much more powerful and organized states, something that Arminius might have been aware of. The reasons for waging war also become more varied. No longer just a matter of revenge or the preservation of personal honour, wars can be fought over control of resources and territory, something which larger and more complex tribes would no doubt wage with some frequency, but would be largely unthought-of by smaller and less-advanced tribes with smaller populations, and therefore, smaller needs to support those populations.[44]

The Germanic tribes appear to fall into both of these categories, those of simple and more complex tribal societies, and aspects of society and warfare bleed across the dividing boundaries between the two. Many of the Germanic tribes had chiefs, and in the case of the Marcomanni a king, who led the tribe as a whole under their single leadership. Other tribes were broken into smaller sub-divisions called clans, each with its own chief which may or may not have been hereditary, and while these clans shared an identical culture and even referred to themselves as belonging to a larger tribal society, there was no chief leading the tribe as a whole; the Cherusci appear to fall into this category, in which Arminius' father Segimerus, although powerful, was merely the leader of one clan out of the several clans which composed the Cherusci tribe. Warfare can be either limited or expansive, depending on the circumstances involved and the needs of the tribe, ranging from small isolated raids to pitched battles between two large bodies of armed men. The reasons for fighting may be vengeance for wrongs inflicted upon members of the tribe or the tribe as a whole, a desire to obtain goods or to kidnap or enslave members of a neighbouring tribe, a need to expand into neighbouring territory in order to accommodate an expanding population, or to gain control over territory and the resources therein. The individual battles may be both highly ritualized, full of bluff and chest-thumping bravado, and at the same time culminate in two hordes of heavily-armed men crashing into each other, inflicting massive casualties on both sides. Family members would accompany the warriors to the battle site, cheering them on and pressuring them to do their best under penalty of being forever shamed as being either cowardly or weak. Prowess would be determined not only by bravery in the face of death, but also based upon how many enemies a particular warrior had slain in a given battle, and as such the warriors would have striven to kill as many of the enemy as possible, resulting in enormous casualties per battle. Trophies taken from the dead bodies, perhaps even dismembered parts from the bodies themselves such as decapitated heads, served as physical proof of a warrior's fighting ability and battlefield prowess, and as such Germanic battles were often accompanied with a great deal of spoil looting, sometimes even while the battle was still taking place. In a warrior-based society, proof of one's abilities and exploits was extremely important in terms of one's social standing, but this practice would rob Arminius of victory against the Romans more than once.

In terms of weapons, spears were the most common. Swords were very few in number, and their quality wasn't especially good due to the poor nature of the metal. 'Bog iron', as it is commonly called, is softer than other irons, which is both good and bad. The softness of the metal means that it is easier for blacksmiths to work with, but it will not hold up in battle and is liable to easily bend or break. There is also at least one report from the Early Middle Ages concerning a Viking duel, in which both parties called a time out in the middle of the fighting so that they might re-straighten their swords. The discovery of a large weapons cache at Nydam, Denmark shows the proportion of weapons usage – over a hundred pattern-welded swords (mostly Roman-made, which were imported via trade into Germania), over five hundred spears and javelins, over forty bows, and over one hundred and seventy arrowheads.[45] The fact that most of the swords were manufactured by outside sources and were then imported into the country shows just how scarce iron was in Germania, so scarce that iron weapons had to be bought rather than natively manufactured.

It was a disgrace for a chief to be surpassed in deeds on the battlefield, and also a disgrace for any of his 'followers' (presumably his retinue) to fail in imitating the chief's bravery – the message here was 'do your best, but don't be better than the chief'. This was important because a battle leader was placed in that position due to displays of personal glory in warfare. Having someone accord himself better made the leader lose face and look weak. As was the case in many tribal societies, the worth of a man was measured in prowess on the battlefield. Tacitus even states that if a tribe is peaceful for too long, the young warriors will seek service in another tribe which is at war in order to show off their skills.[46]

Chiefs were chosen by birth while commanders were chosen by merit. Commanders were expected to lead by example rather than merely issuing orders, and it was a commander's unspoken duty to stand in the front ranks. The commanders, however, were not permitted to punish warriors – punishment was the job of the priests. Each chief had a subordinate body of a hundred men chosen from the community, whose duty it was to act as a council and to help carry out the chief's wishes by helping to administer the territory. According to Tacitus, young men can become leaders if they are from the highest levels of the tribal nobility or if their fathers had done great service in battle or at home. Young men often enroll in the retinues of prominent men of the tribal elite. These retinues are important, and being seen in the company of a high-ranking member of the tribe enhances one's own credentials and social standing. Among the retinues, the followers are organized according to importance, and as such, all of the young men compete with each other as to who shall be regarded as the highest ranking member of the troupe. Not only that, but these nobles also compete with each other in terms of each other's retinues in terms of size (the more important the leader, the larger his band of followers and companions) and the bravery of its members. In this situation, both sides benefit. A chief who has a large retinue is regarded as being important, and a man gains importance if he enrolls in the retinue of an important chief. Such high-ranking chiefs and nobles are regarded as important men both within and beyond his tribe, receiving ambassadors and gaining gifts and tribute. Sometimes, Tacitus comments, even the very mention of such a person's name will be enough to stop a war from occurring – if a certain person of very high standing is fighting against you, then it is better not to fight at all.[47]

This segment of Tacitus' *Germania* concerning the boys who served as retainers for chiefs and other high-ranking nobles sounds very much like the *Antrustiones* ('the Entrusted Ones'), and the *Pueri Regis* ('the King's Boys') which were two types of retainers in Frankish society, respectively those who served the king and those who served the nobles, even though the latter of the two refers to the royalty not nobility.[48]

We tend to think of chiefs essentially like mini-kings. It's only natural for many people to make this comparison, taking a system that we know, ie *kingdom*, and miniaturizing it to fit the parameters of a society which is somewhat less complex than a kingdom, but might be organized roughly along the same lines. In some ways, this is true – there were certainly chiefs and chieftains who controlled powerful realms, had prosperous economies, and had thousands of soldiers serving in their armies. As stated before, the tribal or clan chiefs performed a variety of functions. One of the chief's primary functions was the redistribution of wealth. Many times, loyalty to a chief was secured by how much he gave to his people, a sort of bribery-based loyalty. A chief who was stingy might lose the support of his people. A prime example in Germanic society of the redistribution of wealth is the practice, reported by Julius Caesar, of the annual redistribution of land ownership, in which each year the chiefs decide which family gets to own which particular plot of real estate. When the time came to discuss matters, minor affairs were discussed solely by the tribal chiefs, but more serious ones involved the entire tribe. Legal assemblies were always on certain pre-determined days, except in emergencies, usually during new or full moons for auspicious reasons. Interestingly, those involved in the assemblies had to show up armed, I'm assuming that if one wanted to have the right to have his say, he needed to prove he was willing to fight. The priests acted as heralds, keeping order. When the chief makes a proposal, the people either voice their disapproval by grumbling, or approve by holding up their weapons.[49]

Germanic law was typical of European tribal societies. Serious crimes were punishable by death (as stated in the section on Germanic religion), while lighter offences were punished with fines, in this case by handing over a certain number of cattle, with half being paid to the injured party and the other half paid directly to the tribal government. Tacitus claims that the Germans did not have a monetary system, or even mineral-based wealth. The Germans, it seems, had no concept of money, with Tacitus stating that they regard gold and silver objects just the same as those made of clay. He moreover states that tribes in contact along the Roman frontier have grown accustomed to using coinage, presumably from trade with the wealthy Romans, but tribes in the interior were still using the old-fashioned barter system, trading one item for another.[50]

Germanic Artistic Culture

Much of what we know of Germanic art comes mostly from the Late Antique and Early Medieval periods of European history, with a majority of the subjects being Scandinavian or Anglo-Saxon, but the Germans did have art before this time. The Celts had a profound influence on Germanic artwork. The later *La Tene* style that had become the dominant Celtic art style in the first century BC is seen in many examples of Germanic metalwork, and was especially prevalent, of course, in western and southern Germania – the lands that bordered those of the Celts. Since Germania lacked precious metals, trade with neighbouring tribes or states made silver and gold available to the Germans, although the earliest gold objects, mostly rings and pendants, that can be clearly seen as Germanic rather than Celtic or Roman were produced much later in the late first century BC.[51] Other gold items were torques, the familiar ring-shaped necklaces commonly identified with the Celts. These jewellery items have been found virtually all over the northern world, from Scotland to Russia, though I wonder if all the cultures manufactured them or merely traded them in exchange for other items.

Celtic merchants were trading with the Germans by the mid-first century BC, bringing their own Celtic wares in addition to importing foreign Greek and Roman goods from the south. By the time the Romans came in the late first century BC, more goods became available for purchase, such as glass, pottery, jewellery, and artwork. No doubt the tribal chieftains wished to obtain these goods as a mark of prestige, and the more imported items one owned, the greater his clout. Trade, however, was probably based upon barter rather than buying, with Romans and Germans trading Roman goods for Germanic ones. Certainly those tribes dwelling along the border would have been familiar with Roman currency, but tribes in the interior would have been less familiar with money, and may have viewed silver and gold coins more like decorative items to be made into necklaces than as a medium of wealth.[52]

Chapter Three

Varus

Varus and his Family

Publius Quinctilius Varus (his middle name is sometimes written without the 'c') was born in 46 BC to a long-existing patrician family. There are no busts or statues of Varus which exist, nor is it known if any were created at all. All we have to represent his physical characteristics are coins that bear his image. In spite of their impeccable lineage, the *gens* Quinctilia were never all that powerful or regarded with any eminence. Most of the family's members had been quaestors, praetors, or state priests. The *quaestor* was the lowest level in the Roman bureaucracy. The man in question had to be at least 25 years old and was responsible for maintaining the state archives as well as overseeing the imperial treasury. The office lasted for only one year, and there were ten quaestors elected per year. The *praetor* was one of the higher offices of state, in fact the second-highest in Roman administration subordinate only to the Senatorial consul, and was an office which entitled its bearer to possess *imperium*, 'the power of command', the power and authority to command military units. A man wishing to be elected to the praetorship had to have previously served as a quaestor and had to be at least 39 years old. Six praetors were elected each year and were responsible largely for judicial affairs. Only one man, Sextus Quinctilius Varus, had been elected Consul in 453 BC, but died before his term expired due to a massive and devastating plague which was sweeping through all of Italy that year – this was the only time before Varus' birth in 46 BC that a member of the gens Quinctilia had held the consulship. Two other ancestors had fought against Hannibal's brother Mago during the Second Punic War. As the years passed, the family diminished in wealth as well as political influence and power, and plunged sharply during the twilight of the Republic. The hard times that the Varus family faced in recent years was probably due to, among other things, the loyalties that its various family leaders had shown to various political factions – they always backed the losing side.[1]

We know from Paterculus that Varus' grandfather and father had committed suicide. No information is given about his grandfather or the reasons for his suicide, but we know quite a lot about Varus' father, Sextus Quinctilius Varus. He had been a praetor in 57 BC and had successfully petitioned for the return of Marcus Cicero, who had been banished from the city.[2] Sextus Varus later fought in the civil wars which destroyed the Roman Republic. He was a fervent anti-Caesarian, and cast in his lot with Caesar's arch rival Pompeius. Unfortunately for him, he was taken prisoner by Caesar following his victory at the siege of Corfinium – Caesar lists Sextus Quinctilius Varus as a quaestor, one of several eminent men who were presented to Caesar after his victory. Caesar addressed them all, saying that their taking up arms against him was a poor return for all of the benefits and awards that Caesar had given to them previously, and then set them all free. One would think that after this display of generosity, Sextus Varus would not be willing to tempt fate and rebel a second time, but as said before, he was a loyal supporter of Pompeius, and so after Caesar pardoned him, he fled to Africa. Here, he linked up with another anti-Caesarian named Publius Attius Varus (no relation to Sextus Quinctilius Varus, as the two bear different *nomen*). Caesar sent one of his subordinate commanders, Gaius Curio, from Sicily along with two legions and 500 cavalrymen to seize control of the province. These soldiers were men who had initially fought alongside the pro-Pompeians at Corfinium, but who had defected over to Caesar's side. Some of them were soldiers that Sextus Varus had commanded during that siege. Attempting to appeal to their loyalties, Sextus Varus rode up and around them, exhorting them not to shed the blood of the men that they had formerly fought alongside, nor should they continue to fight in the service of their old enemy. Adding to this, he made promises of pardon if they would abandon Caesar and rejoin the pro-Pompeian side, but his pleas and promises fell on deaf ears. The anti-Caesarians were again defeated in battle. Sextus Varus was again captured and pardoned, which was remarkable since Caesar was unlikely to grant mercy a second time. Publius Attius Varus fled to Spain, and was eventually killed at the Battle of Munda, where his head was presented to Caesar. After Caesar's murder,

Sextus Varus fought against Marcus Antonius and Gaius Octavianus at the Battle of Philippi, a battle that he wouldn't survive. It's been suggested that, given that he fought with those who had assassinated Caesar, he might have been one of those who plunged his dagger into the dictator's body on the Ides of March. At Philippi, when he saw that the battle was lost, Sextus Varus had himself killed rather than surrender to Antonius and Octavianus. 'Varus first covered himself with the insignia of his offices and then forced his freedman to commit the deed.'[3]

With his father dead, young Publius may have been raised by a supposed uncle named Quintilius Varus who was documented as living in the well-to-do town of Tivoli.

He appears to have been a lawyer from [the city of] Cremona in northern Italy, certainly a patron of the arts, a friend of [the poet] Virgil, rich enough to have a house at Tivoli (though of the equestrian, not senatorial class), and well-known enough for Horace to dedicate at least one poem to him...Although there is no direct literary corroboration for a connection with our [Publius] Quinctilius Varus, he has been popularly tied to the town. The Via Quintilio Varo cross the Via Valeria, and the church of S. Maria di Quintiliolo sits on the remains of what is popularly thought to have been his villa. It is at least plausible that Varus inherited the estate in Tivoli on [his uncle] Quintilius' death in 11 BC.[4]

Given that he may have been raised by a lawyer, it shouldn't be surprising that Varus would grow up to be an ambitious bureaucrat. Eager to get into high positions in the Roman political ladder, Varus decided to align himself with Octavianus and the new order. The young man must have made an unforgettable impression on the newly-crowned emperor, since Octavianus was the sort of man who neither forgave nor forgot. Considering that his father had fought against firstly Octavianus' uncle and secondly against himself, one would naturally think that the young Varus would be permanently barred from taking any part in governance due to his association with his father. But Publius Varus must have had something to offer, otherwise Octavianus would have cast him aside. Perhaps his upbringing by a prominent lawyer and art patron helped to enhance his standing as well as his knowledge of law and the arts. So, Octavianus took a risk and took the young Publius under his wings. His loyalty was rewarded handsomely.

Varus also had three sisters, all of them named Quinctilia (Roman women were always named in reference to the family's *nomen*, which makes personal identification rather difficult when there are multiple women with the same name), and thankfully we know something about them, which is unusual since Roman sources usually write about men and mostly leave women out of the picture. Varus' connections with the ruling family in Rome helped to secure his sisters' marriage to many prominent men of the day. The oldest married Lucius Asprenas, a close associate of Caesar Augustus. Their son Lucius Nonius Asprenas, Varus' nephew, would eventually obtain a military command in Germania and act as one of Varus' deputies. The middle sister married Cornelius Dolabella, another man affiliated with the emperor who fought alongside him in the civil war against Marcus Antonius. The youngest sister married Augustus' nephew Sextus Appuleius, a prominent politician and administrator who had a distinguished career, having been appointed as a provincial governor in Spain, Asia Minor, and the Balkans.[5]

Varus' Political Career Begins

When Octavianus triumphed over his one-time ally Marcus Antonius in 31 BC and became Rome's first emperor, afterwards taking the title of Augustus, Varus benefitted from his ties to the newly-placed royal family. We first hear of Varus in 22 BC (he would have been 25 years old) as a *quaestor* accompanying Caesar Augustus on a tour of Rome's eastern holdings. Given that the emperor hand-picked his personal secretaries, and he only chose two, Varus would have considered it a high honour to be one of the two selected to accompany the emperor.[6]

It's also believed that Varus acted as a legion commander, but only for a brief period of time, maybe one year. 'A substantial part of the Nineteenth [Legion] was at Dangstetten on the Upper Rhine between c.15 BC and c.8 BC. Its commander was, at that moment, Varus.'[7] If this is true, then Varus was already experienced in Germania, which would have further given him credit when the time came for Augustus to choose a governor of that land. However, by the time that he became Governor of Germania Magna, it would be twenty years after his brief stint as a legion commander, and chances are everyone there would have forgotten all about him. If it is true that Varus acted as a legion commander, it must mean that, at one time, he had been elected as a praetor, because this was the lowest-ranking office which granted its bearer the right of *imperium*, the right to command troops. Since you needed to be at least 39 years old in order to hold this office, this must mean that Varus must have held this office at the earliest in the year 7 BC. But this is in contradiction with Lendering's assertion that the 19th Legion was under Varus' command sometime between 15–8 BC. Moreover, it is also cutting very close to when Varus was appointed as the Governor of Africa, if he wasn't *already* appointed by this point.

In 14 BC, aged 32, Varus married Vipsania Marcella, who was the sister-in-law to Caesar Augustus' stepson, the famous general Tiberius Claudius Nero, and the daughter of Augustus' best friend Marcus Agrippa. Varus had been married beforehand, but his first wife's name is unknown. The next year in 13 BC, Varus was made a Senatorial consul, the first member of his family in over 400 years to hold the consulship, along with Tiberius. When Marcus Agrippa died in 12 BC, Varus delivered the eulogy. When Vipsania Marcella died, Varus re-married, this time to Claudia Pulchra, Augustus' grand-niece. Together they would have a son named Publius Quinctilius Varus the Younger.[8]

Governor of Africa

In the year 9, 8, or 7 BC, depending on which source you believe, Varus was made the governor of the province of Africa. The name of the province is somewhat misleading; to the system of Roman governance, Africa referred not to the continent, but to a specific province comprised of the northern half of Tunisia and a narrow strip of land stretching along the coast of what is now western Libya. Its capital was Carthage, rebuilt after the first one was destroyed and famously had the surrounding landscape sown with salt to prevent crops from growing there in the future. Technically, Varus' title would have been 'Proconsul of Africa', since a *proconsul* was a governor who had once served as a consul in the Roman Senate in the past. Not much is known about his administration since he occupied this post for only two years and nothing particularly noteworthy or exciting seems to have happened during that time. Africa had been a Roman province since the destruction of the Carthaginian Empire in 146 BC, so the province was thoroughly Romanized by this point. It has been proposed that his former brother-in-law Tiberius, the emperor's stepson, arranged it so that Varus would be made the governor.[9] Varus' connections to the imperial family were paying off.

Africa was a very important province due to the vast quantities of grain that came from that region. People today are baffled by this revelation, and rightly so since today the North African coastline is almost entirely desert, but in ancient times, North Africa was one of the major breadbaskets of the empire. The inhabitants of the city of Rome consumed an estimated 8,000 tons of grain per week, with large cargo ships transporting the grain across the Mediterranean. Julius Caesar reported that the province of Africa exported over 8,800 tons of grain and over 264,000 gallons of olive oil per year. As Governor, it was Varus' job to keep the grain and other goods flowing. Rome's very survival depended on it.[10]

Africa was a prestigious post, but also a politically dangerous one. Some Roman provinces were controlled by the emperor while others where controlled by the Senate, but Africa was jointly controlled by both, and the two often quarrelled. So, Varus was in a precarious position of conducting himself in order to please both parties.[11] Varus also presumably had to conduct diplomatic relations with the western vassal state of

Figure 2. Publius Quinctilius Varus. No known statues or other artwork from ancient times depicts this man. The only physical evidence that we have of him are coins that bear his image. This coin is dated to his governorship of the province of Africa. Römisch-Germanisches Zentralmuseum. Mainz, Germany. (*Photo by Jona Lendering, used with permission*)

Mauretania. I imagine trade extended to this area, which helped to increase the province's wealth, so Varus had to play a diplomatic dance in order to ensure that the trade routes stayed open, and to ensure Mauretania's fealty to Rome.

Not only was Varus' appointment as Governor of Africa a test of his ability, both in terms of pleasing both the emperor and Senate at the same time as well as keeping production and tax collection running like clockwork, but it was a test of loyalty as well. Varus administered a region that was both monetarily wealthy due to trading goods as well as vital for Rome's existence due to the grain supply. A governor in control of such a wealthy province might be tempted to rebel.[12] Augustus must have waited anxiously, testing to see if Varus really was the friend that he professed to be. When no troubles occurred, the emperor must have breathed a sigh of relief. Varus could be trusted. He had passed his audition as a provincial governor. Knowing that he could hold his own, the emperor re-assigned Varus to a tougher post.

Governor of Syria

In either 7 or 6 BC, Varus was made Governor of Syria, its capital in Antioch. Syria had been annexed as a Roman province in 64 BC following Rome's victory in the Third Mithridatic War. Like Africa, Syria was fabulously wealthy due to its strategic location on the east-west trade routes, and was thoroughly Romanized by this time. However, the Syrian governor had to not only take care of affairs within the borders of the province of Syria itself, but also conduct diplomacy with the various client kingdoms that bordered it, trying desperately to keep the peace. A roiling mix of nationalities and political interests, the region seemed to be just a hair's breadth away from chaos at every glance. Syria needed a strong person to merely keep order, let alone make the province profitable for the Roman treasury. Moreover, to the east lay the formidable Parthian Empire, Rome's chief enemy in that region who was far more dangerous than the Saharan nomads that occasionally raided African villages. Not so long ago, a large Roman army had been utterly butchered by the Parthians at the Battle of Carrhae in 53 BC, the result of a high-stakes military gamble gone horribly wrong, and it must have lingered in the minds of every provincial governor of Syria since then. A Cold War tension perpetually existed in the region. As such, Varus needed to constantly be on guard for any sign of conflict.[13]

If Varus was doing a good job as Governor of Africa, why remove him? Why not keep him there in control for as long as he was able to perform? I believe that both the emperor and the Senate were gauging his abilities as an administrator. If he managed to conduct himself well, it would look very good on his political record, and so, Varus was given a shot as Syria's governor. One wonders what his reaction was when he was told of his newest assignment.

As Governor of Syria, Varus had to deal with several problematic states: Cappadocia to the north, Armenia to the northeast, and the Parthian Empire to the east. However, perhaps the most difficult of Rome's regional client kingdoms to appease lay in the south – the Kingdom of Judea (modern-day Israel), its capital in Jerusalem. Judea's leader was the infamous King Herod I, sometimes known as Herod the Great, who had been placed on the throne of Judea by the Romans as a puppet ruler three decades before. Even as far as ancient standards go, Herod was ruthless – some would say unnecessarily ruthless – when it came to exacting his will.[14]

By now, Herod was in his late 60s. In the last years of his life, the paranoid tyrant was suffering in extreme pain from multiple ailments. Some people doubtless thought that it was divine justice. Herod had only recently and narrowly escaped an assassination attempt by his second wife's sons, and afterwards had all of them executed. Now, the heir to the throne, Prince Antipater, was viewed as having a hand in the plot as well. The Jewish historian Josephus says that Varus 'happened to be in the palace'[15] at that time when it was decided that Prince Antipater was to be put on trial. The reasons for Varus' visit to Jerusalem aren't known, but perhaps he was making the rounds of the various territories under his jurisdiction, making sure that all was well before he really got down to business as Syria's governor. Varus would act as one of the judges, and Herod himself would act as the other judge – a clear sign that the trial was a sham. Antipater was found guilty of trying to poison his father and was imprisoned. Herod made another of his sons, Prince Antipas, his heir.[16]

In the year 4 BC, it looked as though the old tyrant was finally on his last legs. Believing that the king was powerless to do anything, the people began to rise up against Herod's oppressive rule. One of the more famous acts of defiance occurred in Jerusalem and was led by two well-educated and well-respected rabbis: Judah ben Sariphai and Matthias ben Margaloth. These two men were especially popular with the youth of the city, and using that influence, they preached sedition among their followers. The two rabbis became even more fervent when they received false information that King Herod had died. They decided that it was time to strike a blow for God.[17]

Several years earlier, as a gesture of his fealty to Rome, King Herod had placed a large gold eagle statue atop the main gate of the Great Temple in Jerusalem – all people who wished to pray there had to walk under it. It was a gesture that was asking for trouble. First, Jewish religious law strictly forbade images of any living persons or things in or on temples. Second, the eagle was the symbol of Rome, and its presence at the most holy Jewish site symbolized that Rome was now no longer just a vague overlord that allowed the Jews to do whatever they pleased as long as they were loyal to Caesar, but was interfering in their personal lives as well. Third, Herod placing the eagle there as a sign of favour to Rome clearly showed that the Jews were no longer in control of their own country. It was Caesar Augustus, not Herod, who was their real master. Everything had to be done by the emperor's consent. The Jews were, in essence, second-class subjects in their own country. This was a sentiment that may have been more-or-less understood by everyone prior to this incident, but with the erection of the Roman eagle atop the temple gate, it was now blatantly obvious. Fourth, since the eagle was placed atop the temple gate, anyone who wanted to pray inside would have to walk under the eagle – a humiliating act of subservience.[18]

As long as King Herod was alive and well, everyone had to grudgingly submit, but now with Herod believed to be dead, it was felt that the time was right to tear down this hated symbol of Roman domination. And so, in broad daylight and in front of an ever-growing crowd of onlookers, a group of young men climbed to the top of the gate and hacked the eagle to pieces with axes – a gesture of *violent* defiance. The soldiers who guarded the temple rushed forward and arrested forty of the demonstrators, who were brought before Herod and thereafter executed.[19]

Herod's physical and mental state became markedly worse after this incident. In one of his final acts, he ordered Prince Antipater (who was still in prison and was hoping to be freed once his father died) to be executed and that his will should be changed. Later that year, after languishing in extreme pain for a long time, his body slowly deteriorating, King Herod finally died. Upon his death, Judea exploded.[20]

Part of the reason why had to do with Herod's last wishes. His will stated that the kingdom of Judea was to be divided up amongst his sons: Prince Archelaus would be officially crowned as his father's successor, but he would only rule over the districts of Judea and Samaria; Prince Antipas would rule over the districts of Galilee and Perea; Prince Philip would rule over the remaining districts of Golan, Trachan, Bathan, and Paneas. Although this was the last will and testament of King Herod, it was not set in stone just yet. As a client kingdom of Rome, it would be up to Caesar Augustus, not the Judean government, to decide who would take the Judean throne after Herod. The old king's will would not be official unless Augustus said it was.

After throwing a lavish funeral festival for his father (which had been ordered by Herod in his will), Prince Archelaus stood before the people and promised to grant their various petitions. But the spectre of the 'eagle incident' still hung over Judea. Certain people lamented that others had been punished for adhering to God's law, and demanded that Herod's associates should be punished. The chief priest was especially targeted for this plan, and it was decided that he should be removed from his post and another man put in his place.[21]

When Archelaus heard about these plans, he was angry but decided not to do anything rash. He'd go to Rome first, be officially crowned, and *then* do something about these plots when he returned. When he and his entourage arrived in Judea's port-city of Caesarea, a man named Sabinus, the procurator of Syria, met them along with a body of Roman soldiers. He told Archelaus that he had been ordered by Governor Varus, who himself was already on his way, to go to the palace and place Herod's personal possessions in safe keeping. But Sabinus wished to claim Herod's treasures for himself. After Archelaus and his company left, Sabinus raced to the palace and seized all of Herod's possessions, and then ordered the fortresses to be handed over to him as well.[22]

At around the same time, the Jews began to launch another revolt, most likely a retaliatory measure against Sabinus' actions, but it had a messianic tint to it, since a man named Simon proclaimed himself King. It was now Pentecost, the holy day commemorating the fiftieth day following Passover, and the Jews began converging on Jerusalem. Sabinus was surrounded. His small body of soldiers fought against the Jewish rebels, but when the Romans began to take heavy casualties, they decided to set fire to the temple, killing many people, and then plundering it afterwards. The reaction was instant – more people came, surrounding Sabinus' stronghold. They told him that if he and his men would leave right now, they would not be harmed. Sabinus decided to stay, hoping that Varus would come with his legions.[23]

This was just the sort of thing that Varus feared would happen ever since he became Governor of Syria two years earlier – Judea was ripping itself apart. Josephus tells us that Varus had a feeling that something was brewing beforehand.[24] When word reached him that a revolt was in progress, he feared that the single legion that was posted in Judea would be over-run, and knew that he had to do something very quickly in order to restore order to the region.

Varus quickly mobilized for battle. Syria was home to the 3rd, 6th, 10th, and 12th Legions. Varus gathered together two legions and all of the cavalry detachments from each of the four legions (roughly 10,000 infantry and 480 horsemen on paper, but likely much less than that in reality) and marched them to Ptolemais (modern-day Acre, Israel). Gathering reinforcements along the way, his men destroyed the towns of Sepphoris and Emmaus. 2,000 Jews were crucified. Sabinus fled and disappeared.[25] Not long afterwards, Varus ceased to be Governor of Syria.

Why had Varus been taken out of his post as Governor of Syria? It certainly wasn't because of his harsh treatment of the Jewish rebels. His actions were perfectly in accord with what was expected of a Roman governor when a region rose in revolt. So if not for this reason, why was he given the boot? One hypothesis is that he may have been engaged in criminal activity. Paterculus states that when Varus first arrived in Syria, he was poor and the province was rich, but when he left, he was rich and the province was poor.[26] Although it isn't stated if he was actually accused by the imperial authorities of lining his pockets, one wonders if he was officially charged with embezzlement and had to stand trial. If he was, regardless of whether he was found guilty or innocent, the trial would have damaged his prestige and credibility in the region. One of the things that lead to a province rising up against Rome is being led by a governor who the people believe is corrupt; that sort of thing is just asking for trouble. So, Varus may have been removed before any further damage could be done there. If he was found guilty of embezzlement, it's likely he would have been barred from any other administrative post to prevent him from taking any more money. The fact that he was given a new job later in life – Governor of Germania Magna – shows that he may have been cleared of the charges if a trial occurred and that his appointment was a safe risk.

Although Varus' treatment of the Jews may have been condoned by the imperial government as a governor merely taking the necessary measures when countering a revolt, word of his actions may have spread throughout the entire East, and the people living there now knew what he would do if he felt the province was in disorder. An accusation of embezzlement would have only escalated the people's dislike for Varus, for if he both robbed the treasury and used force, he would have been seen as a tyrannical administrator, and no one willingly submits to such authority. Resistance and anti-Roman demonstrations would have increased. Moreover, if the situation in the East became too chaotic, the Parthians might use this to their advantage and strike the Roman frontier. Augustus must have realized that as long as Varus remained in Syria, the entire eastern Mediterranean would be put into a position of increasing jeopardy. For the sake of the overall security of the empire, Varus had to go.

Governor of Germania Magna

There are no records of any political positions that Varus held between 4 BC (the date when he supposedly left Syria) to 6 AD. Actually, we have scant record in regards to much of Roman history during this BC–AD transition period. It seems that Varus was not given any administrative posts for a decade, perhaps with the emperor hoping that all would be forgotten if Varus laid low for a while. One wonders what he did during that time. Was he unemployed for ten years, living off of his private fortune? Due to his close connections with the imperial family, it's almost certain that Augustus gave Varus some sort of monetary stipend during this time. And so Varus may have become what many of us would call 'the idle rich', if indeed he was rich. Would Augustus have allowed his patrician friend to live the high-class aristocratic lifestyle that was familiar to him, or would he have had to economize due to a minimal allowance? These are questions that may never be answered. What we do know is that in 3 BC, assumed to be one year after he was fired from his post in Syria, Varus remarried. His newest bride was Claudia Pulchra, Caesar Augustus' grand-niece.[27] This shows that Augustus still kept his old associate close, even if he didn't hold a post within the imperial infrastructure.

But Augustus presumably didn't want to lose a capable and experienced administrator, so what was he to do with Varus? Augustus needed to send him somewhere where he could carry out his duties, preferably a place where no one knew who he was. Perhaps that is the reason why Varus was kept out of the public eye for so long, with the emperor hoping that time would fade the memory of his actions. Possibly in 6 AD, it was decided that Varus could be put to good use by administering one of Rome's newest possessions, across the Rhine.

The region called *Germania Magna*, 'Great/Large Germany', stretched from the Rhine to the Elbe Rivers. There were already two other areas within the Roman Empire that were referred to as 'Germania'. Within the eastern Gallic province of Belgica, which had been taken by Julius Caesar over fifty years earlier, Augustus had established two military operation zones sometime between 16–13 BC, which he dubbed 'Germania Superior' and 'Germania Inferior'. These areas would be controlled and patrolled by the Roman Army, and the commanders would be subordinate to the governor of Belgica. In either 83 or 84 AD, Emperor Domitian split the province of Belgica in half and turned these military zones into official provinces.[28]

The region known as Germania Magna had only been under Roman possession for the past fifteen or so years, since Drusus led his legions into this land. However, it is uncertain as to whether this land was a full-fledged Roman province when Varus arrived, or if it was merely an occupied territory under military jurisdiction. Consequently, it is also unclear if Varus was an actual governor of Germania Magna, or if he was a military commander who was in charge of overseeing affairs there until an actual administration took over.

The exact nature of Varus' job in Germania has been the subject of much academic debate. It certainly doesn't help that the ancient sources don't provide a concrete answer. The ancient Latin word for 'governor' is *praepositus*, but this word is not used anywhere in connection with Varus, or indeed any of the people who came before him. For example, the Roman historian Paterculus uses the phrase '...*ubi ante triennium sub M. Vinicio, avo tuo, clarissimo viro, immensum exarserat bellum*' ('...where three years before under Marcus Vinicius, your grandfather, the most eminent man, an immense war erupted').[29] He doesn't list any office but merely states that the running of Germania was 'under' Marcus Vinicius, meaning that he could have been a governor, but he also could have been a military commandant in charge of administering the region *de facto* until a real full-fledged administration could take over. Paterculus says the same of Varus, where he is described as *praeesse*, which means rather vaguely 'in charge'.[30] The Greco-Roman historian Cassius Dio calls Gaius Sentius Saturninus, the man who presided over Germania immediately before Varus arrived, as 'the governor of Germany',[31] but Paterculus describes Saturninus as being a legion commander, not a governor.[32]

The vague and confusing nature of the ancient sources has led to a multitude of opinions from modern historians. Jona Lendering states Germania Magna was a province since Drusus' conquests, though he states that the 'governor' ruled that land only in name since 'Germania Magna' technically didn't exist yet. According to him, the title of 'Governor of Germania Magna' had been given to Drusus even before he started the war, and the troops that he would use in the battles to come would henceforth be used as the occupying force when the battles were over.[33] Adrian Murdoch doesn't actually state that there were official governors in Germania Magna before Varus; he just says that there were people who presided over the territory.[34] Whether these were governors or simply military commanders entrusted to command the occupying force and keep the peace until civilian officials and administrators could be sent, it isn't clear.

Personally, I believe that Varus was Germania Magna's first official governor, and that those who came before were merely army commanders entrusted as leaders of the territory until it was properly developed into a province. My reasoning for this comes from two points. First, based upon ancient descriptions of what Varus did while there, his work appears to have been mostly administrative, not militaristic. Second, Varus had two military commanders assigned to the province, which clearly shows a division of work between military and administrative personnel.

Record of what had happened to those unfortunates in Judea would have been good news for Varus' credentials – should trouble arise in Germania, this was a man who had no qualms about dispensing the characteristically harsh Roman justice. By all means, therefore, Publius Quinctilius Varus seemed like the perfect man for the job as the first official governor of Germania Magna. When Varus arrived there, he would be helped by a Germanic prince acting as his advisor. His name was Arminius.

Chapter Four

Arminius

The Name

It's something of a hobby for etymologists (people who are interested in the origins and meanings of words) to decipher the meaning of the names of famous historical people, and there has been a long-standing debate among historians and etymologists about what the name 'Arminius' means. Firstly, it must be stated that 'Arminius' was not his real name, or at least modern historians and etymologists don't think so. It certainly wasn't Hermann, as modern Germans claim. His real name might have been Erminameraz,[1] a hypothesis that was first put forward in 1982, and since there's no way to prove or disprove it, I'm going to run with this idea.

It wasn't unusual for barbarians in the service of Rome to have two different names, one that they used among their own people, and one used when in the company of the Romans. For example, the name of the man who slew King Adaulphus of the Visigoths in 415 AD was named both Euervulf and Dubius, the former being his Gothic name and the latter Roman.[2] It's perfectly reasonable, therefore, that Erminameraz used his birthright name when among his fellow Germans and referred to himself as Arminius when among the Romans.

What do these names mean? Since our knowledge of early Germanic languages is understandably limited, translating his two names is difficult. Let's first take his hypothetical name Erminameraz. *Ermin-* is a prefix meaning 'the eminent',[3] and is therefore a title, similar to the modern usage of 'His Highness' when addressing a prince of a royal household. Since Arminius is clearly referred to as a prince in the historic records, this explanation is valid. It is likely that Germanic princes, or at least princes within the Cherusci tribe, had names that began with this prefix. Now for the remainder of his name: *-ameraz*. The first two syllables of *-ameraz*, 'amer', could be related to the Proto-Germanic *hamur*, or 'hammer', but this isn't likely. -*Meraz* and -*merus*, which is a section of his father's name (Latinized as Segimerus, but likely Sigimeriz in original Germanic), look similar and could possibly mean the same thing, but as I state later in this book, changing just one letter in a word can make the two words mean entirely different things. The Gothic (one of the Germanic languages) word -*mers* means 'having great authority, power, fame, and influence'. -*Mers* could be a variation of the Germanic words -*merus* or -*meraz*. The Latin equivalent of this word's definition would be *auctoritas*. The first 'a' in -*ameraz* could be an article meaning 'of, that, which is'. So, the name can be broken down into *Ermin* + *a* + *meraz*, translated as 'the eminent one of great *auctoritas*'. I highly doubt that as a child, the young prince would have been born with a name describing him as having a great deal of influence and power among his people. This means that either it was a name that he took later in life or it is part of his title of *ermin*, 'the eminent'. Perhaps Erminameraz was a title given to a chief's firstborn son, or to the heir of the tribe's throne. Either way, Erminameraz as a whole looks more like a title rather than a name.

As far as the name *Arminius* goes, several ideas have been put forward in the past. One author proposes that his name might somehow be connected to a Roman family with a similar name, the *gens* Arminia. As stated earlier, Arminius served as an auxiliary commander in the Roman Army. While the leaders of small ethnic-based auxiliary units (like an auxiliary century) likely belonged to the same tribe that they led, it was common practice for the overall commander of multiple auxiliary units (like an auxiliary cohort) to be a Roman citizen, usually a former legion officer. Arminius' superior might have been a Roman military tribune with the *nomen* Arminius, and when the young German prince became a Roman citizen, he adopted the name of his commander. It's an interesting and potentially valid hypothesis.[4]

Another hypothesis which has been discarded has been 'the Armenian'. This translation has been laughed at by historians and linguists, though I should warn that this translation should not be so quickly discarded. Obviously, his name doesn't mean 'the Armenian' *literally* since Arminius was a German, but there is another connection to this title. A couple of historians have recently proposed that Arminius' name is a reference to *armenium*, also known as azurite. This is a vivid ultramarine blue dye that was created by processing it from a certain mineral found in Armenia – so there *is* a slight connection. It's been put foward that Arminius was named after this blue colour because of his Germanic blue eyes. It's a view that has credibility. In fact, the Greek historian Strabo, who was the earliest historian to write of the events surrounding the Battle of Teutoburg, writes down the name as Arm*e*nius, not Arm*i*nius. So too does Publius Florus in his *Epitome.*[5]

Arminius might also be a Latinized corruption of the Lombardic word *arimannus*, which means 'army man' or 'fighting man', which would be a fitting name for one who saw military service.[6] However, because this is specifically a term used in the Lombard language, and moreover a term used in the eighth century AD, this makes it unlikely that *arimannus* was the origin for Arminius' name. Another idea is that Arminius might be a corruption of Herimannus, a Germanic god of war.[7] *Herimannus* and *arimannus* look eerily similar. Also, the early Christian cleric Dionysius Afer called the Germans *areimaneis*, meaning 'warlike men' in Greek,[8] and this word is very similar to *arimannus* in how it's spelled, pronounced, and translated. Saint Gregory Nazianzen also used *areimaneis* when describing the followers of Arianism.[9] It seems clear, therefore, that some version or another of *arimannus* existed in Germanic vocabulary, all meaning roughly the same thing.

And now for my own contribution to the debate regarding the name 'Arminius'. I believe that there's no reason to think that these names were exclusive. The Romans, especially their writers, loved puns and plays-on-words, and the similarities between these two words, both of which applied to Erminameraz in terms of his character, would have been immediately noted. Therefore, they would have called him Arminius because both *armenius* and *arimannus* suited him. So, his name essentially would have meant 'the Blue-Eyed Fighting Man'. Very appropriate.

Arminius and his Family

Considering that Arminius has become such a famous figure in the study of ancient and military history, it is surprising how little we actually know about him. Arminius, or Erminameraz as his name actually might have been, was born in 16 BC, the son of Segimerus (his real name was probably Sigimeriz, meaning 'victory-renowned'), one of the clan chiefs among the Cherusci tribe. Despite popular conception, it has never been stated that Segimerus was the chief of the Cherusci tribe as a whole, but was merely the chief of one clan within the Cherusci.[10]

Details on Arminius' family are sketchy. We don't know much about Arminius' father, and we know even less about his mother. All we know about her was that she was still alive during Rome's revenge campaign against the Germans in the years after the Battle of Teutoburg, and that she supported Arminius' cause for the liberation and freedom of Germania from Roman domination. This is the only mention of her in the ancient sources; we have no idea what her name was, or what happened to her afterwards. Arminius also had an uncle named Inguiomerus (possibly an early version of the name Ingmar), and we only know a little about him from Tacitus' writings. He also supported his nephew's cause, and would fight alongside him during his campaign against the Romans, although he was hot-headed and impetuous and often disregarded his nephew's counsel for the sake of glory and bravado. We'll be discussing him in more detail later on.[11]

Arminius had a younger brother who is only known to us as Flavus. Obviously it is a Roman name, or rather a nickname, since the Latin word *flavus* literally means 'yellow', no doubt a reference to the boy's blonde hair. Since his brother was also a tribal prince, it is certain that Flavus would have borne a name that began with the prefix *ermin-*, though it is beyond our knowledge to know what his whole name would have been. The year of Flavus' birth is not recorded, so we don't know how much younger Flavus was in relation to his brother.

Both Arminius and Flavus served in the Roman Army under the esteemed commander Tiberius Claudius Nero in the Great Illyrian Revolt, which lasted from 6 to 9 AD. Tacitus comments that Flavus served as a scout. When Arminius left the Roman Army to go back home, the day he left was probably the last time that he ever saw his younger brother until several years later when they would find themselves on opposite sides of the battlefield. By *that* time, they were bitter enemies because Flavus refused to join his brother in his rebellion and stayed loyal to Rome. Tacitus records that Flavus had lost one of his eyes during a battle, presumably with the Illyrians sometime between 7–9 AD, after his brother had already left the Balkans for Germany – when the two met, Arminius questioned his brother about his injury, indicating that the injury was not suffered when Arminius was still fighting in Illyria, and therefore, Arminius would not have known about it. Later in life, Flavus would have a son named Italicus, who was born and raised in Rome. In 47 AD, Emperor Claudius made Italicus the leader of the Cherusci on the tribe's request because Italicus was the sole surviving member of the royal family.[12]

Strabo also makes reference to another possible brother of Arminius named Sesithacus. He is an enigmatic and frustrating character to understand because there is a great deal of confusion surrounding who exactly this person is. Strabo is the only ancient author who mentions Sesithacus by name, and the historian Tacitus makes a vague allusion to a person who might also be this man. Strabo says in his account that a man named Sesithacus was the son of Segimerus, a chief of the Cherusci. We know that Arminius' father was named Segimerus and that he was a Cherusci clan chief, so that could mean that Sesithacus was Arminius' brother. It isn't known whether this was Arminius' older or younger brother, or if he was possibly a half-brother or step-brother, or maybe an illegitimate son of Segimerus. What is stated is that Sesithacus took part in Arminius' rebellion against the Romans, because he was taken prisoner by the Roman commander Germanicus several years later. Sesithacus was married to Rhamis, who was the daughter of the Chatti chief Ucromir. Both Sesithacus and his wife were taken prisoner during Rome's revenge campaign and were prisoners-on-parade in Germanicus' triumph in 17 AD. History does not record what happened to them afterwards.[13]

Tacitus' account provides some intriguing but vague information. He states that during Rome's revenge campaign following the Battle of Teutoburg, the Roman officer Stertinius was sent to officially receive the surrender of Segimerus and his son – the son's name isn't mentioned in this source. Segimerus is described as being the brother of Segestes (whose name possibly means 'master of victory', derived from the Germanic *sig*, 'victory' and the Old Frankish *gastes*, 'master'). Segestes was one of the clan chiefs of the Cherusci tribe, a staunch supporter of the Roman Empire, and one of Arminius' main antagonists. Stertinius led both Segimerus and his son to Oppidum Ubiorum, the settlement that had been established for the Ubian tribe on the banks of the Rhine years earlier. Here, official pardons were given to both men, although Tacitus states that the Romans were reluctant to grant a pardon to Segimerus' son because he had defiled Varus' body. How he did it isn't described, but we know that after the Battle of Teutoburg, Varus' head was cut off – this un-named nephew of Segestes might have committed this act.[14]

There are two questions that must be answered when looking at these two sources. First, is Arminius' father Segimerus the same as the man named as Segestes' brother? Second, is Sesithacus the same man that Tacitus makes reference to? It seems clear that Arminius' father Segimerus and Segestes' brother Segimerus were not the same person, even though both are called Cherusci chiefs. They were simply two different men who happened to have the same name. There is no mention of Segestes being addressed or referred to as Arminius' uncle in any ancient source. Only Inguiomerus is referred to as Arminius' uncle, and since Segestes is not referred to in that fashion, one can assume that Segestes and Arminius were not related, and consequently, Arminius and Sesithacus were not related to each other either. Furthermore, while Sesithacus' father is named Segimerus in Strabo's account, I have seen earlier editions of Strabo's work in which the name is written not as Segimerus but as Aegimerus. I've seen this spelling used in a few early editions, so I'm confident that it is not a one-off publisher's typo. So, this makes Sesithacus' identity clearer. Sesithacus was _not_ Arminius' brother, and not even a relative. Sesithacus was the son of Segestes' brother Aegimerus, who was a chief among the Cherusci tribe – it isn't stated if he was a village chief or clan chief or whatever, but I'll assume he was a clan chief, since village chiefs weren't that prominent and their social position would not have been mentioned unless absolutely necessary.

What did Arminius look like? The closest thing to an actual description of Arminius' appearance and personal character comes from the Roman historian Paterculus. He describes the future rebel leader as a young man of noble birth, brave, alert, and intelligent.[15] However, he makes no detailed mention of his physical appearance other than he was young, a rather obvious fact considering his birth date. There is a marble bust on display in the Capitoline Museum in Rome, Italy which has been attributed to this Germanic prince. It's likely that this work of sculpture might not be specifically of Prince Arminius at all, but rather a generalized artistic rendering of what a Germanic barbarian was believed to have looked like; the artist is unknown. The bust of this man, whoever he might be, is portrayed with long curly hair covering his ears and reaching just to the chin-line. The head faces towards his right. He has a full face and somewhat thick lips, and there are hints of facial hair forming a moustache and beard, making it appear that he hasn't shaved in a few days. This feature is very telling since Roman men were almost always clean-shaven and had short hair, and regarded long hair and facial hair as primitive and uncouth. He is evidently very strong, with a thick muscular neck and strong shoulders and pectorals. This image appears to have been the Roman archetype of what a Germanic barbarian was supposed to be like – strong and wild.

In the Service of Rome

The date when Arminius entered Roman service is speculative. He may have been taken to Rome as a hostage following Rome's Germanic campaign, which would have been around 6 BC. If so, Arminius would have been 10 years old. It's also possible that Arminius was taken away into the Roman Army following the defeat of the Cherusci in 4 AD by Marcus Vinicius and Tiberius Claudius Nero. If this date for Arminius' entry into Rome's service is true, then Arminius would have been 20 years old. There's no definite way of knowing which the right answer is, but I'm leaning towards the first option, because if he had been taken away in 4 AD, it would have given him just two years to learn Latin and become fully acquainted with Roman military tactics. If it was the latter, Arminius must either have been very bright and passed his studies with flying colours, or else he was rushed into military service, and although Paterculus says that Arminius was unusually gifted for a barbarian, as he puts it, such a crammed time frame doesn't sound believable. Therefore, I believe that the most likely scenario is that he was taken into Roman custody following the end of Drusus' and Tiberius' Germanic campaign, and not following the rebellion which occurred later.

As a hostage of Rome, Arminius would have been educated in Latin if he wasn't knowledgeable in it already, Roman culture, and the Roman military. Given his age, he must have spent a few years in the Army, although we know hardly anything about his military service. His training was soon put to the test, because Arminius served as an auxiliary commander in the Great Illyrian Revolt of 6–9 AD.[16] It's also commonly held that Arminius was an auxiliary *cavalry* commander,[17] which would make sense given the Cherusci's prevalence for horsemen, although I must state that the subject of infantry or cavalry is never explicitly stated in the ancient accounts. It is likely during this service that Erminameraz acquired the name 'Arminius'. He would have led his own men, the Cherusci, into battle, since auxiliary battalions comprised of tribal warriors were often led by their own chiefs. They may have even been allowed to take their own equipment with them, and Rome was more than happy to not spend its money providing things when they could be obtained for free.[18]

Arminius' service in the rebellion, however, must have been quite limited, as he acted as one of Varus' companions during his administration as Governor of Germania Magna. So it's likely that he only saw service for the year 6 AD, and then was dispatched to Germania. Still, he must have distinguished himself greatly during his brief one-year (if even that long; he possibly saw service only for a few months) stint on the battlefield. Not only was he made a Roman citizen, which gave him the right to vote, perhaps taking the name of Gaius Julius Arminius,[19] but he was also knighted into the Equestrian Order,[20] which meant that he could own property within the empire's borders. Given that Cherusci land was now Roman land, I'm assuming that the property in question was in fact the property his family *already* owned, and given that he was a member of the royal family, I imagine that he held a fairly sizable tract of land. These were impressive rewards for a man who was only 22 years old at the time, and one who was not even born a Roman. Most Roman men could only dream of getting citizenship, let alone be knighted. However, something must be stated. According to Roman law, non-citizens like Arminius who acted as auxiliaries in the Roman Army could obtain citizenship only after completing a full term of twenty-five years of military service. Arminius certainly did not spend twenty-five years in the saddle of his warhorse, so it seems that the Romans bent the rules in Arminius' favour, granting him citizenship before his term was completed. His battlefield achievements must have been impressive, even Achillean. However, if Arminius really was the epic horse-riding sword-wielding Wagnerian hero that he's taken to be, the Romans make stark mention of it. Remember that accounts pertaining to Arminius' life were made *after* the Battle of Teutoburg, and the Romans may have been leery about describing how the leader of a serious rebellion against Rome was once a great warrior who performed mighty, almost god-like deeds on the battlefield, and was rewarded handsomely for it. Therefore, mention of his military service is scant, which is understandably frustrating to modern historians. Still, we cannot ignore the fact that Arminius was made a Roman citizen and was made a member of the knightly class. Despite his youth and barbarian ancestry, Arminius was now regarded as one of the higher-ups in Roman society.

Chapter Five

Germania Under Rome

Rome Encounters the Germans

For many years, the only barbarians that the Romans knew of were the Celts, who inhabited the British Isles, Gaul, northern Spain, Austria, and northern Italy. These two peoples had fought many wars against each other over the years, and were familiar to each other. The Romans were completely ignorant of what lay beyond the Celts' lands, and were unaware of any barbarians that lived in central Europe.

The Romans were first made aware that there was another and possibly more dangerous group of barbarians dwelling to the north during the last years of the second century BC. According to Plutarch, the Roman military, commanded by Gaius Marius, had been busily engaged fighting a war in northern Africa against King Juggurtha of Numidia (the northern half of Algeria). No sooner had word reached Rome of the capture of Juggurtha and the war's end when news suddenly arrived of a great invasion from the barbarian north. However, these savages were not Celts, but were an entirely new group that was completely unknown to the Romans – the Germans. This was Rome's first contact with these people.

The invasion force was comprised of two tribes called the Teutons and the Cimbri, both of which came from Denmark. At first, the reports of their vast number were disbelieved, but soon these reports were held to be correct – 300,000 heavily-armed men were marching southwards into Gaul, with even larger bodies of women and children behind them, searching for a new land which would support such a high population. According to Florus, they were forced to leave their homeland because floods had completely inundated their territory.[1] Plutarch states that the Romans didn't know where these people came from, but later ascertained them to be Germans due to their language, tall stature, and blue eyes.[2] The historian Tacitus, writing his *Germania* in 98 AD, years earlier than Plutarch's *Lives*, may have been the first to write about the Germans having blue eyes,[3] considered to be a stereotypical feature of Germanic peoples even to this day.

The first fight between Roman and German came in 113 BC. The Germans had crossed the Danube, invaded the lands of Celtic tribes who were allied to Rome, and then pushed across the Alps into northeastern Italy. A Roman army, led by the Senatorial consul Gnaeus Papirius Carbo, faced down the Germanic invaders not far from the Adriatic port-city of Aquileia, whereupon he ordered the Cimbri to turn around and evacuate the lands that they recently seized. The Cimbri agreed and prepared to depart. However, not content with simply letting the barbarians leave, Carbo went back on his word and attempted to ambush them at a place called Noreia. In the end, the Roman army was almost exterminated and Carbo barely escaped with his life.[4] The Battle of Noreia was the first time that the Romans and Germans had fought with each other, and it was not a fortuitous beginning for Rome. The Germans left, for the time being, but they would return a few years later.

When the Germans returned, they directed their attention westward to Gaul, and in response, another Roman army was mustered to meet them, this time led by the consul Marcus Junius Silanus. The Germans sent representatives to him, asking for land for their people; in exchange, they said the Republic could 'use their hands and weapons for any purpose it wished'.[5] The Romans refused to grant them any land concessions, and so the Teutons and Cimbri decided to take land by force. This battle, likewise, ended in defeat – the Roman army was destroyed and the camp was seized.[6]

As a further blow against the Republic, the Celtic tribes of east-central Gaul, namely the Helvetians, Tougeni, and Tigourini, exploited this recent defeat to begin their own search for new lands to the west. A Roman army sent to restrain them, led by the consul Lucius Longinus, was thoroughly crushed, resulting in the deaths of Longinus, his second-in-command, and other high-ranking officers. The people of the city of Tolosa (modern-day Toulouse, France) were so frightened and incensed by the recent disasters and the Romans' inability to stand up to the barbarians that the population of the city revolted.[7]

The Romans had suffered three defeats – two at the hands of the Germans, and one at the hands of the Gauls. The Romans suffered a third major defeat

by the Germans at the Battle of Arausio, which would go down as one of
Rome's worst military defeats in its entire history. The battle was fought
in October 105 BC on the banks of the Rhone River in southeastern Gaul.
The Roman army was jointly commanded by Gnaeus Maximus and Quintus
Caepio. However, as the story goes, the two men couldn't stand each other
and argued with each other constantly. As a result, the commanders split
the army in half and defended separate sides of the river. The Roman force
was thoroughly destroyed by the Germans. One ancient source reports that
80,000 Roman soldiers and as many as 40,000 Roman camp followers were
massacred within the course of a single day. Caepio escaped, but upon his
return he was arrested and court-martialled. He was found guilty of being
responsible for this catastrophic defeat, and as a punishment, he was stripped
of all of his powers and had all of his property confiscated.[8]

Plutarch states that the advance of the Germanic barbarians could not be
stopped. The Romans had sent three armies against them, but they had all
been destroyed.

> Their courage and daring made them irresistible, and when they
> engaged in battle they came on with the swiftness and force of fire,
> so that no one could withstand their onset, but all who came in their
> way became their prey and booty, and even many large Roman armies,
> with their commanders, who had been stationed to protect Transalpine
> Gaul, were destroyed ingloriously; indeed, by their feeble resistance
> they were mainly instrumental in drawing the on-rushing Barbarians
> down upon Rome. For when the invaders had conquered those who
> opposed them, and had got abundance of booty, they determined not
> to settle themselves anywhere until they had destroyed Rome and
> ravaged Italy.[9]

In desperation, the Senate re-elected Gaius Marius as Consul, even though
it was against Roman law – a man could only be made Consul once every
ten years, and not any time sooner. But the people refused to listen to those
who decried this decision, because they foresaw 'that this would not be the
first time that the law had given way before the demands of the general
good, and that the present occasion demanded it'.[10] Marius returned

to Rome from Africa on 1 January, was made Consul, and celebrated his triumph over Juggurtha, who would be executed six days later. Afterwards, Marius began to train and equip a new army to fight the Germans, and it is here that some of his reforms were first put into place. He forced the men to do all sorts of physical exercises, to prepare their own food, and most importantly to carry their own supplies rather than have wagons or mules carry them, thus creating the endearing nickname of the Roman legionaries, 'Marius' mules'.[11]

After the Germans rampaged through Gaul and even briefly invaded northern Spain, Marius sent out a new army and clashed with the Teutons at the Battle of Aquae Sextae. Unlike previous battles against the Germans, the Battle of Aquae Sextae was a Roman victory, and a major one. According to Titus Livius, 200,000 enemy warriors were killed, and another 90,000 taken prisoner, including their leader Teutobodus. These figures are probably highly exaggerated, especially since Publius Florus states that the Germans only lost 65,000 dead during this battle, but by that same token Florus also states that Roman casualties numbered a paltry 300 dead, which is scarcely believable considering the ferocity of earlier battles against the Germans and the impressive losses that the Romans suffered during them. Regardless of the statistics, the Teutons had been thoroughly smashed as a fighting force. Afterwards, Marius directed his attention against the Cimbri. At the Battle of Vercellae, he once again won a great victory. Livius states that 160,000 Cimbri warriors were killed, including their leader Chief Boiorix, and another 60,000 captured.[12]

After the Cimbrian War, as it came to be known, the Germans disappeared off of Rome's radar until Julius Caesar's war in Gaul half a century later. Caesar, it seems, had no interest in the Germans until he was petitioned by some of the Gallic tribes to aid them in their struggles against a foreign race of people who dwelt east of the Rhine, but had crossed into Gaul and had seized a large portion of their territory.

The story, we are told, went like this: Sometime before Julius Caesar began the conflict that would make him famous, two Gallic tribes called the Averni and Sequani were at war against another Gallic tribe called the Aedui. The Aedui were very powerful, and little progress was being made against them, so the Averni and Sequani asked the Germans for help. The

Germans agreed, and 15,000 of them crossed the Rhine and entered Gaul, but after they saw how good the land was, more and more came into Gaul, until 120,000 Germans were living in that country. The Aedui declared war upon the Germans and fought several battles against them, but were severely defeated by them in all of these fights. The Germans succeeded where the combined strengths of the Averni and Sequani failed, and thoroughly crushed the power of the Aedui to the point that the Aedui were forced to beg to the Sequani for protection. The Sequani must have been pleased, but then the tables were turned when the Germans, led by Ariovistus, seized possession of one-third of the Sequani's territory and demanded that they hand over an additional third. He asked this because a large party of 24,000 Germans from the Charude tribe had recently joined him, and he now needed to provide lands for them. By Caesar's account, Ariovistus was a cruel tyrannical ruler. Representatives of the Gallic tribes went to Rome and addressed the Senate, asking for Rome to assist them in driving the Germans out of Gaul, saying that if they were not expelled, they would soon possess all of Gaul, and the native Gallic Celts would be forced to find a new land to call their home. Caesar agreed to help, not so much out of humanitarian or moral interests, but because he thought that the Germans would become bold and spread into other areas, including Italy. After negotiations failed, Caesar's army met Ariovistus and his Germanic horde at the Battle of Vosges. The Romans were victorious, but although many of the Germans were killed, Ariovistus eluded death or capture and escaped across the Rhine back into Germania. However, he died not long afterwards; the circumstances of his death are not recorded.[13]

Caesar's army moved closer and closer to the Rhine, with the Germans repeatedly sending envoys requesting that he not advance any further, and with Caesar disregarding their requests and pressing onwards. Caesar sent out all of his cavalry, 5,000 horsemen, forward to scout ahead of the main army. After they travelled some way, they came upon a much smaller party of 800 German cavalry. Although the Germans were outnumbered by more than six to one, the Germans attacked the Romans, and after inflicting some casualties, they forced the Roman cavalry to flee. This body of German cavalry was actually the advance guard of a much larger Germanic force located eight miles to the east, mustering their men and preparing to attack Caesar with all of their strength. The day after the cavalry ambush, Caesar's army attacked the large German encampment located near the Rhine, estimated to hold 430,000 men, women, and children, and having a large number of wagons. Apparently, all of the Germans living in Gaul had concentrated themselves in this one spot. Despite being heavily outnumbered, Caesar's army charged the camp, attacking the Germans so suddenly that they had no time to prepare defences. Caesar records that the Germans were thoroughly massacred. Many of them were killed in the fighting; others fled and were chased down by Caesar's cavalry; the rest tried in desperation to escape across the Rhine, and many drowned. A few of the Germanic princes and tribal elders were taken prisoner. By contrast, Caesar's men had suffered hardly any casualties.[14]

All of the Germans who had been living in Gaul were either killed, captured, or escaped across the Rhine into Germania. Caesar and his army now stood upon the banks of the Rhine River. Not content with simply driving the Germans out of Gaul, Caesar became determined to cross into Germania itself and fight the Germanic barbarians on their own soil to ensure that they never threatened Gaul, or rather Rome's future holdings in Gaul, ever again. The Rhine was 400 yards across, and the most obvious way to get to the other side was to transport men by ship. However, Caesar felt that having the infantry-based legions transported by ship was not fitting with Roman dignity, so he resolved to build a bridge. 'Caesar's Bridge', as it came to be known, was an impressive feat of engineering, specifically designed and constructed to withstand the swift currents of the Rhine River. Amazingly, the work was finished in just ten days, but when you have a whole army of highly-motivated and loyal men ready to do any work that you ask them to do, I suppose Julius Caesar could have accomplished just about anything. With the bridge completed, he marched his troops onto German soil. Caesar and his army spent only eighteen days in Germania, scouting the terrain and burning farms and villages. They met no resistance. After they left, his army destroyed the bridge to prevent the Germans from once again crossing into Gaul.[15]

Following Caesar's assassination in 44 BC, and with the Romans preoccupied with civil war and the political position of Egypt, Germania and its peoples fell from the minds of most Romans. But with the defeat

of Antonius and Cleopatra, and with the accession of Gaius Octavianus as
Rome's first emperor in 31 BC, the civil wars had ended and now the Romans
could get back to doing what they did best – conquer.[16]

Tensions Escalate

The German invasion in the second century BC created an air of paranoia
among the Romans. To them, the Germanic tribes were bloodthirsty savages
who would commit every cruelty imaginable. Therefore, keeping the border
secure against these barbarians was a high priority, and it was just as well,
because shortly after Octavianus' accession to the throne, the Germans began
raiding Roman territory in Gaul. From 31–28 BC, the Germans felt confident
enough to launch three large forays across the Rhine into Rome's Gallic
holdings. Moreover, there was still strong anti-Roman sentiment among the
Gauls, who had been conquered by Rome twenty years previously. In fact,
there were still some small rebel factions. In the year 30 BC, the Gallic region
of Aquitania rose in rebellion. Even twenty years after Vercingetorix' death,
Rome's hold on Gaul was still tenuous.[17]

One tactic used by the Romans to keep Gaul safe and to win over the
Germans was to resettle certain Germans in Gaul in order to turn them
into Roman allies, and the archetypal example was that of a tribe called the
Ubians.

> The Ubii had long been supporters of Rome and in the late 30s BC,
> Agrippa relocated them – a tribe from around the River Lahn, east of
> the Rhine – across the river in the sparsely populated low-lying area
> of the Cologne basin. This was not a punitive measure, [because] it
> was at the request of the Ubii themselves. They had suffered numerous
> attacks from a neighbouring and much larger tribe called the Suebi
> for many years. Their relocation was not a gesture born solely out of
> magnanimity on Agrippa's part. As allies, the Ubii could now act as a
> buffer zone…and shield Gaul from marauding Germanic tribes.[18]

As a token of the emperor's favour, the Romans built an entire city for them
from scratch! It was called Oppidum Ubiorum, 'Town of the Ubians'. Many

years later, this settlement was designated as a *colonia*, and was re-named Colonia Agrippina. The modern city of Cologne, Germany is built atop this settlement, and its name is a corruption of the Roman title *colonia*.[19]

But this practice of resettlement didn't mean that the Romans were trying to extend open arms to the Germans. The fact that the Romans were trying to turn certain Germans into allies shows that the Romans were still afraid of the Germans and wished to pit them against each other if hostilities erupted. Moreover, placing these new allies on the border created a buffer zone, and Rome was comforted in the idea that if the tribes across the Rhine *should* attack, they would have to attack Rome's German allies first. In their opinion, it was better that some barbarians die than Romans. Despite all the favour shown to them, the Ubians were seen as expendable. Whether the Ubians realized this or not isn't certain.

The three raids that the Germans had committed showed that the Rhine frontier was unstable. The civil wars had depleted Rome's military, and as such, the border between Gaul and Germania couldn't be protected, and the few soldiers who *were* there obviously couldn't be everywhere at once. Aside from raiding, it also seems that the Germans were conducting deals with the Gallic rebels, engaging in covert arms shipments in order to keep the Gallic resistance movement going.[20]

The Romans tried to stop this, but with too few troops, they couldn't possibly stem the flow of weapons. When one supply route was closed down, the Germans merely re-located their operations to another sector. Until more Roman troops could be brought in to secure the border, the Germans would continue to smuggle weapons into Gaul to supply the Gallic resistance factions. Therefore, forts were constructed along the length of the Rhine and were garrisoned with troops.

Germania remained relatively untouched during this time, with Roman operations being confined to punitive expeditions – reprisals against the German raiders and weapons smugglers. The Romans would attack and chase after the raiders, but then would return back to their base camps. The Romans didn't stray too far from their forts or lines of communication. Besides, in their eyes, Germania was not important. What *was* important was securing Gaul and wiping out the last vestiges of resistance there.[21]

By 27 BC, the Aquitanian revolt had been crushed and Gaul was thought to be more or less pacified, and with that matter settled, Rome could now concentrate on Germania. Troop numbers on the Rhine border steadily increased, and several large forts were constructed between 19–17 BC. By this time, it was clear that Rome's attitude towards the Germans had become more than just preventing raiding into Gaul – the Germans were going to be Rome's next target for imperial expansion. It certainly helped that half of the newly-constructed forts were located in positions that could aid Roman expansion since they guarded important routes into the interior of Germania. The forts were stocked with supplies and the legionaries drilled. Clearly, war was coming, but the Romans had no pretext for an invasion. The Germans, to their misfortune, would provide one.[22]

The Roman-German Wars Begin

The sight of the Rhine border bristling with forts and troops must have left no doubt in the Germans' minds that they were about to be attacked. Then, as a sign of bravado, parties of Roman civilians began filtering across the Rhine and establishing settlements in Germania before it was even conquered. Obviously, the Germans were going to react violently to these trespassers. One might even think that this was what Rome was hoping for all along.

In the summer of 17 BC, three Germanic tribes – the Sicambri, Usipetes, and Tencteri – decided that enough was enough, and they began attacking Roman settlements within Germania. These tribes were located on the Rhine, and as such Romans were squatting more on their lands than other tribes in the interior. Any Roman found east of the Rhine was executed. Then, to further drive the message home, these three tribes crossed the Rhine and attacked Roman border settlements in Gaul. While on one of their forays, these Germans managed to push back a Roman cavalry unit which had been operating in the area. Chasing the fleeing horsemen, they ran into General Marcus Lollius, the commander of the 5th Legion. He and a small party of men had been out on patrol when the Germans found him. In the ensuing skirmish, the Germans managed to capture the 5th Legion's eagle – the highest disgrace for any Roman unit.[23] Years later, Varus' legions would be destroyed in the forests and all three of their eagles would be seized.

Given all the damage that they had done, the Germans might have been confident that the Romans would abandon their plans for conquering Germania, believing that the tribes were simply too dangerous to deal with. On the contrary – the Romans now had their perfect pretext for an invasion. No one could defy Rome and remain unpunished. With war inevitable, in 13 BC, Caesar Augustus sent his stepson to the Rhine – Drusus Claudius Nero. Drusus was Tiberius' younger brother, and like Tiberius he felt that the path to fame was through military victories. His first experience in military command came two years earlier in 15 BC when Augustus ordered him to fight the Rhaetians, who lived north of Italy in what is now Austria, between Gaul and Noricum (which had been conquered the previous year). The Rhaetians had been raiding eastern Gaul and even crossed the Alps and raided settlements in northern Italy. Furthermore, they executed all of their male prisoners. For these reasons, Drusus was sent to fight them. In his first taste of battle, he routed a small party of them, and was awarded the office of Praetor as a result. Eventually, Drusus drove the Rhaetians out of Italy, and Tiberius was sent to expel them from Gaul. After the Rhaetians had been confined to their homeland, both Drusus and Tiberius invaded Rhaetia from different points, and in a short time, the land was conquered. Much of the male population was deported to other areas of the empire so that they could not concentrate their strength and rebel against Roman rule. Now, Drusus was ready for his next military assignment.[24]

The 25-year-old commander arrived on the Rhine in 13 BC. For most of the following year in 12 BC, he conducted reconnaissance and occupied himself with supply and communications. He also commissioned the building of several forts along the Rhine, including Argentoratum (modern-day Strasbourg, France), Moguntiacum (Mainz, Germany), and Fort Vetera (Xanten, Germany). In 11 BC, Drusus established his headquarters at Fort Vetera, which had been completed the year prior. From here, Drusus launched his famous Germanic campaign.[25]

Rome's Germanic Campaign

According to Cassius Dio, Drusus' campaign against the Germans officially began when he waited for them to once again cross the Rhine for a raid,

Figure 3. Tiberius Claudius Nero.
Museo Archaeologico Regionale, Palermo,
Sicily. (*Wikimedia Commons, public domain
image*)

Figure 4. Drusus Claudius Nero. Musee
du Cinquantenaire. Brussels, Belgium.
(*Photo Jona Lendering, used with permission*)

whereupon he attacked them and drove them back. Then, Drusus crossed
the Rhine with his army and invaded the territory of the Usipetes. He then
marched north against the Sicambri and laid the land to waste. Travelling
down the Rhine and landing in what is now the Netherlands, he conquered
the Frisians, who afterwards served as allies in his army, and then attacked
the Chauci, who lived in northwestern Germany in what is now Lower
Saxony. Satisfied with what he had done so far, he returned to Rome as
winter was setting in.[26]

The following spring of 10 BC, Drusus returned to the Rhine to resume the
war. He once again had to subjugate the Usipetes and Sicambri. Apparently,
they had regained their strength, and besides, the Romans didn't occupy
these lands but merely attacked them and withdrew to their winter quarters
on the Rhine. He then invaded the territory of the Cherusci, whose territory
stretched from the Ems to the Elbe, and pushed as far as the Weser. He
would have continued onwards if his army hadn't run out of supplies. With

supplies almost gone and winter once again approaching, he decided to withdraw his army into friendly territory. As Drusus' army marched back to winter quarters, the column was ambushed by the Germans, and the force was very nearly massacred.[27]

> The enemy harassed him everywhere by ambuscades, and once they shut him up in a narrow pass and all but destroyed his army; indeed, they would have annihilated them, had they not conceived a contempt for them, as if they were already captured and needed only the finishing stroke, and so come to close quarters with them in disorder. This led to their being worsted, after which they were no longer so bold, but kept up a petty annoyance of his troops from a distance, while refusing to come nearer.[28]

Cassius Dio states here that if the Germans weren't so overconfident of victory, they could have overwhelmed Drusus and his men. But Drusus managed to drive them back, and afterwards the Germans didn't attack the Romans, but perhaps occasionally shot a few arrows into the column and then frantically retreated back into the forest. The ambush of Drusus' column in the forest when entering a narrow pass is almost identical to when Arminius attacked Varus years later. Moreover, the fact that Drusus managed to turn the tide in the end is similar to what happened on the first day of the Battle of Teutoburg. For Drusus, it was a close escape, and a frightening reminder of just how dangerous the Germans could be.

Once again, Drusus returned to Rome at the campaigning season's end, and this time he was awarded a triumph and had an arch built in his honour. Moreover, it was voted that the doors to the Temple of Janus should be closed, believing that the empire was at peace. Peace, however, didn't last very long, for in the spring of 9 BC, he once again set out for the Rhine and spent the majority of that year attacking the Chatti.[29]

In 8 BC, despite bad omens, Drusus returned to Germania and once again attacked the Chatti and advanced as far as the territory of the Sueves, 'conquering with difficulty the territory traversed and defeating the forces that attacked him only after considerable bloodshed'.[30] Afterwards, he once again attacked the Cherusci, then crossed the Weser and advanced as far as the Elbe River. Ovid states that Drusus extended Rome's dominion to new lands that had only recently been discovered. The philosopher Seneca states that Drusus and his army went into places that were so remote that the natives who lived there did not even know about the existence of the Romans. There is a story that he was warned by a goddess not to cross the Elbe, and so he and his army withdrew. On his way back to the Rhine, Drusus fell from his horse and broke his leg. Languishing in his summer camp, his injury became seriously infected, and after thirty days, Drusus died from the disease, most likely gangrene.[31] Considering his character, exploits, and reputation, it was an inglorious way to die.

When Augustus learned that Drusus was sick, he ordered Tiberius to quickly go to him. Ovid states that Tiberius was in the city of Pavia at the time, and when he heard about his brother's condition, he rode non-stop day and night until he arrived at his dying brother's side. He arrived in time, but it wasn't long before Drusus drew his last breath. The great Drusus, conqueror of Germania, was dead.[32]

Drusus' soldiers wanted his body cremated and have the ashes buried where he died. Only with reluctance did they agree to let his brother Tiberius take the body back to Rome for burial.[33] Out of respect, his soldiers erected a monument to him in the city of Moguntiacum (modern-day Mainz, Germany), a cylindrical tower made of stones, which can still be seen there to this day. Suetonius remarked that it was a custom amongst the soldiers to run around the monument on a certain day of the year (presumably the date of his death), and cities in Gaul were to do honour to him by offering prayers and sacrifices.[34]

Tiberius brought his brother's body back to Rome, walking on foot rather than riding as a gesture of respect and deference to his brother. At first, the body was carried by centurions and the legionary tribunes, but only as far as the army's winter headquarters (it isn't stated where this is). Afterwards, whenever the funeral procession passed through a town, the body was carried by its leading men. Upon the arrival of Drusus' body in Rome, it was laid out in the forum, and orations were made in his honour. All of Rome was in deep mourning, and especially the imperial family. The poet Ovid wrote a long letter of condolence to Drusus' mother Livia, the wife of Caesar Augustus, entitled 'The Consolation to Livia Augusta on the Death of her son Drusus Claudius Nero'. The body was carried by knights and senators to the Campus Martius, the Field of Mars, where it was cremated. Afterwards the ashes were interned in the imperial family's mausoleum.[35]

Suetonius comments that Drusus was a man 'eager for glory',[36] but there's no dispute that his accomplishments were impressive. He was the first Roman to navigate the shores of the North Sea. He conquered western Germania, extending Rome's dominion from the Rhine to the Elbe. He ordered the construction of a series of forts and, interestingly, even canals which were named the Drusus Canals in his honour, connecting the Rhine with the Yssel. He showed great determination and bravery in battle, often at great risk to his own life, although sometimes doing so out of a desire for personal glory rather than out of courage. He was a man that Rome honoured and respected, and although he was a staunch republican and loudly opposed the idea of a monarchy, Caesar Augustus held him in high regard. Suetonius comments that at the time of Drusus' death, there was a conspiracy theory floating around that Augustus had him poisoned due to his opposition to the monarchy, but Suetonius says that this was utterly ridiculous. Augustus had nothing but admiration for his deceased stepson, and stated that he hoped that his heirs would be like Drusus. In reward for his accomplishments, the Senate voted that a marble arch ought to be erected in his honour on the Appian Road. Moreover, due to his great success in Germania, he was given the *agnomen* 'Germanicus', a title that would be carried by his heirs.[37]

But the war in Germania was not yet over. Once the time of mourning had passed, work needed to be resumed in earnest. Tiberius was called in to continue the campaign. Initially, Tiberius concerned himself with securing the lands that Drusus had claimed rather than seeking to gain more territory. Paterculus states that 'after traversing every part of Germany in a victorious campaign, without any loss of the army entrusted to him — for he made this one of his chief concerns — he so subdued the country as to reduce it almost to the status of a tributary province'.[38] In 6 BC, after everything was deemed peaceful, Tiberius retired to the island of Rhodes.[39]

Occupation and Rebellion

Drusus had conquered much of western Germania, and following his death his brother Tiberius finished the job. All lands from the Rhine to the Elbe

Rivers were now under Roman control. The task had taken three years to accomplish, an unusually long length of time, and only one third of Germania's territory was under Roman domination. The greatest cost of this war was unquestionably the death of Drusus, a rising star in the Roman world, who died at the peak of his career. Tiberius had done well in bringing the remainder of the western territory to heel, but with Tiberius now gone, someone was needed to keep the newly-acquired German territories under Roman control. After so much effort, this land could not be allowed to be reclaimed by the barbarians.

Assuming Tiberius' post of governor-general of this land was Lucius Domitius Ahenobarbus. He was an ambitious young man, in his late 20s or early 30s when he took command of the occupation of Germania Magna. A former governor of Africa and married to Augustus' niece, he seemed like a good choice at the time, but his character left much to be desired.[40] Suetonius describes him as 'haughty, extravagant, and cruel'.[41] He was an arrogant uncouth man who showed insulting disrespect both to his superiors and to Roman social conventions. He forced Roman aristocrats and their wives to act on stage (something considered beneath the upper class), he gave beast-baiting performances in all corners of Rome, and had a taste for gladiatorial fights – the bloodier the better. In fact, the fights that Ahenobarbus relished were so blood-drenched that Augustus warned him to tone down the carnage and show some restraint, but after the emperor's warning was flatly ignored (something that was *never* done, which shows the sort of person that Ahenobarbus was), Augustus was forced to issue an official edict against Ahenobarbus demanding that his gladiatorial fights not have 'such inhuman cruelty'.[42] In short, Lucius Ahenobarbus was a tyrant. *This* was the man that was now in charge of Germania Magna. In retrospect, his appointment was asking for trouble.

Ahenobarbus' headquarters were located on the Ister River. Upon his arrival in the region, he began to make his own mark upon the landscape. Germania had virtually no roads or pathways, and the constraints of the terrain made travel in some places difficult. To solve this problem, Ahenobarbus constructed a series of roads which cut through the marshy areas of the country. These roads were made Celtic-style, laying out rows of logs or wooden beams across the swamps. These 'plank roads' were common in the Celtic regions, especially Ireland, and the Romans must have learned about it from contact with the Celts over the years. Ahenobarbus' plank roads were almost certainly meant to be temporary, put in place until proper Roman roads could be constructed, but they continued to be used for many years.[43]

But civic construction was not enough for the fiery Ahenobarbus. He 'had intercepted the Hermunduri, a tribe which for some reason or other had left their own land and were wandering about in quest of another, and he had settled them in a part of the Marcomannian territory'.[44] It seems that this incident ignited that desire common to most if not all Roman military commanders – the desire to conquer, or at least invade. Eager to gain some glory for himself, he (and I'm assuming a sizeable army) crossed the Elbe River with no opposition, 'penetrating Germany farther than any of his predecessors,[45] made alliances with the Germanic tribes on the opposite side of the river, and afterwards set up an altar to Caesar Augustus. For these accomplishments, he was awarded the insignia of a triumph, without actually being given a triumph itself'.[46]

Upon his return, he relocated his headquarters to the Rhine River, probably so that it could be better supplied. It is then that we begin to see the Germans turning against him, and by extension Roman rule. His military adventure across the Elbe was a clear display of Rome flaunting its martial power. Moreover, his pushy manner alienated and upset many of the tribes, especially Arminius' tribe, the Cherusci.[47] Tensions were growing among the natives.

Ahenobarbus was replaced by Marcus Vinicius, but the damage had already been done, and not long after Vinicius arrived, the Germans rebelled. This rebellion took three years to put down, lasting from 1–4 AD. Cassius Dio states that the rebellion began when some Germans kidnapped and murdered some Roman traders who had entered their tribal lands to trade with them. Maddeningly, no further information is given about this rebellion other than Vinicius fought in it for three years and was awarded a triumph for his efforts. This native rebellion must have been a major event in the area, but what is most telling is the fact that the war lasted for three whole years. Apparently, no progress was being made in Germania, so Tiberius was once again called in to correct the situation, arriving to the cheers of the troops. Tiberius got to work right away, crushing the last remaining pockets of resistance that remained.[48] This must mean that the rebellion was not going well for Marcus Vinicius, due to perhaps excessive strain or even incompetence on his part. Regardless of the reasons, the war was dragging on far longer than it should have and Tiberius was sent in to bring it to a close. It isn't recorded how many people were killed in this rebellion, but I can imagine how many casualties, even from a guerilla-type war, could result from three years of fighting, with the Romans presumably exacting punitive retributions on the populous.

Marcus Vinicius may have been awarded a triumph, but he ceased to be the military governor of this territory, and that certainly says something as well – he may have been fired from his post, possibly a punishment for not bringing the rebellion to an end sooner. Tiberius took over as a temporary interim commander until another governor-general could be officially appointed. His name was Saturninus, and he'll be discussed in more detail later.

Consolidation and Control

After the Romans took over the western half of Germania, they set about making sure that it became Roman. Part of that process was the stationing of military units either in Germania proper or along the border in Gaul within the forts which had been constructed along the River Rhine years before. The most famous of these units were the 17th, 18th, and 19th Legions – the three legions that were defeated in the Battle of Teutoburg. These veteran units were responsible for keeping the peace and enforcing Rome's laws in the years following the conquest. There were five legions in total stationed either along the Rhine or in Germania Magna itself in the years between Drusus' Germanic war and the Battle of Teutoburg – the 1st and 5th Legions, which comprised the Upper Rhine Army,[49] and the 17th, 18th, and 19th Legions, which comprised the Lower Rhine Army.

The 1st Legion *Augusta*, 'Augustus' Own' (there were about five or so 1st Legions throughout Rome's history, differentiated only by their nicknames), was created by Julius Caesar in 48 BC in order to fight his rival Pompey. It's interesting to see that the 1st Legion performed terribly in a war in Spain against a tribe called the Cantabrians, and as a punishment for its disgraceful conduct, the legion was stripped of its title 'Augusta'. According to Cassius Dio, '[Marcus] Agrippa…after losing many of his soldiers, and degrading many others because they kept being defeated (for example, he gave orders that the entire Augustan legion, as it had been called, should no longer bear that name), he at length destroyed nearly all of the enemy.'[50] A similar event may have happened to the defeated legions of Teutoburg, where they were regarded as having disgraced the name of their unit and the empire by their defeat, as I'll describe in the seventh chapter. During the BC–AD transition period, the 1st Legion was moved to the Rhine, where it served with apparent distinction in Germania during Drusus' campaign of conquest, thereby acquiring the honorific nickname *Germanica*, 'of Germania'. During the time of the Battle of Teutoburg, the 1st Legion *Germanica* was stationed in Cologne.[51]

The 5th Legion *Alaudae*, 'the Larks', was created by Julius Caesar in 52 BC, made up entirely of Gauls, and therefore was the first legion to be composed entirely of foreigners and not Roman citizens. They were called 'the Larks' because they may have decorated their helmets with bird feathers, as per Gallic fashion. Despite the avian nickname, their unit emblem was an elephant. This was in reference to the legion's involvement in the Battle of Thapsus, fought between Julius Caesar and his rival Quintus Scipio in the year 46 BC in modern-day Tunisia, in which the legion bravely stood its ground against a charge of war elephants. After service in the Gallic Wars, they moved to Spain, and afterwards fought with Marcus Antonius. Following Antonius' defeat, the 5th was placed under the leadership of Gaius Octavianus. After relocating to northern Gaul, the 5th suffered a humiliating disgrace when the Germans ambushed a party of them led by the legion's commander Marcus Lollius and captured the legionary eagle. It afterwards fought in Drusus' Germanic campaign, and I assume that they fought with singular vigour and ferocity in order to restore their honour.[52]

As for the 17th, 18th, and 19th Legions, the ones which were apparently destroyed by Arminius and his Germanic warriors in the Teutoburg Forest, not much is known about them. No information is known about these units' nicknames or emblems, if they had any. It is commonly held that these three legions were created by Gaius Octavianus around the year 40 BC following his victory at the Battle of Philippi. The legions may have been created to invade Sicily, which at that time was under the control of Octavianus' enemy Sextus Pompeius. The need for soldiers was especially pressing since one of Pompeius' subordinates had seized control of the island of Sardinia, which was formerly one of Octavianus' main strongholds of support. However, the invasion of Sicily was delayed and eventually cancelled because Pompeius was forced to abandon the island following a devastating naval defeat at the Battle of Naulochus in which his entire fleet was destroyed by the pro-Octavianus navy, commanded by Octavianus' closest associate Marcus Agrippa. It has been proposed that the men from these three legions were recruited from northern Italy. Pompeius himself was later captured and executed. So these three legions were presumably never used for the original purpose that they were raised for.[53]

We know scant information about the individual histories of these legions. It has been proposed by one modern source that the 17th Legion took part in suppressing the Gallic rebellion in Aquitainia which occurred shortly after Octavianus seized complete power.[54] To further add to the confusion, during the civil wars of the late Republic, army commanders raised their own legions, resulting in different legions on different sides having the same numbers. To illustrate this point, it has been mentioned that the 17th Legion purportedly raised by Octavianus in 40 BC might be somehow connected to another 17th Legion, which was created by Octavianus' arch rival Marcus Antonius, and was given the nickname *Classica*, meaning 'of the Fleet'. This could be taken by some to refer to the Battle of Naulochus, and if so, it would be established that at least one of the three legions took part in military operations concerning the conquest of Sicily. However, the evidence supporting this hypothesis is very flimsy. The 17th Legion *Classica* is likely a completely different unit, and should not be mistaken as being synonymous with the 17th Legion that Octavianus raised.

Of these three legions, we have the most information about the 19th, and it isn't much. An iron catapult bolt-head stamped with 'LEG XIX' was found in Döttenbich (near Oberammergau, Bavaria, Germany), indicating that the 19th Legion participated in the conquest of Rhaetia in 15 BC. This legion might have been bestowed with the title *Rhaetica*, 'of Rhaetia', due to their participation in this war, but titles such as this were only given if this unit had performed with great distinction, and there is no specific mention of the 19th Legion acting with particular heroism and bravery during the conquest of this region. Moreover, titles, especially ones related to battlefield prowess, were highly regarded and would have been mentioned. The fact that no title is mentioned for the 19th Legion indicates that it never possessed one, despite its military service. Afterwards, between 15–8 BC, the 19th Legion was posted to Dangstetten, located in southwestern Germany. This time corresponds with Varus' possible but unlikely brief stint as a legion commander in the area, possibly as the one-time commander of the 19th itself, and it also corresponds with the oldest-known specimen of the *lorica segmentata*, the characteristic Roman infantryman's armour made of several overlapping metal strips, found at Dangstetten and dated to the year 9 BC.[55] It's been stated by one source that the 19th Legion used to be stationed at Cologne, then known as Oppidum Ubiorum, and later as Colonia Agrippina. This is almost certainly the location where the legion was stationed from the time immediately after Drusus' Germanic campaign, from 8 BC to the earliest years of the first century AD – the exact date isn't clear. By the time of Varus' governorship of Germania Magna, the 17th, 18th, and 19th Legions had fought in Drusus' Germanic campaign, and were based in either Xanten, Oberaden, or Haltern, or possibly different sections based in all three locations.[56]

In order to house the soldiers, several large forts were used as bases for these military units operating in Germania. These forts were designed and constructed in accordance with a more-or-less standardized blueprint (no two Roman forts were exactly alike). The outline of a Roman fort is easily recognizable because almost all of them are shaped like playing cards – rectangular in shape with rounded corners. They were also constructed in a specific order of steps. The first thing that would be laid out would be the main roads inside the fort, almost always laid out in the form of a cross, corresponding with the fort's four gates, one on each side of the fort. The gates were taller than the walls, and always consisted of two sets of double-doors with a large tower on each side of the gate.[57]

The buildings constructed within a fort included the administrative headquarters building, the houses of the high-ranking officers, hospital, granaries, storehouses, and various craft and maintenance workshops, but arguably the most important buildings within the fort were the soldiers' barracks. These buildings would have occupied at least half of the space within the fort's walls. The barracks buildings were long and rectangular in shape, and arranged in rows. The rooms were small and cramped. Each contuburnium squad had two tiny rooms – one for their armour, weaponry, and equipment, and another to sleep in. Each sleeping room had a small fireplace with a chimney to provide heat, which was important in colder climates, and especially since these barracks buildings were constructed of concrete which doesn't retain heat very well. Officers such as centurions and standard-bearers would have had rooms to themselves (and as such they would have been slightly better furnished), and there would have been other small rooms on the barracks' far end for offices and storage areas.[58]

In contrast to these hovels was the *praetorium*, or 'commander's house', although the words 'mansion' or 'palace' would be a more accurate description of this spacious abode. This was the home of the commander of the unit stationed within this fort, along with his family. In contrast to the tiny rooms that the ordinary legionaries occupied, the commander (always an aristocrat) and his family lived in luxury. It was one of the largest buildings within the fort, and needed a large staff of servants or slaves to run. The layout of the praetorium uncovered at Xanten, Germany, the location of Fort Vetera (one of the main locations in our story), is one of the best examples of what a fort commander's house would have looked like. The building that was uncovered at this site is dated to a later time period than the one discussed in this book, since only a small portion of the original fortress built here has been uncovered, but it is nevertheless an impressive structure. It's absolutely enormous, measuring 74m x 94.5m in area. There are at least six open courtyards, and one of them measures 18m x 82m in area, shaped very much like a horse racetrack, and encompassed almost all of the west side of this building complex. Other high-ranking officers, such as the legionary tribunes and the camp commandant, would have also had their own houses, although not nearly as large as that of the commander.[59]

Another of the main buildings within the fort was the *principia*, or 'headquarters building'. This was the administrative hub of the fort where most of the work of running the fort and governing the day-to-day activities of the soldiers would have taken place. It was a square building consisting of rooms built around a central colonnaded courtyard, very much in the style of a Roman villa. The rooms built on three sides served as the offices for various clerks, secretaries, and other administrative staff members, as well as for storage rooms. The far side directly opposite the entrance was the large hall, much taller than the rest of the building, and would have acted as a court-house as well as a place to receive emissaries. It also acted as a pseudo-temple, and as such was the religious centre of the fort.[60]

After all of the streets and buildings were laid out, a wall would be constructed. The walls of Roman forts were almost always perfectly vertical, and very rarely sloped. When forts needed to be quickly constructed, as during war-time or just prior to the beginning of a war, the Romans would construct walls out of blocks of sod. These blocks would be cut to a standardized size of 1 x 1.5 Roman feet, laid on top of each other grass-to-grass, and the walls were ten to fifteen feet thick, sometimes thicker. Several examples of Roman turf-cutters have been uncovered by archaeologists, and look virtually identical to turf cutters seen today – a blade shaped like a half-circle mounted on a pole in a T-shape. Although sod walls were relatively easy and quick to construct, they needed to be constantly repaired due to the weathering effects of wind and rain, and even the sun, which would dry the blocks and make them brittle.[61]

If more time was allowed, the Romans could construct walls out of timber and earth. These were much stronger and more resilient than walls made of sod blocks, but it was, of course, necessary to construct forts of this design in areas where there were wide expanses of forests. In heavily forested areas like southern and central Germania, finding large supplies of wood was not a problem. Construction methods regarding timber-and-earth fortifications varied. One method was to construct two parallel palisade walls (walls made of tree trunks stood up vertically and placed in a line with one tree directly against the next one) and then fill the empty space in between the two walls with dirt. Another construction method used a more compartmental design – the two palisade walls were constructed, along with smaller bracing walls which extended between the two, forming a series of square or rectangular-shaped compartments, which were then filled with dirt. Timber fortifications could also be of a more 'finished' appearance than the simple crude log palisades, in which thick squared timbers served as the framework, and the walls themselves were constructed of flat planks of wood nailed horizontally to the framing structure, creating a flat surface. One problem is that timber rots, and in wet humid conditions like Germania or northern Gaul, this rotting process is accelerated, and as such timber fortresses needed to be constantly repaired. Another problem is that wooden walls can be set on fire, unless they were covered with some sort of protective substance.[62]

The strongest walls were, of course, made of stone, but quarrying and cutting them took time and the use of skilled masons. As such, stone forts could only be built in areas where firstly stone was available and secondly where there was minimal or no risk of hostilities, and as such the men could take their time and not rush.

The tops of wooden and stone walls had crenellations – the alternating squares of stones extending upwards from tops of walls which are often seen on medieval castles; the square blocks are called 'merlons', and the space between each merlon is called a 'crenel'. The crenellations atop sod walls were often made of wicker wattles. The crenellations always extended to a maximum of 6 feet above the allure (wall's catwalk), with the crenel spaces measuring 2 to 3 feet square.[63]

In order to provide even more protection, one or two V-shaped trenches would be dug outside the walls, corresponding exactly to the perimeter of the wall, and going all around the fort, except the pathways which led to the gates. Sometimes, one of these trenches would be filled with water, forming a moat. These trenches or moats were usually 10 to 12 feet wide and 6 or 7 feet deep.[64]

Now let's look at some examples of Roman forts which feature prominently in our story. First, we will look at Fort Vetera, modern-day Xanten, Germany. This initially served as the main base for running the province of Germania Magna, even though it stood on the *western* side of the Rhine in eastern Gaul – it wasn't even on Germania's soil. This military post would serve as Governor Varus' headquarters when he first arrived. The fort was originally built as a legionary camp by General Drusus for his great Germanic war. Construction began in 13 BC (interestingly, the year that Varus was serving as a Senatorial consul) and was completed the following year with characteristic Roman speed. The fort's location was excellently positioned, built on the southern slope of a low hill now known as Fürstenberg near the confluence of the Rhine and Lippe Rivers. Its strategic position meant that it commanded a broad flat view of the surrounding countryside. It would have also served as an ideal base camp for Roman riverine naval forces travelling up the Lippe River and pushing further into the interior of Germania.[65]

Fort Vetera was continuously rebuilt and enlarged during the early imperial period. At its largest size, it was truly massive, covering 138 acres in area and was big enough to house two legions, a total of 10,000 men. During the time of the Battle of Teutoburg, this fort was smaller, although how much smaller is difficult to say. So far, archaeologists have identified five layers of construction, dating of course to five different time frames. Archaeological excavations in the oldest layer, the one on the bottom, the layer that indicates when Fort Vetera was first constructed, have yielded frustratingly few results: a ditch (likely the one surrounding the fort), the remains of a timber-and-earth wall, two pottery kilns, and various vague post holes indicating where buildings once stood. It's not much to go on, but it does conclusively prove that a Roman fort was built on this site. The presence of pottery kilns indicates that the buildings here consisted not only of barracks which housed the soldiers but also various craft workshops. A legionary base was, after all, a small self-contained city, and needed various commodities. Workshops such as blacksmiths, carpenters, bakeries, and tailors would have been a standard component of a base's layout.[66]

A description given by Tacitus gives us some impression of the fort's dominating nature on the terrain, and its intimidating presence to Rome's enemies. The description comes from a much later date than the time period focused on in this book, describing how the fort appeared in the mid-to-late first century AD, but it is nevertheless worth taking a look at. In his *Histories*, he describes the fort as being built partly on a gentle slope, and partly upon flat ground. It was large enough to hold two legions, and was surrounded by a palisade (a wall made of logs) with towers constructed along the wall's length. A sizeable civilian settlement had grown up around the fort during the peacetime years to the point where it could have been considered a town. He also describes Fort Vetera as a 'winter quarters' for the Roman soldiers – this will be of some importance later on when the Battle of Teutoburg is discussed.[67]

Which legions were stationed here? It's highly likely that at the time of Varus' governorship, and possibly a little beforehand, Fort Vetera was the base camp for the 18th Legion, considering that the gravestone of Marcus Caelius, the commanding centurion of the 18th, was found here.[68] It is not recorded what the second legion stationed here was. It may be possible that the 18th shared the fort with a large force of auxiliaries, since we know that Varus took six cohorts of auxiliaries with him on campaign.

Civilian settlements tend to gradually emerge around military installations, and Fort Vetera was no different in that respect. What *was* different about this particular small village was that the people who lived here were neither Romans nor Gauls, but were Germans. These were people from the Sicambri tribe, which had given the Romans so much trouble in recent years. Following Drusus' death, his brother Tiberius took over the Roman conquest of western Germania, and among his exploits, he attacked the Sicambri, crushing them. After this tribe was beaten into submission, he deported a staggering 40,000 people across the Rhine into eastern Gaul and settled them in lands along the Rhine River. These displaced Sicambri were collectively known as the Ciberni, which may be the name of a particular clan within the Sicambri tribe. Pliny the Elder mentions them as the 'Cugerni' in his description of the peoples of northeastern Gaul, dwelling between the Ubians who lived in the town of Cologne and the Batavians who lived on the islands in the Rhine Delta. The Ciberni were, therefore, settled on a fairly sizeable tract of riparian territory. One of their newly-established settlements was near Fort Vetera, as recorded by the historian Tacitus, who states that the Ciberni, or Cugerni as he calls them, live on plots of land around the military base.[69]

The village located the nearest to the fort was called Cibernodorum, literally 'marketplace of the Ciberni'. These people were forced to swear peace and loyalty to Rome, adopt Roman customs, and pray to Roman gods. Many of them likely spent their whole lives supplying the needs of the Roman soldiers in the nearby fort. Later on, some of the Ciberni would serve as auxiliaries in Emperor Claudius' invasion of Britain, and would take part in the Batavian Revolt of 69 AD, which would culminate in the destruction of both Fort Vetera and the nearby village of Cibernodorum. Both sites would eventually be rebuilt, although the new fort, which archaeologists have given the rather unimaginative designation of 'Castra Vetera II' (*castra* is the Latin word for 'fort' or 'castle'), was built a little distance from the site of the old one. In the early second century AD, Emperor Trajan designated the town of Cibernodorum as a *colonia*, and renamed it Colonia Ulpiana Traiana. The modern-day *Archäologischer Park Xanten* is built on top of the remains of this Roman town. Here, visitors can see the impressive town's gates, sections of the town's walls, the amphitheatre, and the bath-houses, among other things.[70]

Another major military base was Fort Aliso. No one is precisely sure where this camp was, but presently, there are two strong candidates – Haltern, Germany and Paderborn, Germany. It should be noted, however, that there is currently no physical evidence of a Roman fort having been built at Paderborn. As for Haltern, located 30 miles east of Xanten, it was unquestionably the site of a large Roman military camp. The fort at Haltern was founded in 5 BC as a naval post on the Lippe River. Over the years, however, it became much more than that, and by Varus' arrival, it had ballooned in size into a massive military complex. It was 47 square acres in area and surrounded by a timber-and-earth wall, which was in turn ringed by two parallel trenches, one of which was presumably filled with water, as Caesar had done when he constructed his fortifications for the siege of Alesia. Like Fort Vetera, this camp was large enough to hold two legions. Aside from the standard military buildings, there were a large number of administrative buildings here as well. It has been hypothesized that Haltern was being developed to serve as an administrative centre,[71] and I believe that Haltern was going to replace Fort Vetera as Germania Magna's administrative centre in the near future. Fort Vetera was, after all, not even within the 'province' itself.

The reason why some historians believe that Fort Aliso was located where Paderborn is today (even though, as stated before, there is currently no evidence that a fort was built there) is due to linguistics. It is believed that Fort Aliso was built on the confluence of the Lippe and Alme Rivers, since the Alme was known as the Eliso River in ancient times. Eliso is very similar to Aliso. This would place Fort Aliso near modern-day Paderborn, Germany.[72] Grammatically, this would make sense. However, until archaeological excavations can be conducted at Paderborn, and until definitive proof of a Roman fort is found at that site, we cannot be absolutely certain.

It's believed that the 19th Legion, or at least a portion of it, was posted in Haltern because a large lead bar weighting 140lbs was found there with the letters *CCIII L.XIX* stamped onto it. *L.XIX* stands for 'Legio XIX' – the 19th Legion. *CCIII* is the Roman numeric for 203. This lead bar belonged to the 19th Legion and weighed 203 Roman pounds.[73]

It is currently unknown where the 17th Legion was stationed. Both Xanten and Haltern were large enough to accommodate two fully-manned legions, and we are almost certain that the 18th was stationed at Xanten and the 19th was at Haltern. This leaves room for one extra legion at both locations.

One modern source states that there was a large Roman fort built on the Lippe River north of Dortmund. This corresponds with the Roman fort found at Oberaden, located on the Lippe River, located about 10 miles northeast of Dortmund. It was large enough to hold one full-sized legion, and also possessed a large number of administrative buildings. Some believe that this location, not Haltern, served as the capital of the province of Germania Magna. But Oberaden had a very short life; it was only operational for three years, having been constructed in 11 BC, and abandoned in 8 BC.[74] There is no way that Oberaden could have served as the administrative centre for Germania Magna.

Another location where Rome established a military presence on the Lippe River was Holsterhausen. This site was occupied from 11–7 BC, located 15 miles east of the main legionary camp at Xanten, and located halfway between Xanten and Haltern. Another site was Anreppen, built in 4 AD after the end of the Germanic rebellion, and located over forty miles east of Oberaden. Further to the east along the Weser River was a fort at Hedemunden, which is the easternmost Roman fort discovered in Germania so far. Archaeologists have also uncovered a road extending from Anreppen east towards Paderborn. This is the only real evidence, however slight, that the Romans might have had a presence there. However, the road might have actually been made to connect Anreppen with the fort at Hedemunden, and there might have been no Roman presence in between, so this road should not be used as direct evidence of the existence of a Roman fort at Paderborn. Other forts were established south along the Main River, including Mainz-Kastel and Marktbreit.[75]

One Roman site of particular interest is Waldgirmes; unfortunately, we don't know the ancient Roman name of this location. Built on a peninsula of land jutting into the Lahn River, it was a splendid site for defence. Indeed, if one saw Waldgirmes, you would think that it was a fort. But it wasn't – it was an entirely civilian settlement. Waldgirmes began as a fortified trading post, but soon mushroomed into a bustling town thanks to an influx of settlers and merchants. It is the only Roman town that has been discovered east of the Rhine. Forensic analysis of preserved wood used to construct the town's well, likely one of the first structures built, was dated to 4 BC. Both Roman and Germanic pottery have been found here, and it has been suggested that Romans and Germans must have coexisted peacefully in this town. There have also been found fragments of a large gilt bronze equestrian statue, likely of Caesar Augustus, which would have stood in the middle of the forum. The image of the emperor was ever-present, and the emperor was Rome. Waldgirmes is an example of how Rome cemented its claims on newly-conquered lands. Initially occupied by the military, the Romans began to construct the new province's infrastructure, and obviously felt confident enough to build a town, which demonstrates that the Romans believed that the area was secured.[76]

Well, we've discussed in detail the Roman side of this story, but what about the Germans? How were they coping with their country becoming a part of the empire? I think Cassius Dio sums it up best...

I shall now relate the events which had taken place in Germany during this period. The Romans were holding portions of it — not entire regions, but merely such districts as happened to have been subdued, so that no record has been made of the fact — and soldiers of theirs were wintering there and cities were being founded. The barbarians were adapting themselves to Roman ways, were becoming accustomed to hold markets, and were meeting in peaceful assemblages. They had not, however, forgotten their ancestral habits, their native manners, their old life of independence, or the power derived from arms. Hence, so long as they were unlearning these customs gradually and by the way, as one may say, under careful watching, they were not disturbed by the change in their manner of life, and were becoming different without knowing it.[77]

Rebellion in Illyricum

In the year 6 AD, the Romans were preparing for their next big military campaign. This one was to be directed against the Germanic Marcomanni tribe, located in what is now the Czech Republic. As stated in an earlier chapter, the Marcomanni, led by King Maroboduus, were a formidable foe, possessing a professionally-trained army numbering 74,000 strong. To counter this threat, eight Roman legions were amassing on the Danube, commanded by Tiberius. Roman troops were just five days march from the Marcomanni border. The invasion was scheduled to start in a few days. But then, a massive rebellion broke out in the Roman province of Illyricum, the Roman name for the western Balkans, roughly corresponding to Yugoslavia in the twentieth century.[78]

The uprising took everyone by surprise. The native Illyrians, like many of the Germanic tribes to the north, had been subdued and were now under the jurisdiction of Rome. But the effort to pacify them had lasted more than two centuries. The Romans had fought five wars against them, and they were hardly one-sided. The Illyrians were formidable opponents, and Rome suffered many bloody defeats at their hands. After Augustus launched his campaign against them, it seemed that the Illyrians had finally been brought into line. Wrong.[79]

> The Dalmatians, chafing under the levies of tribute, had hitherto kept quiet, though unwillingly. But when Tiberius made his second campaign against the Germans, and Valerius Messallinus, the governor of Dalmatia and Pannonia at the time, was sent out with him, taking most of his army along, the Dalmatians, too, were ordered to send a contingent; and on coming together for this purpose and beholding the strength of their warriors, they no longer delayed, but, under the vehement urging of one Bato, a Desidiatian, at first a few revolted and defeated the Romans who came against them, and then the rest also rebelled in consequence of this success.[80]

> [Tiberius] Caesar had already arranged his winter quarters on the Danube, and had brought up his army to within five days march of the advanced posts of the enemy [the Marcomanni]...when all Pannonia,

grown arrogant through the blessings of a long peace and now at the maturity of her power, suddenly took up arms, bringing Dalmatia and all the races of that region into her alliance.[81]

The Romans were utterly terrified when word of this rebellion arrived. The historian Suetonius called the Great Illyrian Revolt the greatest threat to Italy itself since the Punic Wars, a sentiment that is probably an exaggeration. But there's no denying that this revolt was a serious threat, as one group was advancing towards the Italian passes and threatened an invasion. Paterculus states that the rebel force had swelled to 800,000 strong and was rampaging all over the countryside. Augustus, frantic to the point of paranoia, organized a levy, drafting every available male into the Army in order to meet the growing threat, including retirees and newly-freed slaves, and addressed the Senate that the rebels would be at the gates of Rome within ten days. Augustus had an understandably similar reaction when word of the disaster in Germany reached him three years later.[82]

The invasion of Bohemia, therefore, had to be postponed while this crisis raged in the Balkans. Tiberius took command of the forces dealing with the Pannonian rebels while his nephew Germanicus, a rising star in the Roman Army, was sent to deal with the Dalmatians – Augustus had ordered Germanicus to go because he was suspicious that Tiberius was acting too slowly.[83] It was around this time of crisis that Publius Quinctilius Varus was made Governor of Germania Magna.

Enter Governor Varus and Resentment Escalates

Before Varus arrived, Germania Magna was presided over by the esteemed military commander Gaius Sentius Saturninus, a former Senatorial consul who had taken over as the governor-general of the region after the German rebellion of 1–4 AD ended. Paterculus describes him as an illustrious virtuous man of energy, action, and foresight who was intolerant of vice and corruption and performed his martial duties very well but also had a fondness for the finer things of life, and was a pleasant character to know.[84] Saturninus made certain that peace was kept in the territory he presided over. Apparently there were some disturbances, but he conducted himself well and brought these minor uprisings to a stop, forcing the Germans to swear for peace not once but twice. He received triumphal honours for his efforts.[85]

Saturninus was a capable administrator and military commander, and men such as him were desperately needed. It was decided by the higher-ups that he should act as one of Tiberius' subordinate commanders in the war against the Marcomanni. However, with the eruption of hostilities in the Balkans, Saturninus was sent south to fight the Illyrian rebels. With Saturninus taken away from his administrative duties, someone was needed to fill the vacuum of Roman governance in that region, and so Publius Quinctilius Varus was called in.[86]

It's uncertain whether Varus was Germania's governor in 6 or 7 AD.[87] Varus was certainly at his headquarters in Fort Vetera by 7 AD. I believe that Varus may have been given the position of 'Governor of Germania Magna' by the emperor in late 6 AD, but didn't arrive there until the spring of 7 AD. However, I have no way to prove that, and besides, the debate as to which year Varus was made Governor is purely academic.

Varus was assigned two deputy governors to help him with his duties: Lucius Nonius Asprenas and Gaius Numonius Vala. Lucius Asprenas was Varus' nephew, the son of Varus' sister and Lucius Asprenas Sr., who was 'a close friend of Augustus'[88] – again, Varus tried to maintain good relations with the imperial family. Lucius Asprenas junior was born around 28 BC, so he would have been in his mid-30s by the time his uncle became Governor of Germania Magna. He was in command of the Upper Rhine Army (1st and 5th Legions) in general and was the legate (legion commander) of the 5th Legion specifically, stationed at Moguntiacum (modern-day Mainz, Germany). In fact, Varus may have arranged it so that his nephew would be the legion's commander. It helps to have friends in high places, and it certainly helps if the governor just happens to be your uncle! We know that Asprenas oversaw the 1st and 5th Legions, and served as the commander for the 5th Legion specifically because the 1st, 5th, 17th, 18th, and 19th Legions were posted to defend Germania Magna, and since Vala commanded the 17th, 18th, and 19th, Asprenas must have commanded the remaining two, a fact confirmed by Paterculus who says that Asprenas led 'the two legions under his command'.[89] Asprenas was married by this point to a woman named

Calpurnia. Paterculus makes an accusation that Asprenas was something of a profiteer, because after the Battle of Teutoburg he seized much of the property and inheritances of those who were killed in the battle.[90]

Varus' other deputy governor, Gaius Numonius Vala, Commander of the Lower Rhine Army, was *not* a relative.

> Vala had a less straightforward career and was several years older than Asprenas, possibly in his early forties. He was from an upwardly mobile, if not well-known, family that originally came from the region of Campania, south-east of Naples. His father appears to have been a coiner of some repute...His age would suggest that his command in Germany was not his first military posting...This suggests that Vala was legate and in position before Varus and Asprenas appeared...Going down the chain of command, while nothing is known of Asprenas' camp commanders in Upper Germany, we know that Vala commanded three camp commanders in Lower Germany: Lucius Eggius, Ceionius and Lucius Caedicius.[91]

Vala might have been the 18th Legion's legate, a hypothesis based on the facts that the 18th was most likely located at Xanten, Varus' headquarters was located at Xanten, and Vala was present with Varus at the Battle of Teutoburg. Aside from Asprenas and possibly Vala, we don't know the names of any other legion commanders.

I imagine that not long after Varus arrived, Arminius stepped in.

> Thereupon appeared a young man of noble birth, brave in action and alert in mind, possessing an intelligence quite beyond the ordinary barbarian; he was, namely, Arminius, the son of Sigimer, a prince of that nation, and he showed in his countenance and in his eyes the fire of the mind within.[92]

Arminius definitely saw service in the Great Illyrian Revolt in 6 AD, and was afterwards sent to Germania, probably arriving the next year in 7 AD after Varus, which would make Arminius 23 years old at the time of his newest post. What sort of work would Arminius have done for Varus? No one actually states Arminius' job specifics, but I dare say we can make some educated guesses. It is certain that he would have performed several functions. Firstly, he would have acted as a translator, knowing how to speak both Latin and Germanic, and possibly even a little Greek if he was well-schooled. I wish to state, though, that it's very likely that he had been in Rome's service for over half of his life, and during that time he might have forgotten how to speak his native Germanic language. This is referred to by linguists as 'language attrition'. A bilingual person who is forced to continuously use their second language more often than their first language often forgets parts of their original first language. Language skill and proficiency deteriorates and is sometimes completely forgotten altogether. In order to determine if this might have happened to Arminius, it all depends on whether or not he would have been in frequent contact with fellow Germans who still spoke Germanic as a native language and whose proficiency had not deteriorated due to excessive use in speaking Latin. It is known that Arminius led a cohort of Germanic auxiliaries, so he would have been around fellow Germans, and almost certainly members of the Cherusci tribe, but these men might have been under Rome's care for just as long as he had been, and they too might have forgotten large chunks of their native language due to long periods of disuse and the dominant usage of Latin. The best way for Arminius to retain his native tongue would be for him to regularly go back to Germania and be around people who spoke the native language as a first language. Would Arminius have been allowed to go back to Germania on a regular basis to visit his family? Possibly, but there's no way we can be certain.

Secondly, he would have been an advisor to Varus on Germanic society, customs, and culture. Fellow Romans might give biased and overly-outlandish reports on what sort of people the Germanic barbarians were. Roman soldiers fighting in Germania likely had contemptuous disrespect for the people they fought against, and would have had an axe to grind. Colonial and imperial powers, or even other cultures who regard themselves as being more civilized than others, look down upon people that they regard as primitive. Native tribal cultures especially feel the brunt of this air of superiority, and are often regarded as backward savages engaging in all manner of heathen rituals, many of which are attributed to be overly-superstitious or even demonic in nature. Outlandish stories are often believed due to people's ignorance of the truth and common popular perceptions about what tribal peoples are supposed to be like, preconceptions which have endured even to this day. Images of people either semi-naked or fully naked, face paint, bones through noses, animal skins, feathers, war drums, dancing, and human sacrifice are potent in the minds of modern people just as much as they were to the imperialistic Victorians, the American colonists, and the ancient Romans. Having an actual German, a 'civilized' German by Roman perceptions, would help to put aside all of the stereotyped nonsense and give true information about his people. His knowledge on Germanic society, customs, and culture would help Romans understand their newfound subjects and act appropriately. Too often, rebellions had occurred because Romans blundered their way into things and chose not to act tactfully. With a person fully knowledgeable on Germanic society, the Romans could act with more finesse and not step on anyone's toes. Unfortunately, it has been demonstrated more than once in the past that having thorough and complete knowledge of your enemy's ways helps to conquer them more thoroughly, the idea being that you can figure out the best ways to subtly twist his thinking around to your way and not his. Cassius Dio clearly states the effects of this subtle practice of gradually converting (for lack of a better word) the Germans to living a more Roman lifestyle.

> The barbarians were adapting themselves to Roman ways, were becoming accustomed to hold markets, and were meeting in peaceful assemblages. They had not, however, forgotten their ancestral habits, their native manners, their old life of independence, or the power derived from arms. Hence, so long as they were unlearning these customs gradually and by the way, as one may say, under careful watching, they were not disturbed by the change in their manner of life, and were becoming different without knowing it.[93]

Arminius would provide information of the Germanic way of life, and the Romans would act upon that information, exploiting it for their own advantage. One wonders if the Romans had every intention of using Arminius as a tool in this way. Moreover, one wonders if Arminius himself realized that the Romans were using his cultural expertise for their own purposes. If so, it may very well have been one of the causes for his rebellion.

Thirdly, and most important of all, he would have acted as Rome's ambassador to the Cherusci tribe specifically and perhaps to all nearby tribes by extension, luring the barbarians over to the Roman way of doing things. No doubt Arminius would tell them of the benefits of being under Roman rule – technology, education, social advancement, and a chance for glory via military service, which was very important for a warrior-based society. Arminius, therefore, acted as Rome's official public relations representative to the Germans. He would have answered questions and served as an intermediary in disputes. Arminius would have acted as part arbitrator, part PR man, part spokesperson, part recruiter, engaging in the common colonial or imperialist practice of dangling the carrot. He was a man who wore many hats.

Arminius must have performed his new duties very well. In fact, because he was entrusted with performing so many functions, he must have been regarded as a figure of great importance within Varus' staff. This is corroborated by Cassius Dio, who states that Arminius soon became an important member of Varus' inner circle, and one of his most trusted friends.[94]

None of the ancient authors who discuss the events leading up to the Battle of Teutoburg go into any length on Varus' administration of Germania Magna, but from the few fragments that exist, we can develop a picture of what Varus' three years as the governor of that province were like.

> It is more difficult to retain than to create provinces; they are won by force, they are secured by justice. Therefore our joy was short-lived; for the Germans had been defeated rather than subdued, and under the rule of Drusus they respected our moral qualities rather than our arms. After his death they began to detest the licentiousness and pride not less than the cruelty of Quintillius Varus. He had the temerity to hold an assembly and had issued an edict against the Catthi (sic), just as though he could restrain the violence of barbarians by the rod of a lictor and the proclamation of a herald.[95]

Florus says here what many conquering armies have discovered – conquering a country is easy; holding onto it is the hard part. Only Florus speaks of 'cruelty' when describing Varus' administration; no other author speaks of him as being brutal towards the Germans, which makes me wonder if this claim by Florus is an exaggeration. Florus does, however, state what other authors have stated about Varus – that he ruled Germania as though it were a firmly–established province, which it clearly wasn't.

Cassius Dio comments that once in power, Varus tried to step up the process of Romanization among the Germans. Previously, the discarding of native customs and the adoption of Roman ones had occurred at a slow, almost imperceptible pace, which is probably the best way for one culture to become assimilated into another.

So long as they were unlearning these customs gradually and by the way, as one may say, under careful watching, they were not disturbed by the change in their manner of life, and were becoming different without knowing it. But when Quintilius Varus became governor of the province of Germany, and in the discharge of his official duties was administering the affairs of these peoples also, he strove to change them more rapidly. Besides issuing orders to them as if they were actually slaves of the Romans, he exacted money as he would from subject nations. To this they were in no mood to submit, for the leaders longed for their former ascendancy and the masses preferred their accustomed condition to foreign domination. Now they did not openly revolt, since they saw that there were many Roman troops near the Rhine and many within their own borders; instead, they received Varus, pretending that they would do all he demanded of them, and thus they drew him far away from the Rhine into the land of the Cherusci, toward the Visurgis, and there by behaving in a most peaceful and friendly manner led him to believe that they would live submissively without the presence of soldiers.[96]

When placed in charge of the army in Germany, he entertained the notion that the Germans were a people who were men only in limbs and voice, and that they, who could not be subdued by the sword, could be soothed by the law. With this purpose in mind he entered the heart of Germany as though he were going among a people enjoying the blessings of peace, and sitting on his tribunal he wasted the time of a summer campaign in holding court and observing the proper details of legal procedure. But the Germans, who with their great ferocity combine great craft, to an extent scarcely credible to one who has had no experience with them, and are a race to lying born, by trumping up a series of fictitious lawsuits, now provoking one another to disputes, and now expressing their gratitude that Roman justice was settling these disputes, that their own barbarous nature was being softened down by this new and hitherto unknown method, and that quarrels which were usually settled by arms were now being ended by law, brought Quintilius to such a complete degree of negligence, that he came to look upon himself as a city praetor administering justice in the forum, and not a general in command of an army in the heart of Germany.[97]

Based upon the preceding passages by Florus, Dio, and Paterculus, it appears as though Varus was a very black-and white person in the area of governance – a certain land either *was* a Roman province or it *wasn't*. In his mind, Roman provinces were safe, militarily secure, and had a taxable population, whereas non-Roman lands were dangerous and full of hostile natives who needed to be brought into subjugation. So Varus, due to his way of seeing things, didn't recognize Germania Magna as unstable since, at least in his mind, if the Romans controlled it, it *was* stable. This is probably due to the fact that he was the governor of Africa and Syria for several years, both of which had been under Roman control for generations and were more or less safe and fully assimilated into the Roman Empire. Germania Magna, by contrast, was still in a hazy transitionary state from independence to subjugation. Germania was a new experiment and therefore the standard rules governing established regions didn't apply there, but Varus didn't understand this.

No wonder, therefore, that upon his arrival, he treated the Germans as though they were subjects and had been so for generations, as opposed to what they really were, which were people who were still in the process of being gradually assimilated into the Roman way of doing things. Social changes for the Germanic people had until then occurred in a somewhat sporadic jerky pace, with little bits of Roman-ness gaining ground here and there. With Varus, Romanization crashed in like a roller coaster. If Rome controlled it, it needed to be *entirely* Roman.

Varus began by levying taxes. All Roman subjects paid taxes, and since the Germans had submitted to the Romans a couple of years prior, taxes would have been familiar to them, but I'm assuming that the taxes involved were both small and seldom collected, perhaps only once a year. Varus naturally assumed that the Germans were now Roman subjects like everyone else, and as such, they were expected to pay the same taxes as everyone else. Such an assumption makes perfect sense, at least when viewed through his eyes and his beliefs regarding Roman provincial control. If people in Spain or Gaul had to pay a certain amount each month, then the Germans had to do so as well. One set of rules for everybody. I believe that, since the Germans surely must have been paying taxes before, they would have gotten used to the idea of taxation, and perhaps would have tolerated it if the amounts expected were small enough. But Cassius Dio clearly states that upon Varus' arrival, he exacted large sums of money from them, so that must mean that the Germans were now expected to pay higher taxes than before and to pay them more frequently, perhaps once a month as opposed to once a year as had been the case before. In *their* eyes, such a radical change would have been seen as intolerably oppressive, especially considering that the Germans as a culture did not acknowledge monetary worth. Taxes and money were something new to them, and now, they were being ordered to collect more and more for the imperial treasury.

In regards to money, some of our best archaeological evidence for Varus' governorship of Germania Magna comes from recovered coinage. It was, after all, the discovery of a substantial amount of Roman coins which first alerted archaeologists and historians that Kalkriese, the location where one portion of the Battle of Teutoburg took place, almost certainly the fighting which occurred on the second day, was the site of a large Roman presence within northwestern Germany. Varus' presence in the area of the Rhine River between the years 7–9 AD, the years of his governorship of the province, is proven by the presence of large numbers of coins counter-marked with his name. Most of these are copper *as* (pl. *asi*) coins, which were minted in the city of Lugdunum (modern-day Lyon, France), where a mint had been established on Caesar Augustus' orders around the year 13 BC as a means for the empire to pay its soldiers. Many of these coins were stamped at the military bases that these soldiers were posted at with the names of the unit commanders. The reason why was because commanders would sometimes give bonuses to the troops, and they stamped their names on the coins to perpetually remind the men of their generosity. Many of the coins found in Roman military bases along the Rhine and in the western German interior have the letters VAR stamped on them, and it's obvious who the letters VAR stand for.[98]

Another way that we can see that Varus thought Germania was secure was that he dispersed the troops under his command. Rather than concentrating them around forts, he spread them throughout the countryside manning smaller but still vital posts, and their duties were changed from defending the province from attack, to enforcing the law by arresting criminals, overseeing trade, and so forth.[99] Again, this isn't odd, considering that Varus viewed Germania Magna as a standard Roman province where everything was secure and duties pertained now solely to administration. In his eyes, now that hostilities were over, the legions could be put to use acting like a makeshift police force. To the Germans, who were accustomed to seeing the soldiers largely confined to areas around army camps, having squads of heavily-armed men being sent all over the countryside enforcing the governor's will (which was already seen as oppressive due to the sudden increase in taxation) must have seemed like the actions of a tyrannical government. A governor uses the legions as his law enforcers, his muscle? It was an unheard of level of authoritarian control. Only tyrants used soldiers to get their way.

Heavy taxation and having armed men at practically every trading post, river crossing, and supply route was unsettling for the tribes. This sort of crack-down control, which was apparently far harsher than the firm-handed approach employed by Varus' predecessor Saturninus, was something which was brand new to the Germans, and understandably, they didn't like it. Cassius Dio sums up their sentiments: 'The leaders longed for their former ascendancy, and the masses preferred their accustomed condition to foreign domination.'[100] Well, what to do? Resistance was futile, that was obvious. But the liberty-conscious Germans felt it insufferable to continue as they were.

The Germans who had long been regretting that their swords were rusted and their horses idle, as soon as they saw the toga and experienced laws more cruel than arms, snatched up their weapons under the leadership of Armenius.[101]

It isn't stated in any of the accounts how or why Arminius changed his loyalties from pro-Roman to anti-Roman, but something must have happened that made Arminius question where his real loyalties lay. Attempts made at reconstructing the events which were to change him forever are probable but purely fictitious, and there's no way we can ever know if these guesses are actually correct. It's probable that Arminius' sentiments changed over a period of time, and was not a quick transformation, the result of a long series of many little things which occurred gradually, the anger and the bitterness against Rome steadily and imperceptibly accumulating and building up inside him. Regardless of exactly how it happened, Arminius had begun to seriously entertain the idea of launching a rebellion against the Romans.

At first, then, he admitted but a few, later a large number, to a share in his design; he told them, and convinced them too, that the Romans could be crushed, added execution to resolve, and named a day for carrying out the plot.[102]

The reason why Arminius didn't tell more people at first was because there were many pro-Roman Germans, like he once was, and if they learned of Arminius' treasonous plot, then his death warrant was signed. One of them was his own uncle, Inguiomerus, 'whose influence with the Romans was long-standing'.[103] Eventually, he joined sides with his rebellious nephew. Among the more influential pro-Roman Germans was Segestes, who might have been Arminius' uncle (again, this idea is disputed). Segestes was a high-ranking nobleman from the Cherusci tribe, just like Arminius, although he may have been from a different clan. Like Arminius, he had been granted Roman citizenship, and also his son Sigimund as well, who at that time was serving as a priest in Cologne. Segestes was also the father of the woman who would later become Arminius' wife – Thusnelda. Arminius was passionately enamoured with this woman, even though she was already betrothed to another man, but Arminius didn't care. In the future, the two of them would elope, with Thusnelda disregarding her father's intentions for her, such was Arminius' love for her. Arminius, though, had no love for Thusnelda's father; he and Segestes couldn't stand each other. Segestes let his pro-Roman feelings be very well known. Tacitus records a speech that he delivered to Germanicus several years after the Battle of Teutoburg:

> This is not my first day of loyalty and steadfastness towards the Roman people. From the time when I was presented with citizenship by Divine Augustus, I have selected my friends and enemies in accordance with your interests—and not through hatred of my fatherland (traitors are resented also by the side which they prefer) but because my verdict was that one thing was advantageous to Romans and Germans alike, namely peace rather than war.[104]

In the end, Segestes' people, clamouring for battle against the Romans, out-voted Segestes and his calls for Roman friendship and opposition towards Arminius. Segestes was forced to throw in his lot with Arminius and his rebel supporters, and was brought into the fold under protest. Segestes' son, Sigimund, also joined the rebel cause, although he would later have second thoughts and ask the Romans to show mercy to him.[105]

Some tried to remain neutral. The powerful and war-like Chatti, possibly the strongest tribe in western Germania, don't appear among the roster of tribes that pledged themselves to Arminius' cause. Due to the Chatti's power, they had long been a target for Roman aggression. Drusus attacked them several times during his campaign in Germania, and the tribe suffered greatly. The historian Strabo refers to the once-powerful Chatti as being one of the impoverished tribes of Germania,[106] no doubt a reflection of the constant warfare and destruction which was inflicted upon them. The Chatti may very well have had enough of bloodshed, and so when Arminius raised his war banner, once again calling the Germans to arms, the Chatti tried to stay out of the fighting. The last thing that they wanted was *another* war. However, war soon found them, and the Romans attacked them in the years after the battle. The Marcomanni, the most powerful tribe in southern Germania, also tried to remain neutral, possibly because its leader Maroboduus was a Roman citizen, or possibly because Maroboduus knew that if he joined Arminius it might very well be the death sentence for his nation. Following the battle, Arminius tried to sway the Marcomanni over to his side by sending Varus' decapitated head to Maroboduus as a gift. Instead of accepting it, which the Romans would have interpreted as an act of collaboration and thus make the Marcomanni a target for Roman aggression, Maroboduus sent the head back to Rome for proper burial. Eventually, Arminius would declare war upon the Marcomanni for refusing to support him.

Other tribes openly refused to go along with Arminius' plan. One of those who rejected Arminius' call for rebellion were the Ampsivarians (different from the Angrivarians, who *did* support Arminius's cause). They were one of the Cherusci tribe's neighbours, located to the northwest of the Cherusci's territory, near the modern-day Netherlands-Germany border. The Ampsivarians were led by Boiocalus, a pro-Roman chief, who recounted years later that Arminius had him imprisoned for refusing to help him in his war against the Romans, known as 'the Cheruscan rebellion',[107] fully showing that the Cherusci tribe, the tribe that Arminius belonged to, was the main force behind this uprising. Chief Boiocalus afterwards joined sides with the Romans during their revenge campaign against Arminius following the Battle of Teutoburg. Interestingly and ironically, fifty years later during the reign of Emperor Nero, the Ampsivarians would launch their own rebellion against Rome. The Chauci, another pro-Roman tribe who lived in what is now Lower Saxony in northwestern Germany, also refused to help Arminius. In fact, during the revenge campaign, the Chauci sided with the Romans and even provided them with auxiliary troops to fight Arminius' rebels.[108]

Regardless of the objections of some and the outright defiance of others, Arminius' call to arms had stirred enough passion in enough men to make his plan possible. The Cherusci were behind him, and so were the Marsi, Bructeri, and Angrivarians. The decision was made – Rome would be driven out of Germania, and the Germanic people would be free once again. All that was needed was to decide when and how. It was one thing to decide to make war upon the Romans, but it was another thing entirely to come up with a good plan as to how to do it. Although the Roman military no doubt suffered its share of defeats, its successes far outnumbered them, and the Germans had long memories about the massacres inflicted upon them by the Romans in years past – Gaius Marius, Julius Caesar, Drusus Claudius Nero, and Tiberius Claudius Nero. How do you not merely defeat but completely destroy the Roman presence in Germania? In response to these imposing questions, which must have gone through everyone's mind at that time, Arminius, an experienced veteran of the Roman military and well-seasoned in battle, drew up a plan on how to overpower the best military in the Western world, and it was an absolute gem.

Chapter Six

The Battle

Prelude to Disaster

It had been decided that the Romans had to pay with their lives for their unjust treatment of the Germans. The organization of the rebellion must have taken considerable time and even more secrecy to avoid the Romans detecting their intentions. But just exactly how do you keep secret an entire population mobilizing for war? I haven't the faintest idea, but however he managed to do it, Arminius did it very well.

The way that the Germans thought to lure Varus and his men into the battle was to have an isolated tribal rebellion. It isn't certain whether this was an actual planned uprising or if it was just a tale that was invented to get Varus to march there with his men.

> Then there came an uprising, first on the part of those who lived at a distance from him, deliberately so arranged, in order that Varus should march against them and so be more easily overpowered while proceeding through what was supposed to be friendly country, instead of putting himself on his guard as he would do in case all became hostile to him at once.[1]

It isn't stated in any ancient source which tribe was to begin the revolt, but Adrian Murdoch believes that it was the Angrivarians,[2] a hypothesis that I agree with. The Angrivarians were the Cherusci's immediate northern neighbours, and as such were far away from the main encampment of Fort Vetera. A rebellion there would lure the Roman soldiers far away from their base, stretching their supply and communication lines. If something went wrong, they could be easily cut off, surrounded, and destroyed. If the Angrivarians indeed *were* the ones who began the revolt, it was extremely fitting because their tribal name was a fantastic pun for this situation –

'Angry at the Varians'; in other words, opposing or attacking those who were with Varus.

Where was Varus when all of this was happening? This is important because we know that Varus had a large portion of the army with him, and determining where everyone was helps to deduce Varus' path of advance through Germania. Several modern accounts state that he and his army were at Minden, but this cannot be true because Minden is where the Angrivarians lived! It doesn't make any sense to go on a journey to attack the Angrivarians if they are in your own backyard. So, Varus and his men must have logically been in a different location during this time. There are two main choices on hand – Fort Vetera, located on the Gallic side of the Rhine, and Fort Aliso, located on the Lippe River slightly into the interior of the province. It is unlikely that they would have been at Fort Vetera While this legionary stronghold had originally served as Varus' headquarters when he first arrived to preside over the province, his new administrative centre would have been re-located to Fort Aliso. This establishment was much better suited as a summertime base camp than Fort Vetera, being closer to where the action was, necessary when going on campaign. Although it wasn't too far away, being only a little more than thirty miles west of Fort Vetera, it was far enough into the interior of the country to allow Varus to spread out his men and his influence into Germania better from this location than from a small fort on the other side of the Rhine. Fort Vetera was too far west to have been an effective centre of administration and communication within the province, let alone as a forward military base. It would also mean having to travel a very great distance from here to Minden, a much longer and more arduous journey than if he had set out from Fort Aliso. Therefore, the most likely answer is that Varus and his men were at Fort Aliso just prior to this battle, and it was from here that he would set out from.

Sometime prior to the unfolding of this fake rebellion, Varus was met by Segestes, who repeatedly warned Varus of Arminius' plot, and urged Varus to place Arminius under arrest.[3] However, Varus refused to believe him, stating that Arminius and the other Germans were his friends. Paterculus ominously notes 'After this first warning, there was no time left for a second'.[4]

Many historians have crucified Varus for this as an unforgivable error in judgment, but let's be fair. Segestes and Arminius' father Segimerus were rival clan chiefs among the Cherusci tribe, and Segestes and Arminius had a long history of ill-feeling. Later in his life, after this battle, Arminius would elope with Segestes' daughter Thusnelda, and Segestes was adamantly against Arminius marrying his daughter, let alone eloping with her. That being said, one wonders if Arminius was even now showing his love for Thusnelda, and Segestes was trying to think of a way to stop it. The last thing that Varus wanted was to get himself involved in another family dispute which could have wide-reaching repercussions, like what had happened in Judea. He didn't seem to be particularly eager to repeat what had happened those many years ago with Herod's heirs. Besides, Cassius Dio states that Segimerus and Arminius were good friends of Varus, and Varus became very upset whenever anyone suspected these two Germans of ill will.[5] Although it isn't recorded what Varus' exact response to Segestes' warning was, Paterculus says that Varus dismissed Segestes' warning, saying that he had been good to the Germans and he trusted them. I can also imagine him citing the rivalry between the two clans with each thinking of a way to undo the other, of Segestes' hatred of Arminius due to his feelings for his daughter, and with Varus stating once more that he had known Arminius for the better part of three years and was a trusted advisor and friend, and that he didn't want to hear anything more said about his character. Varus, therefore, had no reason to suspect Arminius of conspiracy or treachery. Florus writes 'Varus was so confident of peace that he was quite unperturbed even when the conspiracy was betrayed to him by Segestes, one of the chiefs.'[6] Segestes himself later commented that he was 'put off by that leader's sluggishness',[7] meaning Varus and his refusal to act on his repeated warnings.

Then, word arrived of the Angrivarian uprising. Varus acted quickly. In response, he sent the 17th, 18th, and 19th Legions to deal with the revolt. Varus could have easily dispatched just one legion to take care of the situation. Why send three? Moreover, why did he himself have to go? Couldn't he just send one of the legates, or perhaps one of his two deputies to command the troops?

Firstly, let's deal with the question of why Varus sent so many men to deal with this tribal uprising, and to do that, we have to talk about communication. People who live in modern society are accustomed to almost instantaneous communication, but this is only a recent development. For almost all of human history, communications were slow to arrive and full of tense anxiety in between dispatches. Therefore, by the time the news of the Angrivarian uprising reached Varus, the revolt may have been in progress for a week or possibly longer, considering that Germania had few roads at the time and dispatch riders may have had to cross stretches of wilderness. Within those seven days, the situation could have become much graver, and Varus knew that. If he sent men to deal with the uprising, by the time they would get there, which could be *another* seven days, the rebellion could have spread to the surrounding tribes. Anticipating that the enemy strength might have increased, Varus decided to send many more men than actually necessary, just in case things were more serious than first reported.

There would have also been a secondary purpose to sending so many men. If no other tribes had joined the Angrivarians, which I'm assuming that Varus was hoping for (I don't think that he would have wanted a repeat of the earlier Germanic revolt of 1–4 AD), Varus could always station the other legions around the neighbouring tribal lands in order to make sure that the rebellion wouldn't spread and the area would be kept pacified. So, whether or not other tribes had joined the Angrivarians, Varus needed many more men, either to fight a larger-than-suspected enemy or just to keep the peace.

Now comes the question of why Varus himself had to go with the men instead of someone else. He could have easily entrusted matters to the legion commanders, or perhaps to one of his two deputy governors, but Varus had to come with the men. It was expected that in times of hostility, a governor had to take care of military affairs within his own province. Varus had led his men in Judea when he suppressed the revolt there. Other governors in other provinces commanded troops stationed in those provinces whenever unrest flared up. Commanding troops was one of the tenets of a successful Roman life, and a person who did not flex their military muscle was regarded as weak. Politicians did (and still do) use records of their military service, either as soldiers serving in war or as the leader of militaristic expeditions and missions, just as Varus was doing right now, in order to garner support during elections or to gain royal favour. To not command troops yourself would be a break of tradition, as well as being seen as a sign of weakness – you were either too lazy, too incapable, or too cowardly to lead the men yourself, so you had someone else do it for you. Such tongue-wagging gossip could ruin a man's reputation, especially if he was in a high social position. Aside from keeping to form, as well as keeping a good image, another reason that Varus would have accompanied his men was to provide morale. The governor was a very important person, perhaps *the* most important person in the province. Varus came to provide assurance to his men that there was no reason for them to fear for their safety. If the governor was coming, then it must be safe, right? This idea perhaps contributed to the legions' abhorrently lax and undisciplined conduct during the march, as I will describe further on.

Popular history states that three whole legions were massacred during the Battle of Teutoburg, but exactly how many Romans were journeying to Angrivarian lands? Paterculus states that there were three legions, three cavalry detachments, and six cohorts of auxiliaries.[8] How many men would this be? The basic unit of a legion was the squad called a *contubernium*, which consisted of eight men. Ten contubernia created a *century* (eighty men). Six centuries made a *cohort* (480 men). Ten cohorts made a *legion* (4,800 men). Keep in mind that these numbers do not include officers. Also, the 1st Century of the 1st Cohort would always be double-strength, numbering at 160 men instead of eighty (later on around 50 AD, the 1st Cohort would be re-organized so that there were only five centuries in it, but each of these five centuries were double-strength). All this means that, on paper, a legion constituted around 5,000 men. Each legion had a detachment of cavalry to act as scouts and pursuers. The detachment was divided into four platoons consisting of thirty horsemen each, totalling 120 cavalrymen per legion. With three legions, that means there were 360 legionary cavalrymen on this mission. Also accompanying the legion were artillerists. In addition to cavalry, each legion also had sixty 'scorpion' catapults (large crossbows which could shoot arrows) accompanying it, one for each century of infantrymen, each with a crew of perhaps two men, totalling 120 artillerists per legion. Although Paterculus does not mention artillery being brought along on the expedition, archaeologists have uncovered artillery ammunition at the battle site, indicating that catapults *were* brought along, although how many is completely unknown. Auxiliaries were not organized into legions, but standardized at the cohort level. With each auxiliary cohort at around 500 men, there would have been a maximum of 3,000 auxiliaries in the battle. This would bring the total number of Roman soldiers to 18,360 men, not including officers.[9]

Many popular accounts of this battle from modern times depict the Romans as losing their entire force, with casualty estimates ranging from 15,000 to 20,000 men. This range would fit perfectly with the full-strength force of 18,360 men which Varus purportedly brought with him. But this is with the understanding that the units in question were at their full-strength and were all present on hand to deal with the rebellion. In reality, the legions were almost always undermanned. One example of what the true numbers of those fit for duty at any given time comes from a document found at Fort Vindolanda, located on Hadrian's Wall, and dated to the late first century AD.

The document says that the first cohort of Tungrians from northern Gaul was 752 men strong, commanded by six centurions…Of those 752 men, forty six were on secondment to the governor of Britain's guard; 337 men and two centurions were at Corbridge, another camp on the Wall; and one centurion was in London on business unknown. It is impossible to read where the others where, but in the end, there were only 296 men left in Vindolanda under one centurion – of whom thirty-five were unfit for duty, either ill or wounded. That leaves thirty-five per cent of the men on active service. This state of affairs was not exceptional and is corroborated by a daily report on a detachment of soldiers found on an ostracon in Bu-Njem in Tripolitania in the third century. Of the fifty-seven men stationed at the fort, over half were away on exercises, sick, or seconded to other projects.[10]

Even if a legion did not have men dispersed to other locations, there were still deficiencies in the ranks created by bribery. Many people are always trying to get out of doing work, and Roman soldiers were no exception to this. This may be shocking to some to learn that a substantial percentage of the Roman military was made up of goldbricks who evaded work at every opportunity. This contrasts sharply with our popular conceptions of a Roman soldier, who purportedly joined the ranks either out of patriotism, a sense of duty as a Roman, in search of adventure and conquest, or even for the lucrative benefits that would await him, including a substantial cash bonus upon discharge equivalent to several years' salary. But keep in mind that Romans who entered the legion were expected to devote twenty-five years of their life to the military, most of it being front-line service. Their pay was rather minimal, even by modern standards; even today, a soldier's salary is rather small, and it is sometimes said that no one joins the army to get rich. While life for the higher-ranking officers could be considerably plush, the living conditions for the ordinary soldiers were rather Spartan. Work, toil, and hard labour occupied a majority of a legionary's service. Discipline was harsh, and you could be severely beaten for what we would consider to be relatively minor infractions. Serious offences would often result in executions. And then there was the constant risk of dying in battle, and to some legionaries it must have seemed to be an impossible task to stay alive for the full duration of their twenty-five year service contracts. For those who had joined the Army seeking to gain personal glory on the battlefield, the real life of a soldier in the emperor's legions must have been a disheartening shock. No wonder, therefore, that people tried to escape from it, but a temporary reprieve from duty came at a high price. According to Tacitus, legionaries who wanted leave had to pay high bribes to their centurions in order for them to approve their requests. It got to the point where paying for leave amounted to a form of taxation, which was often very steep and excessive. Of course, those who had the money could afford to buy their way out of doing work, but since the pay rates for Roman soldiers were minimal, the way that they got such large amounts of cash was usually by stealing, outright robbery, or perhaps by earning some small wage from a second job that the legionaries had on the side, which in itself indicates how low army wages were for the ordinary infantrymen, and how desperate they were for money. One out of every four men in a century, twenty out of every eighty men, would be either away on leave or loafing around the camp on 'excused duty'. Thus, Tacitus concludes, the legions were ruined by idleness, laziness, and lack of discipline.[11]

The fact that Varus' legions were not up to full strength is corroborated by Cassius Dio, who states that Varus had not kept his force concentrated in one spot, but had scattered the men everywhere, dispersing them throughout the province.[12] So, there is absolutely no way that he would have had the complete 18,360 men immediately available to him. Even if he had wanted to collect everyone for this expedition, he would have had a very difficult time rounding them up. Tracking down where they all were and collecting them would have taken weeks, time which Varus' didn't have. The Angrivarian rebellion needed to be crushed quickly, and Varus could not afford to sit around for weeks while small parties of his soldiers slowly dribbled into his main encampment from here and there. In that time, the rebels might become too strong for him to handle. He needed to march on the rebels now with the men that he already had. So, Varus did not take three whole fully-manned legions into the forests of Germania, as per popular conception – the number was actually much less than that. As to how much less, this cannot be determined with any certainty. If only around three-quarters to one-third of a legion was available for duty at any given time, then this means that out of the estimated full-strength 15,000 men in the three legions, there would have only been between 5,000–11,200 legionaries available for duty during this mission, not including the cavalry or artillerists. The difference between thirty-three per cent and seventy-five per cent is a very wide gap, and regrettably there's really no way that we can further refine this number to a more compact percentage bracket. Let's assume that all of the cavalry were present, bringing the minimum number to 5,360, and the maximum number to 11,560. Auxiliaries were often stationed as police and security forces, so their percentage might have been substantially less, perhaps one-third to one-half. Out of 3,000 auxiliaries, this leaves a minimum of 1,000 men, and a maximum of 1,500 men. Adding the auxiliaries to this brings the total number of soldiers to a minimum number of 6,860, and a maximum number of men to just over 13,000. So, the number of Varus' soldiers would have been somewhere between roughly 7,000–13,000 men. Just to be on the safe side, selecting the number directly in the middle gives us 10,000 men, although I must state that this number should not be accepted as a definite statistic but as an educated guess.

Added to this number would be a considerable number of support staff in addition to the actual rank and file – administrative clerks and secretaries, craftsmen, engineers, doctors, veterinarians, cooks, and regimental chaplains. Roman records enumerate the numerous types of jobs these people held, called *immunes* because they were exempt or 'immune' from doing manual labour. These men would have been fairly substantial in number, and based upon the records that we have of this expedition, it seems that Varus took along everything including the kitchen sink. Also, large numbers of non-military artifacts have been uncovered by archaeologists at the battle site. Such objects include surveying tools, shovels, pick-axes, medical instruments, metal pens, dispatch cases, bronze platters and vases, eating utensils, buckets, and game pieces. Carrying all of this extra equipment would be pack animals such as donkeys and mules, and even supply wagons pulled by horses, mules, or oxen. Since Varus presumably had no idea how long he and his men would be in the field, he likely brought a large supply of food, drinking water, and wine with the expedition as well, which would have served only to further add to the already straining burdens of marching through relatively uncharted territory over rough terrain.[13]

In addition to the soldiers and their support staff, there would also be camp followers. These were persons who were not enrolled in the military, but served as workers or companionship. Many of them would have been members of the soldiers' families, while others would have been itinerant workers doing manual labour around the fort or marching camps in exchange for a few coins, or possibly just a meal and a roof over their heads. Where soldiers are located, prostitutes are sure to be nearby, and there were likely a few women of the oldest profession plying the men for silver in exchange for sex.

Cassius Dio makes a passing reference to the presence of camp followers among the marching column, stating that there were more than a few women and children accompanying the expedition, and even a large number of servants. Evidence of the presence of women in the marching column is attested by the discovery of several pieces of female jewellery, hairpins, and one disc-shaped brooch. If this was meant to be a purely military expedition, and one which required a great degree of urgency, why bring these non-military personnel with you, which could be more of a liability than a benefit? Why bring such a large number of non-combatants to a battle? Part of the reason might be that the soldiers would fight all the harder knowing that their families were watching them, and they would be forced to not show any cowardice or hesitation in the fight. Another reason would be that bringing their families so close to the battle would deliberately put their women and children in harm's way, and thus the soldiers would fight all the harder to make sure that they did not fall into the hands of the enemy, either as captives or as casualties. Both of these explanations are attested in Roman accounts of the barbarians that Rome faced, such as the Celts and

Germans, who brought their families with them on campaign so that they could watch their warrior menfolk conduct themselves in battle – those that acted with singular bravery and audacity were honoured and praised, while whose who held back or even showed fear in the face of the enemy were held in dishonour.[14]

As shown earlier, a large number of servants accompanied the column. These persons would have attended upon the aristocratic tribunes and other high-ranking officers, who were presumably accustomed to being waited upon. They would have also acted as pages or squires in helping the men put their armour on, and would have been responsible for keeping their weapons, armour, and clothing in good condition.

How many camp followers would there have been accompanying the Roman soldiers as they advanced through the Germanic countryside? At the Battle of Arausio, fought more than a hundred years previously, 80,000 Roman soldiers and 40,000 camp followers were killed. I refuse to believe that this large number of camp followers would be made up entirely of women and children. This is likely a number which encompasses not only the women and children of the soldiers' families, but also the support staff which was required to travel with any large military force. Still, it seems like an unusually large number, and I can scarcely believe that a third of any Roman military force would be made up of these people – the number is simply too high. It's certainly possible that these statistics are exaggerated. It's also possible that these numbers may be a special case, and that most of the time the percentage of camp followers compared with the soldiers would have been much smaller. Regrettably, there is no way that we can even begin to come up with a rough estimate of these people, as we can do with the Roman soldiers. No hints are given by any ancient source as to the number of people accompanying the Roman troops. The number of camp followers is incalculable, and any attempt made by any author to come up with a number is a blind unsubstantiated guess.

The Romans marched towards Angrivarian lands. Is there any way that we can determine what route Varus and his men would have taken? Minden, the capital of Angrivarian territory, was located northeast of Fort Aliso; the distance between the two, in a straight line, measured eighty miles. Considering that an infantryman's average marching pace is twenty miles per day, this means that on paper it would have taken Varus and his army a minimum of four days to reach their destination, but the route taken couldn't have possibly been that direct. Naturally, Varus would try to take the most direct route possible in order to put down this rebellion as fast as he could, but the route would never have been in a straight line. He would have likely travelled east up the course of the Lippe River as far as he dared before changing course and turning northwards. The town of Paderborn, which was one of the probable sites of Fort Aliso, is located on the easternmost part of the Lippe River. This might have been the army's last stop before turning northwards.

Between Haltern and Minden, although located closer towards Minden, is a strip of rugged hills and ridges known as the Lower Saxon Hills, and Varus would have had to cross through this broken territory in order to get to his destination. This terrain is characterized by two high parallel ridges called eskers, which were deposited by the retreating glaciers following the end of the Ice Age. The northern esker ridge is called the Wiehen Ridge, or the Wiehen Hills. The southern esker ridge is called the Osning Ridge, which was later renamed in the nineteenth century during an upsurge in German nationalism as the Teutoburg Ridge following an earlier erroneous belief that this location was the site of the famous battle. Although this location has been proven to be the incorrect site of the battle, the name has remained unchanged. In between these two prominent ridge lines, the territory is dominated by steep mountains, hills, and ravines, also formed through glacial activity. Interestingly, these ridges correspond with the boundaries of Cherusci territory. These ridges stretch for hundreds of miles until they terminate in the Harz Mountains, located in the southeastern part of Cherusci territory – 'Harz' is probably a modernized corruption of the name 'Cherusci'. Immediately north of the northern ridge line, the land flattens out, forming the vast North German Plain. This landscape would have been almost entirely marshland during ancient times. Indeed, even today, there are large areas of swamps and marshes in this area, such as the Großes Torfmore (located right next to Minden on the west), the Uchter Moor, the Ochsenmoor, and many others, along with several lakes and many small ponds. It would have been a wet soggy environment, one which was ill-suited for battle. Through careful study of the topography of this area,

I'm absolutely certain that Varus and his army entered this rugged landscape via a gap in the southern ridge line, located where the town of Bielefeld now stands; this pass is located north/northwest of Paderborn. After his army travelled through this pass, he would travel in a northeastern direction through the hill country (although his progress would have been slow) until he reached the Porta Westfalica Pass, the exit point on the northern ridge line. The Porta Westfalica is located four miles directly south of Minden; the Weser River runs from east to west through this hilly country until it makes a sharp northern turn through the pass and flows near Minden. After exiting the Porta Westfalica Pass, Varus' army would have easily been able to reach Minden within a day's march.

Thus, if one were to retrace Varus' planned route, he would have started off at modern-day Haltern after collecting as many men as he could within a short time. From there, he would have marched east along the Lippe until he reached the area near Paderborn. Then he would have sharply turned northwest, travelling roughly along the line of the modern A-33 autobahn highway until he got to Bielefeld. After entering through the southern pass located there, he would have travelled though the jagged hill country in a northeastern direction, more or less along the same route as the modern Federal Road 61, passing where the towns of Herford and Bad Oeynhausen stand today, until he reached the Porta Westfalica Pass. From here, he would have turned directly northwards and attacked Minden. This, I believe, was the route that Varus and his army would have taken, or at least the route that he intended to take.

How would Varus' army have advanced? We have several different accounts from a wide range of time periods concerning the marching orders of a Roman army. According to Julius Caesar, writing in the mid-first century BC, his own army advanced with the cavalry, archers, and slingers (all missile troops were auxiliaries) in the front with himself leading the way, followed by six legions, then the baggage, and then two inexperienced legions which had recently been raised guarding the rear against attack. According to the Jewish historian Josephus writing over 100 years later in the late first century AD, the Roman army led by Titus advanced in the following manner: the auxiliaries led the way, followed by the engineers and surveyors, then the commander's baggage, then a small body of infantry, then the commanding

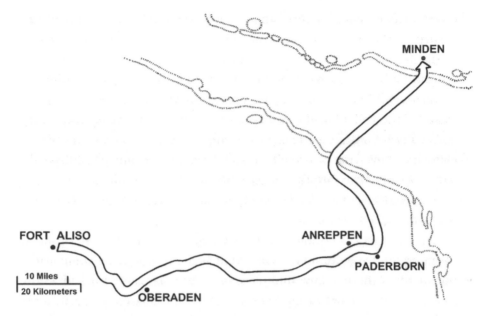

Map 3. The intended route of Varus' march. Commencing at Fort Aliso (Haltern, Germany), travelling eastward along the course of the Lippe River until reaching Anreppen or Paderborn, then marching northwards towards the Bielefeld Pass, and then marching northeast across Teutoburg towards the Porta Westfalica Pass in order to attack the Angrivarians around Minden. (*Illustration by Jason R Abdale*)

officer in the middle of the column accompanied by his bodyguards, and then the legionary cavalry, then the artillery and other siege engines, then the tribunes and high-ranking officers, then the trumpeters and standard-bearers, then the remainder of the infantry, then some more baggage, then the legionary support staff, and the mercenaries last. In Arrian's account of his battle against the Alans, a nomadic equestrian tribal culture from the Caucasus Mountains, written following the Alanic invasion of Cappadocia in 135 AD, he states in his battle orders that the vanguard of the army ought to be comprised of two 'contingents' (likely *turmae*) of mounted scouts along with their commander. After these should come various auxiliary units, including infantry, cavalry, and missile troops. After these should be the infantry. The legionary cavalry should be placed on either side, guarding the flanks, with more cavalry in the rear. In the far rear should be the catapults. The forces of Rome's allies in the region brought up the rear. In all of these accounts, the auxiliaries march first. In Caesar's account, these men are accompanied by cavalry, although it is not specifically stated if the cavalry in question are auxiliary, legionary, or both. Arrian states that the army ought to be led by cavalry scouts, followed by auxiliaries. This arrangement is similar to Caesar's battle order. Josephus states that engineers followed close behind the auxiliaries. Both Josephus and Arrian state that the artillery ought to be in the rear. Arrian makes no reference to baggage or supply wagons [15]

Considering all of these accounts, I believe we can construct Varus' march in the following manner: First, leading the way, were the auxiliary cavalry acting as scouts for the army. After them were the engineers, needed to cut a path through the German wilderness, as attested by Cassius Dio. After them was the remainder of the auxiliaries, consisting of infantry and missile troops, and a portion of the legionary cavalry. Behind the auxiliaries was a body of infantrymen. After these men was the baggage accompanied by Varus and the other high-ranking commanders. After these would be another body of infantrymen. The remainder of the legionary cavalry followed behind, and the artillery lumbered in the rear. However, as we shall see, while this might have been the intended arrangement, the army soon lost its order and different units became entangled amongst one another.

Cassius Dio says that in order to get to the rebel tribe's lands, Varus and his men needed to cross friendly territory, and therefore he hadn't put his men on guard as they would have been if they had been in hostile territory. Strabo also makes mention of this, by saying that when the Romans did come under attack, they were in the territory of the Cherusci tribe, the tribe that Arminius belonged to, and the tribe which served as the backbone of his rebellion. This makes sense, considering that the Angrivarians lived to the north near Minden, and in order to get there, the Romans had no choice but to pass through Cherusci territory. Since Varus regarded the Cherusci as being friendly to Rome, he had no reason to be on guard, and therefore the Roman soldiers were not on guard either. Little did they know what awaited them, fully vindicating Paterculus' ominous statement that the most common beginning to a disaster is a false sense of security.[16] In addition to not having his men being lax due to being in friendly territory, Cassius Dio goes further and states that they marched in no regular order.

They had with them many waggons and many beasts of burden as in time of peace; moreover, not a few women and children and a large retinue of servants were following them – one more reason for their advancing in scattered groups.[17]

The Roman column had, evidently, lost its discipline. Roman legionaries, even when travelling in peacetime or through friendly lands, marched in formation. How Varus, who had previously commanded legions in Judea, would allow his men to march as a disorganized mob with the troops intermixed with the supply wagons and the camp followers is completely beyond my comprehension.

With the column advancing through Germania the way that it was, it's easy to see why Arminius' rebels attacked the Romans when and how they did. But Arminius' strategy was much more complex than simply ambushing a stretched-out Roman column while on the march. He needed to whittle down the Romans' strength as much as he could to further put the odds in his favour. Cassius Dio remarks that even as Varus and his column marched through the German wilderness, with Arminius accompanying them, the Germans began killing Roman soldiers, stating 'Each community had put to death the detachments of soldiers for which they had previously asked.'[18] Apparently, the Germans had asked for small numbers of Roman soldiers to be quartered in their villages, presumably to act as protection from attacks by rival tribes and even criminal activity within the villages themselves. This also corroborates Dio's earlier statement that while Varus was Governor, he had scattered his military forces across the province.

He did not keep his legions together, as was proper in a hostile country, but distributed many of the soldiers to helpless communities, which asked for them for the alleged purpose of guarding various points, arresting robbers, or escorting provision trains.[19]

It is perfectly reasonable to think that among the various assignments that the legionaries received when Varus became Governor was the duty of acting as a makeshift police force or village militia. Besides, the presence of Roman soldiers in villages would ensure that the villages would be loyal to Rome and pay their taxes on time. I find it interesting, though, that the Germans were the ones who asked for these soldiers, and that it was not Varus who merely ordered them to occupy the villages. This shows that Varus was much more responsive to the concerns of the Germans than other authors have previously supposed, who have depicted him as an authoritative administrator who didn't bother listening to the Germans' requests or complaints. Instead, he seems to have been rather open to hearing requests and petitions, especially if they suited Rome's needs.

Arminius took full advantage of this. The detachments of Roman soldiers to the German villages were likely only a handful of men in number, and could have been easily overpowered and killed by the entire village population. It isn't unreasonable to think that Arminius specifically planned for this to happen on a given day as part of his attack strategy. With a large portion of the legions scattered throughout the province, with only small numbers of men in any one location, the Roman security force would have been destroyed one small piece at a time, resulting in the cumulative effect that a large number of Varus' men were massacred *en masse* within the first few hours of the rebellion, and Varus and his men were completely unaware of it. The countryside was now firmly in control of the Germanic rebels. The nearest Roman base was miles away. Unbeknownst to Varus and his men, they were now cut off in enemy territory and completely surrounded. There was little chance of escape.

The Battlefield

For centuries, the site of the infamous 'Varian Disaster' had remained hidden. Several hypotheses had been proposed throughout the years by many historians, but most of these were based upon Roman coins found in one area or another. While the discovery of coins does indeed show a Roman presence, it is hardly evidence for a battlefield. But in 1987, a British Army officer stationed in Germany named Tony Clunn uncovered the battlefield. Clunn had been an enthusiast of the battle's history for quite some time, and in March 1987, Clunn contacted Professor Wolfgang Schlüter, a German archaeologist working for the Department for Preservation of Archaeological Monuments, asking permission to search for Roman artifacts around Osnabruck. Schlüter consented, but he was sceptical that the British lieutenant would find anything. Clunn proved him wrong.[20]

Although Roman coins had been found in a number of other locations, Clunn decided on a hunch to investigate the site where a single Roman *denarius* coin was discovered in 1963 near Kalkriese Hill. Realizing the strategic importance of the site with a hill on one side and an area that was once vast swampland on the other, forming a perfect bottleneck, he began excavating at the site, and eventually found large numbers of Roman coins, which greatly intrigued Professor Schlüter. However, it's hard to look inconspicuous when you're walking up and down a field carrying a metal detector, and naturally Clunn's actions began to attract unwanted attention. Worried that the site might be plundered by souvenir hunters, Clunn worked feverishly. He found even more coins, far more than he'd ever thought that he'd uncover, but as stated earlier, coins do not show the presence of a battlefield. But along with the coins, Clunn also discovered three slingshot projectiles made of lead – distinctly military weapons. After years of subsequent excavations and piles of other uncovered artifacts, in 1998, German archaeologists officially declared that Kalkriese was indeed the correct site for the Battle of Teutoburg.[21]

Well, that's only partially true.

It should be made clear that the battlefield of Teutoburg was not a single location of a couple of hundred square yards, but stretched over many miles, and was fought over the course of several days. Many people today, especially those who are not as informed about the battle as they should be, often use the names 'Kalkriese Hill' and 'Teutoburg Forest' interchangeably. This is because many people have the mistaken idea that the entire battle took place on this one spot. That's not true. Kalkriese Hill was the location of the fighting that took place only on the second day of the multi-day battle. This means that there should be massive amounts of skeletons and artifacts located far away from this site, though trying to pinpoint the exact route that the battle took is nearly impossible. Moreover, modern development has altered the landscape considerably, likely destroying many artifacts in the process. Today, there are modern roads, a canal which runs through the route that Varus and his men are believed to have travelled, and there is even a 'Varus Golf Club'! So it is unfortunate but highly likely that the remainder of the 'battlefield' may never be uncovered.

Kalkriese Hill is located 10 miles northeast of the city of Osnabruck, Germany, just north of the westernmost point of the northern ridge line, the Wiehen Ridge. It's a small hill, being only 157m high, but its northern side is steep, making climbing difficult. Moreover, it's scarred by deep stream-cut ravines, emptying out their contents into the boglands to the north

Kalkriese Hill sits on the northern fringe of the vast Teutoburg Forest. This name has been used since ancient times, called *Teutoburgiensi saltu* in Tacitus' *Annals*, more commonly re-written as *saltus Teutoburgiensis* by secondary authors – apparently, the exact placement of the words doesn't matter.[22] The epic battle between the Romans and Germans fought in this region in 9 AD is commonly referred to as the Battle of the Teutoburg Forest. It has earned this name for two reasons. Firstly, Tacitus mentions it. Secondly, Kalkriese Hill is located right on the northern edge of the Teutoburg Forest. There has been much academic argument about the exact nature of the location's Latin name, because *saltus* can indeed be translated as 'forest', but it can also be 'pass'. To further add to the confusion, the Latin word for 'forest' is *silva*, not *saltus*. If the Roman authors wished to write 'Teutoburg Forest', why didn't they write *Teutoburga silva*?

Clearly, the Latin authors differentiated between the two, and they specifically chose *saltus*, not *silva*, to describe the landscape. Due to their obvious spelling differences, these are not words which can be easily confused. This leads one to think that the commonly-used name 'Teutoburg Forest' has been incorrect all along. So, if the Latin phrase *Teutoburgiensi saltu* doesn't mean 'Teutoburg Forest', then what does it mean?

The word *saltus* is a tricky word in Latin, since it's both a noun and a verb; it means 'jump' or 'leap', but it can also mean 'forest' and 'pass', as in a mountain pass. More appropriately, it probably means 'forested pass', 'wooded pathway', or 'a route in which people travel through woods'. The wooded connotations associated with this word have been the basis for people associating the name Teutoburg with a forest. It may also mean 'a place where people sally out from'. The English word *sally* comes from *saltus*, and means 'to emerge from; to rush or burst forward; to break out from'. It therefore implies the action of emerging out from a confining feature to more open space – from out of a forest or mountains into open areas. *Saltus*, in this case, may mean 'the location in which people travel through and emerge from a forest', which may be the most correct translation of this word. This definition gains a great deal of credibility when we read Tacitus' account of the battle, in which he describes the opening phases of the battle occurring in a forest, but by the end of the battle, the fighting had occurred in a field. This will be discussed in greater detail later in this chapter.

But there's another problem – the exact definition of the word *Teutoburgiensis* – and it is analysis of this definition that leads me to hypothesize that 'Teutoburg' was not the name of a specific geographic feature such as a forest or pass, but rather the name of the area in general. Therefore, the argument concerning whether this battle should be appropriately called that of Teutoburg Forest or Teutoburg Pass should be discarded since I feel that the Germanic name applied to both locations. The reasoning behind my hypothesis comes via Latin translation. If Teutoburg was the name of a geographic feature, the forested pass, it would have been written as *saltus Teutoburgus*, but it isn't. The Latin suffix *ensis* means 'of', specifically used in the context of 'some*thing* of some*place*', so the translation of *saltus Teutoburgiensis* would be 'the forest/pass of Teutoburg', which indicates that this wooded pass was located in an area called by this name, and that this name didn't specifically apply to either the forest or the pass itself.

But there's another problem. The suffix that is used at the end of the word is not *ensis*, but *iensis*, which denotes 'some*one* of some*place*'.[23] One example would be *Hannibal Carthaginiensis* ('Hannibal of Carthage'). This sort of grammatical device can only be used if 'saltus' is a person, not a feature of geography like a forest or a mountain pass. Therefore *saltus Teutoburgiensis* translates to 'Saltus, the person from Teutoburg', but that just can't be right! My only conclusion is that Tacitus made a slight grammatical mistake, and that it should have been written as *saltus Teutoburgensis* – 'the forest/pass of Teutoburg'. That is why this book is sub-titled *The Battle of Teutoburg* rather than *The Battle of the Teutoburg Forest*.

Now that that's out of the way, let's focus on the meaning of *Teutoburg*. *Teut* was the proto-Germanic word for 'tribe/people'. Several Germanic tribes incorporated this word into their tribal names, although in corrupted forms – the Teutons, Chatti, and Jutes. In fact, Deutschland, the German name for Germany, means 'land of the people/tribes'; *Deutsch* is a corrupted version of *teut*. In fact, in many tribal cultures, the tribal names usually mean 'people, the real people, the true people and so on'.

There have been two ways of spelling the name of this location: Teutoburg and Teutoberg. Only one letter was changed, but it could make all the difference because it is very critical in terms of our understanding of the geography of the landscape and the relationship that its native inhabitants had with it. *Burg* means roughly 'settlement', while *berg* means 'hill' or 'mountain'. Although these two words refer to different things – a settlement or a hill – Theedrich Yeat says that they could, in an abstract way, be identical, because settlements, particularly ones for defence, were usually located atop hills. Hilltop fortified towns were a common feature in non-Roman Europe. So, Teutoburg would have essentially meant 'the Tribal Stronghold', or something to that effect. It was a mountainous heavily-forested area, a good place for warriors to hide and strike out from on raids or guerilla attacks. A modern comparison to Teutoburg, 'the Tribal Stronghold', could be the so-called 'Apache Stronghold', a rugged mountainous region in the American Southwest. A part of the Sierra Madre range, it stretched for hundreds of miles, and it was here where the last free remnants of the Apache conducted their raids against the Americans and Mexicans in the late 1800s.[24]

With all of that being said, can we determine what the geographic boundaries of 'Teutoburg' were? The name and the German landscape explain it clearly. As stated in an earlier section of this chapter, in between Fort Aliso and Minden were two steep esker ridges formed by retreating glaciers at the end of the Ice Age. The glaciers carried rocks, boulders, and all sorts of debris within them and atop them, and as the glaciers melted, this debris was dropped to the ground. This process evidently occurred in two distinct phases, since two eskers, somewhat parallel to each other, are located here. In between the two eskers, the terrain is very rugged and mountainous, also formed by the glaciers dropping their payloads of rocks here, and covered in dense forests. This geographic feature extends for many miles to the east in a belt, eventually terminating in the high Harz Mountains. The boundaries of this feature correspond almost exactly with the boundaries of the territory of the Cherusci tribe, which shows that these dominant geographic features were established as marking the border between the Cherusci and their neighbours to the north and south. The terrain south of this expansive geographic feature is low rolling hills, and to the north the landscape is flat and swampy. The topography of this terrain absolutely fits with the idea of Teutoburg as 'the Tribal Stronghold', and is certainly analogous with the mountainous 'Apache Stronghold' of the Sierra Madre. These esker ridges and the mountainous territory between them constitute the region known to both the Germans and the Romans as Teutoburg, 'the Tribal Stronghold'.

What about the pass? Is there such a thing as a *saltus* in this territory, a place where people emerge from a tight confining area into more open space? The *saltus* in question is certainly the Porta Westfalica Pass, located just south of Minden, the gap in the northern esker ridge where a person exits the rugged forest-covered hills and mountains of Teutoburg and enters the flat and open expanse of the North German Plain.

The Battle's Time

We already have estimates of the numbers involved, but what other statistics do we know about the battle itself, such as the length or time of year? Cassius Dio gives the most detailed account of the battle, which he states lasted for four days. His account is the only one that gives a time-frame for the battle.

It is common knowledge among ancient and military historians that the battle took place in the year 9 AD, but during what time of year? At the excavation of the site, the skeleton of a mule was found with a bell around its neck. The bell had been stuffed with straw, presumably to keep it from making noise. Forensic analysis of the straw showed that it had been cut in late summer or early fall, placing the battle in late September.[25] So, not only did the battle's date have a year, but also a month – September of 9 AD. The battle is popularly conceived as being begun on 9 September 9 AD, but this is a date that seems to be chosen at random. Forensic evidence places the battle at late summer/early autumn, which would make it fall somewhere in late September, not early September.

The Roman Soldiers

What exactly did the Roman soldiers that fought in this battle look like? What were their weapons, armour, and equipment? I wish to state right away that despite what many of us, including myself, have been repeatedly told, the weapons, armour, and equipment of Roman soldiers were *not* standardized, at least not as far as the Roman Army as a whole. Standardization probably pertained only to the legion, so all of the soldiers in a certain legion would be equipped according to certain standards, but soldiers in different legions would have looked different from each other. For example, soldiers in one legion might wear a different type of helmet than soldiers in another legion. That being said, even the soldiers in a single legion, say the 17th which accompanied Varus into the Germanic wilderness, would have looked different from each other depending on what type of soldiers they were. Auxiliaries wore different armour than legionaries, and the infantry wore different armour and had different weapons compared to the cavalry. Regular troops wore different clothing and armour from the officers.

Let's begin with their clothing, specifically their uniforms. Roman soldiers wore short-sleeve tunics which just covered the deltoid muscles of the shoulder and came down to just above the knees. The tunics themselves were probably made of wool for the ordinary soldiers, and perhaps finer and more expensive linen for the officers. For many years, people have automatically assumed that all Roman soldiers wore red uniforms because that was what has been portrayed in popular culture, but recently, this dogmatic view has been challenged. The truth is we really aren't 100 per cent certain what colour were the uniforms worn by Roman soldiers.

The *sudarium*, also known as the *focale*, was a scarf worn around the neck to help protect the neck from chaffing while wearing body armour. It is commonly portrayed as being tied in a knot in the front. Roman soldiers also had a wool hooded cloak called a *paenula* which was worn in cold or perhaps rainy weather. There was also a non-hooded cloak called a *sagum*, although it might be better to call it a smock rather than a cloak. It's unknown what colour these items were. They might have been natural colour or dark. Many reconstructions which I have seen often show them as being brown. Records state that these cloaks, capes or whatever they might have been were worn by officers. One record from Vindolanda in northern Britain mentions an officer with a white cloak. Julius Caesar wore a red cloak or cape on the battlefield, which made him instantly recognizable to his men.[26]

Another easily-identified feature of the Roman soldier were his sandals, called *caligae* (singular *caliga*). It was made of a series of leather strips attached to a sole, which were then tied together on the top of the foot using a thin piece of leather. The spacing between the straps allowed for air to circulate, and for water to drain out. Iron hobnails were fixed into the underside of the sole to better grip the surface. Although Roman soldiers are often thought to have not worn socks, evidence from the Vindolanda Tablets discovered at Hadrian's Wall clearly shows that Romans wore socks in colder climates.[27]

The Legionary Infantry

Some scholars and historians refer to the Roman infantry of this time period as 'legionaries'. Technically speaking, *any* soldier within a legion, from buck-private to legion commander was a 'legionary'. The ordinary soldier was referred to as a *miles* (MEE-laiz), which means literally 'soldier'; the modern word 'military' comes from this. They were sometimes referred to as *gregarii*, meaning literally 'herd animals' or 'livestock'.[28] That pretty much sums up what certain officers must have thought of their men, or perhaps what the men depressingly thought of themselves – sheep blindly following their shepherds, going to the slaughter.

A crucial piece of a Roman soldier's kit was his helmet, called a *galea* or a *cassis*. There were many different kinds of helmets that the legionaries could have worn, with several types being in service at the same time. Archaeological evidence from sites in Germany dated to the Roman occupation, and from the site of the Battle of Teutoburg, show that the Romans who were in Germania during this time wore two different types of helmets: the 'Gallic' type and the 'Coolus' type.[29] However, these are rather broad categories, since both of these helmet designs underwent many changes as the decades went by. Can we refine this any further?

The 'Imperial Gallic type-A', whose usage is dated from 25–5 BC, would have certainly been worn by Drusus' soldiers during his famous Germanic campaign. This hypothesis is based on the fact that a helmet of this type was discovered at Nijmegen, which Drusus used as a military base. It also might have been the helmet worn by the Roman legionary infantry at the Battle of Teutoburg. It is more embellished than helmets supposedly worn by the auxiliaries, for it had a brow ridge, E-shaped cheek-pieces, ear holes, and a more decorative neck protector. There is a helmet of this type on display at the Axel Guttman Collection. It is made of bronze and is covered all over with polished tin, giving it the appearance of polished steel.[30]

Another possible contender for the helmet worn by Roman infantrymen was the 'Imperial Gallic type-B', which dates from 5 BC-14 AD,[31] which would place this helmet within the time of the Battle of Teutoburg. This helmet was more elaborate and embellished than the plainer type-As which came earlier, but would this helmet have been worn by the legions in question? The Imperial Gallic type-A dates to the first century BC, and surely to Drusus' Germanic campaign. Would the soldiers have continuously updated their helmets and other pieces of equipment every single time a new model came out? Nowadays, that goes without saying, but in ancient times, this might not have been the case. As an example of this, the original version of the *lorica segmentata* armour was superseded by a new variety invented sometime around 30 AD, but the older model continued to be used by front-line troops at least thirteen years after it was supposed to have been replaced by this newer model. Many times, the differences in gear were purely a matter of style and not improved functionality. That being said, it is highly unlikely that the type-A helmet would have been completely discarded as soon as the type-B was issued. More likely, the transition was gradual rather than abrupt and immediate. It might be safe to assume that ordinary legionaries would have been equipped with the slightly older but still usable type-A helmets, while the officers were equipped with the newer and more decorated type-Bs. Due to their shape, it's likely that the 'Imperial Gallic type-B' would have been used by the legionary cavalry, which will be discussed later on.

In addition to the Gallic-style helmets, there were also the Coolus-style helmets, which were made of brass or bronze, fitted with cheek-pieces and neck protectors, and had a small spike sticking up from the top of the head, reminiscent of the early First World War German helmets (the Germans probably modelled their helmets on these Roman ones). The helmet that could have been worn at this time was the 'Coolus type-D'. Helmets of this type have been found at Bonn, Leiden, Nijmegen, Mainz (the base camp for the 5th Legion), Xanten (the location of Fort Vetera, the supposed base camp of the 18th Legion), and Haltern (the probable site of Fort Aliso, where the 17th and 19th Legions might have been stationed).[32]

It's possible that different legions would have had slightly different gear. For example, it's possible that the men of the 17th Legion wore Coolus helmets, but the men in the 18th Legion wore Gallic helmets. Another possibility, and one which I personally favour, is that different types of soldiers within the same unit had different helmet styles. This is in keeping with the fact that different types of Roman soldiers had different armour, weapons, and equipment, either specialized for their specific roles or purely for the purposes of easy identification within the army. Certain soldiers within a legion might have worn the Gallic helmets and others might have worn the Coolus helmets as part of their specific uniforms.

Following Roman contact with the Celts in Gaul, Roman soldiers wore chainmail armour, which the Celts had invented. The Romans called it *lorica hamata*. It was composed of a sleeveless or marginally sleeveless chainmail shirt, composed of an interlocking meshwork of small riveted steel rings, extending down to either halfway down the thigh or two-thirds down the length of the thigh. The shoulders were further protected by the addition of a shoulder piece which was attached to the front by a pair of S-shaped brass hooks looking like a flattened W. From the front, the shoulder piece looked like a pair of Greek-style shoulder lapels trimmed in leather, and it was squared in the back, extending down the back about a quarter or a third of the way. The chainmail armour had both benefits and drawbacks. In terms of pros, chainmail armour was very flexible and allowed for a wide range of movement (very important in a battle), the open rings allowed the body to breath rather than be stifled and over-heated by solid armour, and the armour offered a sufficient degree of protection against slashing cuts. In terms of cons, each chainmail *hamata* took a very long time to manufacture, since each individual ring had to be interlocked and riveted with the other rings, requiring a steady hand, an infinite amount of patience, as well as the ability to deal with aggravation and frustration. Making a chainmail *lorica hamata* was a slow, tedious, and likely expensive process. It was also surprisingly heavy. Moreover, although it afforded decent protection against slashing cuts, it could not withstand powerful thrusts or chops. The *lorica hamata* was always worn by standard-bearers, musicians, most centurions, and the auxiliaries.[33]

During the reign of Augustus, the *lorica hamata* began to be replaced by a newer form of armour. The *lorica segmentata* – the characteristic Roman armour made of several overlapping steel strips – was invented almost twenty years prior to this battle, at least. The oldest known specimen of this type of armour was discovered at Dangstetten, Germany, located not far from Lake Constance, and dated to 9 BC. Although it is known to have been worn by soldiers at the Battle of Teutoburg (a single piece of the armour, a left pectoral, was found at the site in 1994), it's believed by some that the usage of this armour among the legionaries may not have been widespread, and may have been worn by only a few selected units in the Army. However, I wish to point out again that this type of armour had been in use for almost twenty years by this time. This was *not* a prototype or experimental armour. In 9 BC, the date that the oldest specimen of this type of armour was discovered, the usage of the *lorica segmentata* had already spread to southwestern Germany; I'm assuming that troops stationed in Italy received this armour first. One wonders about how quickly the adoption of this armour spread. If this armour was already being used by Roman soldiers in southwestern Germany in 9 BC, what about 9 AD? It seems perfectly logical that the *lorica segmentata* had reached troops stationed along the Rhine well before this battle. Furthermore, since the 19th Legion was one of the three legions marching with Varus on this day, and since the 19th Legion used to be based in Dangstetten from 15–8 BC, and since the oldest known piece of *lorica segmentata* armour was found in this location and was dated to within this time frame, it is absolutely certain that the infantry of the 19th Legion were armoured in this fashion, and possibly the 17th and 18th Legions were as well by the time of this battle.[34]

But it's difficult to determine if the regular Roman foot soldiers wore one armour type or the other because artifacts uncovered at Kalkriese show both types of armour were worn. As stated before, we have the left pectoral for a *lorica segmentata*, but we also have the S-shaped hooks used to attach the shoulder pieces on a *lorica hamata*. I will be discussing this find in greater detail in the section on auxiliary infantry, since I believe that the owner of this armour was an auxiliary. Based upon the current evidence, I have come to the conclusion that the majority of the ordinary legionary infantry would have been wearing *lorica segmentata* armour by this time, not *lorica hamata* as is often supposed and portrayed. The ones who did wear chainmail, not including the auxiliaries who always wore chainmail, were the standard-bearers, centurions, the centurions' subordinate officers, and trumpeters.

The exact style of *lorica segmentata* worn by the legionary infantry is distinctive. This type has been named 'Kalkriese-type' by armour experts and Roman historians. It appears to have been the very first style of *lorica segmentata*, and remained in service until it was replaced by the 'Corbridge type-A' *lorica segmentata* around the year 30 AD, although the Kalkriese-type continued to be used for many years, even worn by soldiers in Emperor Claudius' invasion of Britain in 43 AD. The Kalkriese-type armour is unadorned with the fancy round brass studs featured on later styles. The edges of the pectorals which the wearer's neck would have gone through are curled up slightly, forming a very short collar, which was trimmed in a thin layer of brass. The neck hole is circular in shape, in contrast with the somewhat V-shaped neck hole in the Corbridge armour.[35]

Like the chainmail *lorica hamata*, the *lorica segmentata* also had its benefits and drawbacks. In terms of pros, the large plates offered much better protection to the wearer than open rings. Secondly, although this type of armour was composed of overlapping solid steel plates, the plates were rather thin, and as such the armour weighed considerably less than the chainmail tunic. Thirdly, this type of armour was quicker to manufacture than a chainmail tunic, and thus it could be mass produced, which would make it cheap to manufacture, thereby increasing its distribution. In terms of cons, the solid plates covering the torso and shoulders didn't allow the body to breathe, and in the hot climates of the Middle East and Northern Africa, its wearer would roast inside like an oven. Secondly, its complex structure of multiple layers of overlapping plate sections connected with buckles and straps meant that its wearer needed help to put it on and take it off. Thirdly, it didn't have the wide range of motion and the flexibility of movement that the chainmail armour had. The shoulder pieces, in particular, restricted the upward movement of the arms, and they would dig into the neck whenever the arms were raised up, hence the presence of the scarf around the neck.

Another type of armour that was occasionally seen in the Roman Army was the *lorica squamata*, literally 'lizard armour'. This was a cuirass made of layers of overlapping metal scales, shaped either like upside-down Gothic arches or like upside-down round-topped tombstones. The scales themselves were fairly small, being perhaps only two inches long, and they provided decent protection. Scale armour was rarely seen, but there are several examples of this type of armour being worn by centurions, auxiliaries, and standard-bearers. Scale armour was never worn by the legionary infantry or cavalry during the Republican or early Imperial periods. It would, however, become more popular in later centuries, especially the Late Antique period of Roman history.

Underneath their body armour, Roman soldiers would have worn a *subarmalis*, a leather vest worn between the tunic and armour, meant to provide some protection against chafing as well as some additional minimal protection. There were cushioned pads on the shoulders, which provided some degree of comfort for the soldier, as the heavy armour would pull down on the shoulders and collar bones. Sometimes, the whole *subarmalis* would be padded. In the case of officers, long leather straps called *pteruges* ('feathers') would be fitted to the shoulders and waistline to give a more Classical appearance. These *pteruges* might be decorated with polished metal rivets or coloured fringe.[36]

The *cingulum militare*, or 'military-issue belt', also known as a *balteus*, was one of the few pieces of kit which was not standardized. Although it was required to have and wear, and although its shape was based on an established general form, its actual appearance varied widely, and was likely in deference to the wearer's own personal aesthetics. Archaeological finds show that this accessory came in a wide variety of styles to suit personal tastes. It consisted of a leather belt faced with square or rectangular metal plates. These plates had a myriad of different designs to choose from. Dangling in front was a short apron of a similar style consisting of between four to eight leather straps, each one being twelve or so inches long, decorated with circular metal plates and with each one terminating in a round or teardrop-shaped disc slightly larger than the ones on the belt. Often believed to have protected the groin, this feature was, in actuality, purely decorative. During the republican and early imperial periods, it was common for soldiers to wear two belts

– one to suspend the sword, and a second for the dagger. By this time, however, it was common to wear a single belt to suspend the dagger from. The sword would be suspended from a belt which ran diagonally across the chest. Several specimens of *cingulum* sections have been found at Kalkriese, and some of them are plated with silver, indicating that the person who wore this particular item had some money, and was likely an officer.[37]

In terms of weaponry, each Roman infantryman, be he a legionary or auxiliary, carried a 2-foot shortsword called a *gladius*. The *gladius* had originally been a weapon carried by the Spanish tribes, but the Romans quickly adopted it into their arsenal. By the time of the Battle of Teutoburg, the earlier 'Spanish-style' design had fallen out of use, and was replaced by the 'Mainz-style' *gladius*, first introduced around 20 BC. The Mainz *gladius* had a wider blade and a more triangular point than the earlier Spanish-style sword, but still retained its elegant wasp-waisted curves. The Mainz-style *gladius* saw service until it was accompanied by the slightly modified Fulham-style *gladius*, which was in turn eventually replaced by the straight-bladed Pompeii-style *gladius*, considered by many to be the definitive *gladius* style. The dating of the Mainz-style *gladius* places it at the time of the Battle of Teutoburg, and it is of little doubt that this was the type of *gladius* carried by Roman troops. The *gladius* was carried on the right hip, hung from a belt that ran diagonally across the chest and back called a 'baldric'. Only centurions or officers of higher rank carried their swords on the left hip as a mark of status. On the left side was a dagger called a *pugio*, with a wide blade the size of a person's hand, and strengthened by a thick central rib to prevent the blade from becoming bent.[38]

The legionary infantry also carried armour-piercing javelins called *pila* (singular *pilum*), which would be hurled at enemy formations to disrupt them and cause havoc before rushing at them with their short swords. The *pilum* is believed to have been invented by the Etruscans sometime prior to the fifth century BC, originally nothing more than a small spear, fitted with a long iron shaft to keep the head from being chopped off. Over the years, it underwent a considerable amount of evolution. Each legionary carried two *pila*; originally one was larger than the other, but by the reign of Caesar Augustus, they were the same size. At least one *pilum* head has been discovered at the Teutoburg battle site. The *pilum* type carried by Roman soldiers at Teutoburg would have had an elongated pyramidal head attached to a long metal shank which was a third of the *pilum*'s length. The shank would be attached to the *pilum*'s shaft by fixing it onto a trapezoid-shaped block at the head of the shaft with two large bolts arranged vertically and a square metal cap which fitted over the trapezoidal block – this particular feature of the strengthening square metal cap was incorporated into the *pilum*'s design in response to the tendency of the *pilum*'s shaft to crack or even break in half upon impact. The butt end of the *pilum* would be fitted with a small conical point. Many people believe that the *pilum* was designed with the specific purpose of getting stuck in an enemy's shield, thereby rendering it unusable. This is false. The real reason behind the *pilum*'s design was to penetrate the shield and impale the man standing behind it. Getting stuck in the shield and rendering the shield unusable was an afterthought, but it was a useful side-effect. The thin iron shank, made of soft porous metal, would bend under the weight of the heavy wooden shaft pulling it down, making it difficult to pull out and be thrown back at the Romans.[39]

With regards to shields, the legionaries fighting at the Battle of Teutoburg would have carried the 'Augustan type-1' *scutum*. It was a large half-cylindrical shield that had curved side-edges, as opposed to later *scuta* that would have straight sides – the characteristic shield of the Roman legionary – which appeared somewhere between 40–50 AD and became the dominant legionary's shield for the next two centuries. The Augustan type-1 was, by best estimates, first adopted by 10 BC, but it might have appeared earlier. In terms of size dimensions, it was 26 inches wide (straight across from point to point, not along the length of the rim, which measured 34–36 inches) and 4.5 feet tall. The Augustan type-1 still retained the long central rib which extended up the height of the shield, a feature found in earlier Roman shields and in the shields of the Celts and Germans. The shield boss was also oval in shape, another feature retained from earlier shield designs. Beginning with the Augustan type-2, which was first adopted in 20 AD during the reign of Emperor Tiberius, the shield boss became circular, mounted on a square metal frame, and the central rib was done away with.[40]

A *scutum* consisted of several thin wooden rods which formed the basic framework for the shield. These wooden rods were curved to form the distinct half-cylinder shape of the *scutum*. Over these wooden rods were several thin layers of wood glued on top of each other, which was then covered over with a tight leather skin (it may or may not have been dyed red; if it wasn't, then red paint would have been added later), and secured with a brass or steel strip nailed around the edges to keep the whole thing from splitting apart. A hole was cut in the middle, making sure not to cut through the wooden rod that ran horizontally across the middle of the shield. This rod would act as the handle. To protect the hand, the open hole was then covered over with a brass or steel boss – a metal half oval-shaped bowl with a flat rectangular rim around its edge. It would be attached to the shield by driving nails through the flattened rim of the boss. The shield was then painted with the familiar yellow 'eagle wings and lightning bolts' design on a red background; this familiar design first appeared during the reign of Caesar Augustus, and became almost standard by 100 AD.[41] When fully assembled, an Augustan type-1 *scutum* weighed somewhere between twelve to fifteen pounds. While on the march, the *scutum* may have been carried using a shoulder strap that ran diagonally across the chest, since I can't imagine carrying a shield by hand for hours at a time – your fingers would go numb.

The Legionary Cavalry

Accompanying each legion was a unit of 120 cavalrymen, a paltry number compared to the almost 5,000 infantrymen which comprised a legion, which emphasizes the importance that the Romans placed upon their foot soldiers. This company-sized unit was divided into four platoons called *turmae*, consisting of thirty men each. Each platoon was commanded by an officer called a *decurio* (also spelled *decurion*), and a second-in-command called a *duplicarius*, literally 'duplicate commander'; the word also refers to an officer who was given double-pay. The legionary cavalrymen were recruited from the ranks of the infantry, although what the requirements were or how the selection process took place isn't stated. The legionary cavalry acted as messengers, scouts, and travel escorts, and conducted policing and routine patrols.[42] But their primary roles were of a strictly battle-orientated nature, either stationed on the flanks or in the rear, protecting the infantry from attacks, and for chasing down fleeing enemy troops.

The legionary cavalryman's kit was substantially different from the ordinary infantry. For starters, they wore Gallic-type helmets that were fitted with iron face masks, mounted on a hinge on the forehead. The 'Imperial Gallic type-B' helmet fits into this time period, so this was likely the helmet worn by the legionary cavalry. Specimens of this 'Kalkriese-type' masked helmet, named after the most famous specimen discovered at the Teutoburg battlefield, have been found in several places, and demonstrate that the masks were fitted onto Gallic-style helmets, not Coolus-style helmets. Although made of iron, it seems that these masked helmets were covered in a second metal sheet. One specimen previously on display at the Museum Carnuntinum in Austria, and now owned by a private collector, has pieces of a brass covering still attached to it, while the famous mask uncovered at Kalkriese, arguably the most recognizable artifact to have been unearthed at the excavations at that site, clearly had a silver covering – there is still some silver around its edges.[43] The reasons for covering the helmet, or at least the face mask, in a second metal aren't clear, but I'm assuming it was to prevent rust. Iron rusts easily, especially in the damp conditions of ancient Germania, and covering it in a second non-corroding metal like silver would protect the inner iron base. Also, if left unpolished, the silver would tarnish to an almost black colour, giving the wearer a sinister appearance.

They only wore chainmail armour, but the *lorica hamata* which they wore differed in one way from that supposedly worn by the infantrymen. The shoulder piece was much larger, so that it draped well over the shoulders, coming halfway down the upper arm. This was the Gallic-style *hamata*, as opposed to the Greek-style *hamata* worn by the infantrymen. Although vambraces for the arms and greaves for the legs were certainly available, there is no evidence that the legionary cavalry, at this time anyway, wore any body armour aside from the helmet and the chainmail *hamata*.

The Roman cavalry carried an 8–foot spear that had a steel point on both ends, both to provide balance as well as to act as a secondary weapon in case the first point was chopped off. The cavalry also carried a sword with a blade measuring 3 feet called a *spatha*. It looked like the *gladius*, but it had a much longer blade due to the soldier sitting high up on horseback and having to be able to strike at soldiers on the ground. He also carried an oval *clipeus* shield, measuring approximately 50 inches long by 24 to 30 inches wide, which would have likewise been decorated with the eagle wings and lightning bolts design common to soldiers within the legion.

In a traditional Roman battle fought on open fields, the job of the legionary cavalry was to protect the flanks and the rear against attack, to charge in as shock troops to disrupt and disorganize the enemy, and to chase down fleeing enemy troops. However, in the confined spaces of the German forests, there was very little that the cavalry could do. In fact, they might have been more of a hindrance than a help.

The Auxiliary Infantry

Auxiliaries were soldiers serving in the Roman Army who did not have Roman citizenship. They could, however, be awarded citizenship after completing a full term of service, and during this time, it would have been twenty-five years: twenty years of front-line service, and five years in the reserves. However, auxiliaries could, on rare occasions, be awarded citizenship early, as was the case with Arminius himself. Unlike the legionaries, whose unit identity centred around the legion (of course), auxiliary infantry were standardized at the *cohort* or battalion level, numbering approximately 480 men, not including officers, and the officers themselves were usually Roman citizens. There was no such thing as an auxiliary legion. The auxiliaries performed a variety of functions, including garrisoning forts and settlements, conducting routine patrols, collecting taxes, and acting as local police, but their primary duty was to augment the fighting capabilities of the Roman military by supplementing the legions with specialized troops composed of locals who were experts in military fields which the regular Roman military was not.

The auxiliary infantry would have been armoured, armed, and equipped in much the same way as his legionary counterparts, but with a few differences. The auxiliary infantry at this time might have worn a helmet that Roman military scholars have termed 'Auxiliary Infantry type-A'. My reasons for saying this is that there is an 'Auxiliary Infantry type-B' helmet, but this particular design is dated to a later period, to the mid-to-late first century AD,[44] which would place this helmet's use during the reign of Emperor Nero. A specimen of the Auxiliary Infantry type-A helmet is currently on display in Rheinisches Landesmuseum in Bonn, Germany. It is similar to the Coolus type-D, but it is simpler in design. It looks like a bronze dome slightly flattened on the top with a flange neck protector sticking out from the back, sort of like a metal baseball cap worn backwards. There's a single hole on each side, which most likely accommodated a leather chin strap and not a metal cheek-piece, since cheek-pieces were attached to the helmet via hinges, and there are no hinges on this specimen.

Of course, I wish to point out that we have no way at all of knowing if the 'Auxiliary Infantry type-A' was indeed used by auxiliary infantrymen in the Roman Army. In reality, auxiliaries might very well have worn another type of helmet. The designation 'Auxiliary Infantry' was apparently given to these helmets because they were plain-looking and didn't have any noticeable mounts for helmet crests, and scholars automatically made a pre-conceived assumption that plain ordinary-looking helmets were worn by the auxiliaries, which I imagine some historians regarded as second-class troops even though their skills were just as good as the regular legionaries, and that somewhat more embellished gear was worn by the legionaries. This is assumption, not fact. It's possible that both auxiliaries and legionaries wore the same gear. It's also possible that different gear was worn by different military units, not different classes of soldiers. However, I admit I have no way of proving any of these ideas, and for the sake of simplicity, until someone is able to prove otherwise, I'm sticking with the modern classifications currently used and assuming that these helmets were worn by the soldiers that they're named after.

In addition to his *gladius* sword, each auxiliary carried two *lanceae* ('little spears') javelins, likely adopted from the Gauls, which were lighter and plainer than the legionary's *pilum*. It's uncertain what types of shields the auxiliaries carried. Some recreations show them carrying circular *parma* shields. The *parma* was similar to the familiar Viking shield – a circular shield measuring 2 to 3 feet in diameter with an outer brass rim and central boss. Other recreations show them carrying the oval *clipeus* shield used by cavalrymen. The oval *clipeus* shield seems to be the prevailing shield type used.[45]

It is also unclear as to what the patterns on the auxiliaries' shields were. Several reconstructions which I have seen show the legionary infantry and cavalry carrying shields patterned with the characteristic eagle wings and lightning bolts associated with Roman soldiers, while the auxiliary infantry and cavalry carry shields decorated with a simple laurel wreath design on a plain background. The idea that the auxiliaries' shields were decorated in this fashion comes from Trajan's Column, dated to more than a century later. On this monument, meant to commemorate Emperor Trajan's conquest of Romania, known in ancient times as Dacia, the story of the conquest is told in relief form, illustrating Roman soldiers, Dacian warriors, battles, and sieges. The majority of patterns seen on the shields of the auxiliaries show one variant or another of this wreath motif, and due to the prevalence of this design, it has become almost granted that Roman auxiliaries always had their shields decorated like this. But it must be stated that the Dacian Wars took place over a hundred years after the Battle of Teutoburg. It is unknown if the auxiliaries who fought alongside the legionaries at Teutoburg would have had shields decorated in this fashion, but the design is appealing to the eye, and it makes for an easily-noticeable contrast, which would have been helpful to Roman commanders.

As stated in an earlier section, archaeologists excavating at Kalkriese have uncovered a pair of brass S-shaped hooks, which were used to attach the shoulder cape onto a *lorica hamata*. In fact, we even know the name of their original owner. Both of these fasteners have the owner's name and the unit he belonged to carved into the surface – 'Marcus Aius, 1st Cohort, Fabricius' Century'.[46] Unfortunately, it doesn't state which legion he belonged to, but it may be irrelevant, since I do not believe that Marcus Aius was, in fact, a legionary. Auxiliaries were organized at the cohort level, not the legionary level. Auxiliary cohorts were made of non-citizens, and while they were usually commanded by their own native officers, they could also be commanded by Roman citizens, many of whom had served in the regular legions. If Marcus Aius was a member of the 17th, 18th, or 19th Legions, then he would have written his legion number rather than his cohort number (example: *LEG XVIII* for '18th Legion'). His emphasis on his cohort indicates that his unit identity was focused on the cohort, not on the legion, and this implies that Marcus Aius was an auxiliary, serving in a century commanded by a Roman centurion named Fabricius (his first name is not recorded), which was a century within the 1st Cohort. This would have been one of the six auxiliary infantry cohorts that Varus took with him on his expedition. It isn't just the exact wording of the inscription that leads me to believe that this man was a non-citizen. Even the name *Aius* arouses suspicion – it doesn't even sound like a Roman name. In fact, it's Aquitanian, a language spoken in southwestern Gaul and northern Spain, although it was more closely related to the ancient Spanish languages than to the Celtic languages to the north and east. According to one source, there are some Roman-era inscriptions which contain names that are rooted in the Aquitanian language, which is believed by some to be the ancestor of the Basque language. The name *Aius* is a Latinized version of the Aquitanian masculine name *Aio.*[47] This would indicate that Marcus Aius, or at least his family, originally came from the area of France now known as Gascony, or possibly the Basque lands of northern Spain.

Now comes the crucial question – was there ever an all-Aquitanian 1st Cohort? The answer is yes. In fact, there were two: the *Cohors I Aquitanorum* ('1st Cohort of Aquitanians') and the *Cohors I Aquitanorum Veterana* ('1st Veteran Cohort of Aquitanians'). Both of these units were auxiliary infantry cohorts raised in southwestern Gaul. It is possible that Marcus Aius was an Aquitanian or proto-Basque from southwestern Gaul in the shadow of the Pyrenees who was serving as an auxiliary infantryman in the Roman Army, under the command of a Roman centurion named Fabricius within either the *Cohors I Aquitanorum* or the *Cohors I Aquitanorum Veterana*, which was stationed on the Rhine.

However, there are three problems with this idea. The first is a matter of dating. The sources which I have seen claim that these two units were created during the reign of Caesar Augustus shortly after taking power, but the dates in which they are confirmed to have existed are much later than this. This dating problem bleeds into the second problem, which is concerned with the fate of units involved in the Battle of Teutoburg. If it is true that Marcus Aius was a member of either the *Cohors I Aquitanorum* or the *Cohors I Aquitanorum Veterana*, and if it is true that both of these units were first created shortly after Augustus took power, and continued in service for at least two centuries, this would be in contrast to the fate of the 17th, 18th, and 19th Legions, which were disbanded. If one or both of these auxiliary units fought at the Battle of Teutoburg, then these units, too, should have been permanently disbanded just like the legions they fought alongside. Why disband the legions but keep the auxiliary units? There's no logic for this. The third problem pertains to the ethnic makeup of the units themselves. Would Marcus Aius, an Aquitanian auxiliary, have been posted to a non-Aquitanian auxiliary unit? There is strong evidence that he could have been. We have the discharge diplomas of two members of the *Cohors I Aquitanorum*, a unit supposedly comprised entirely of Aquitanians from southwestern Gaul and northern Spain. Both of the men in question were *not* Aquitanians – one man was a Thracian from Bulgaria, and the other was a Galatian Celt from central Turkey.[48] So the auxiliary cohort that Marcus Aius belonged to might not have necessarily been an all-Aquitanian unit; he might have been a member of any Augustan-age *cohors prima*, which makes the specific unit that he was stationed with much less likely to be pinpointed, and may in fact never be conclusively known.

Auxiliaries were frequently specialist soldiers, using weapons which the regular Roman military didn't touch. A legionary was first and foremost a swordsman. Missile troops were *always* auxiliaries. The three lead sling stones, which first gave archaeologists a clue that Kalkriese had a Roman military presence, would have been carried by an auxiliary slinger. Auxiliaries also served as archers, and at least one triple-bladed arrowhead has been discovered at this site in 1993, indicating the presence of auxiliary archers on Varus' expedition.[49]

The Auxiliary Cavalry

The Romans were never particularly good horsemen. This is evident with the high emphasis that the Romans placed upon their infantry. The Romans relied upon outsiders, native tribesmen who served as auxiliaries in the Roman Army, to act as specialized fighters within the military. This included the tribes which placed special emphasis upon cavalry warfare, and who were very adept at fighting in the saddle, such as Arminius and his horse-riding Cherusci warriors.

The auxiliary cavalry, like the auxiliary infantry, were standardized at the cohort level, with a full cohort numbering around 500 cavalrymen. An auxiliary cavalry cohort was referred to as an *ala* (plural *alae*), or 'wing', likely named in reference to the common practice among Roman military tacticians of placing the cavalry on the flanks, but auxiliaries, including cavalry, usually led the Roman column while on the march, and if the column came under attack, the auxiliaries would be the first to take casualties. Auxiliary cavalry acted as scouts for the army, leading the way for others to follow behind. Since the auxiliary cavalry were composed of men who had spent their whole lives riding horses, these were men of exceptional skill and ability, not raw fumbling fighting farmers who needed time to find their courage in battle. They would have had an air of elegance and dash about them, like the knights of the Middle Ages. Due to their skill and prowess, the auxiliary cavalry were regarded with great importance, and being the commander of an auxiliary cavalry cohort was something to aspire to. Auxiliary units were often led by their own tribal leaders, and due to the elite position of an auxiliary cavalry leader, it would have greatly helped his personal prestige, which was very important in warrior societies where men commanded through force of personality, charisma, and battlefield prowess. Such a man would have been Arminius.[50]

The visible differences between the legionary cavalry and the auxiliary cavalry were minimal. For starters, it isn't certain if the auxiliary cavalry wore any helmets at all at Teutoburg, since the first type, which is rather unimaginatively classified as 'Auxiliary Cavalry type-A', a brass helmet decorated with a design made to resemble the boar-tusk helmets described in Homer's *Iliad*, only came into use during the reign of Emperor Tiberius, which began in 14 AD, five years after the Battle of Teutoburg.[51] I believe that the auxiliary cavalry either wore the 'Auxiliary Infantry type-A' helmet, or went bare-headed, and I'm leaning towards the latter since there's no record of the auxiliary cavalry wearing any helmets prior to the introduction of the Auxiliary Cavalry type-A helmet during the reign of Tiberius.

The auxiliary cavalry also didn't carry the long *hasta* spear used by the regular legionary cavalry. Instead, he carried a quiver filled with smaller *lancea* javelins, the same kind used by the auxiliary infantry. Like the Norman knights at the Battle of Hastings, the Roman auxiliary cavalry would harass enemy forces by lapping around their formations and hurling javelins at them, killing as opportunity allowed, breaking the momentum of their advance and decreasing their morale. For close-in fighting, he would have also carried the *spatha* long sword.[52]

Legionary Structure and Personnel

Roman military structure is complex and can be a bit difficult for modern students and history buffs to understand, so to help ease the transition, I have provided modern rank equivalents for Roman military ranks. These invented modern ranks are based upon the soldier's position in the Roman legionary hierarchy, their pay rates, and the duties that they performed.

The ordinary legionaries could be considered Privates. The basic legionary received a pay rate of 225 silver *denarii* per year, and pay was only given out three times per year. Legionary infantry were grouped into a squad of eight men called a *contubernium*, who shared a tent and a mule to carry extra supplies. In command of a *contubernium* squad was a man called the *decanus*. The name means 'leader of ten', which is misleading since a contubernium only has eight men. This is because in the past, a century was made of a hundred men, hence the name, divided into ten contubernia of ten men each, but during the late Republic, this number was downsized to only eighty men in a century with eight men per contubernium, but for some strange reason the rank of the squad leader wasn't changed. In modern armies, this Roman squad leader would hold the rank of Sergeant. He received the same pay rate as the ordinary legionary, and looked almost identical except for one difference – his helmet had a pair of feathers, one on each side, to denote his rank.[53]

The most famous Roman officer is arguably the *centurion*. There were sixty per legion, and they were some of the most experienced soldiers within the unit. Centurions served as commanders of both the company-sized centuries and the battalion-sized cohorts. The Roman military, strangely, did not have officers who were specifically in command of a legionary cohort and who had been specially appointed to command the legionary cohort. Instead, legionary cohorts were commanded by the senior-ranking centurion within a cohort, who would act as both company commander and battalion commander simultaneously; only an auxiliary cohort had its own commander, called rather unimaginatively the *prefectus cohortis*, 'cohort commander'. Centurions were ranked in an internal and confusing hierarchy according to seniority. In modern times, they would have held various grades of the rank of Captain. The centurion commanding the 1st Century of the 1st Cohort was the commanding centurion of the legion, the *primus pilus*, and would have been Chief Captain. It should be stated that the man who held the title of *Primus Pilus* only held this position for a one-year term. It may be best stated that the *primus pilus* was in charge of the 1st Cohort *in general*, and the 1st Century of the 1st Cohort *specifically*. He was also responsible for guarding the eagle-bearer of the legion. The other five centurions in the 1st Cohort came second in the hierarchy, and would have been regarded as senior captains. The remaining fifty-four centurions were classified in the following manner: The centurion commanding the 1st Century of the remaining nine cohorts acted as the cohort commanders and their specific century commanders, and also would have held the rank of Senior Captain. The remaining forty-five centurions within the legion were the lowest-ranking centurions, and would have held the rank of Junior Captain. Centurions were recognized by several identifying features. Firstly, they wore a helmet crest which ran from side-to-side as opposed to front-to-back. Secondly, they wore their sword on the left hip, in contrast with lower-ranking soldiers who wore their swords on the right hip. Thirdly, a centurion carried a staff made of vine wood called a *vitis*, which was used to enforce discipline. Fourthly, a centurion never wore the *lorica segmentata*, wearing chainmail, scale, and in some cases muscle cuirasses if it was a high-ranking centurion. Sometimes, the centurion would wear leg protectors called greaves.[54]

Directly under the centurion was the *optio* or 'chosen one'. He acted as the centurion's second-in-command and therefore would have held the modern rank equivalent of Lieutenant. It was his job to supervise the training of all soldiers who were conscripted into the legion, so he would have acted as part-lieutenant and part-drill instructor. In battle, the *optio* stood in the rear left. As a mark of rank, he carried a staff with a metal ball on one end. Under him was the *tesserarius*, the century's third-in-command, standing in the front right, who was in command of the watch-duty sentries and would have held the rank equivalent of Sergeant-Major.[55]

Above the centurions were the high-ranking officers. Unlike the centurions and the men below, most of these men were *not* career soldiers who had spent their lives in the army and worked their way up the ranks. Instead, they were senators and other politicians who were using their military posts to augment their political image and clout. They were always of the aristocratic classes, and their service was done through politically-based appointment or commission rather than through military promotions for courage and ability.

The cohort-commanding centurion's immediate superior was the *tribunus angusticlavus*, the 'tribune of the narrow stripe', named for the thin strip of purple fabric which decorated his tunic. This was an officer who held command over two cohort battalions. Since there were ten cohorts in a legion, there were five *tribuni angusticlavii*. The *tribunus angusticlavus* was of equestrian or knightly rank, and would have formerly been a magistrate or other low-ranking government personnel.[56] They would have held the modern rank equivalent of Major.

The commanding officer of a legion was the *legatus legionis*. A 'legate', the modern English word derived from the original Latin, is a title for a person who has been appointed and possesses special authority to act reliably in a superior's name. Traditionally, the monarch commanded his armies in wartime, but what happened if the emperor wasn't available? The emperor directly appointed his legion commanders, who were always senators, and essentially served as the emperor's stand-in. The official title of a legion commander during the reign of Caesar Augustus was *legatus Augusti legionis*. Legionary command was usually a brief affair, perhaps lasting only a few years before moving onto other things.[57] Since unit identity within the infantry has been traditionally centred on the regiment, and since regiments were commanded by colonels, a Roman legion commander would have held the modern rank equivalent of Colonel.

The legate's second-in-command was a man called the *tribunus laticlavus*, the 'tribune of the broad stripe', so-named because of the wide purple stripe on his tunic, indicative of a man of the senatorial class. He was a young senator, usually in his early or mid-20s, just beginning his political career and looking to get his foot in the door, as it were, with some military experience to further enhance his standing within the Senate and with the Roman public. He essentially acted as the legate's apprentice, learning the ropes of being a legion commander. Due to his youth and inexperience, it is almost certain that he was not entrusted with any serious military matters.[58] In today's armies, he would have the modern rank equivalent of Lieutenant-Colonel.

The legate's third-in-command was the *prefectus castrorum*, 'the camp commandant', a man of equestrian rank. He was the man in charge of the legion's base camp, seeing to it that it was properly maintained and equipped. Unlike the legate and the legionary tribunes, this man was not a young politician who had been appointed to high rank as a means to furthering political ambitions. He was a grizzled old veteran, usually in his 50s, who had formerly been a *primus pilus* centurion and had been knighted in reward for exemplary battlefield service.[59] He would have held the rank of Major.

Arguably the most important soldier in a legion was not the legate or the centurion, but the *aquilifer*, the eagle-bearer. This was the man who carried the legion's golden eagle standard, and who always marched at the front. To lose your eagle was the highest disgrace for a legion. Gaius Marius, the man who reformed the Roman Army at the end of the second century BC, is the one attributed with making the eagle the official emblem of the legion. According to Pliny the Elder, this practice was put into place in 104 BC; before then, legions used a variety of emblems.[60] I like to think that the eagle-bearers wore the *lorica squamata* scale armour instead of the chainmail armour common to standard-bearers because the scale armour was reminiscent of feathers. This would have been especially effective if the scale armour was made of brass or polished bronze, because its gold-like appearance would have fit with the golden colour of the eagle standard. I have no way to prove this statement – it's just an interesting idea which appeals to me aesthetically.

The *signifer* was the standard-bearer for the century, garbed in either a wolf or a bear pelt, and required to stand at the front of the unit where there was the most danger. He was armed with a sword and a round *parma* shield for protection. He carried a tall pole capped with a large open hand, possibly symbolizing the oath of loyalty taken to Caesar Augustus or as a reference to the earlier *maniple* or 'handful' unit. All along the length of this pole were silver disc decorations; these silver discs denoted the century's number within the cohort, from Century No. 1 to Century No. 6 (a cohort was made up of six centuries, and no *signum* has ever been seen with more than six of these discs). Many times, the *signum* would have a small metal plaque fitted onto it, stating the legion and the cohort number for easy identification. Occasionally, a metal wreath would be fixed onto the *signum*, showing that the century had been given a special award for bravery in battle. Standard-bearers like the *aquilifer* and the *signifer* would have held the modern rank of Ensign.[61]

The Germanic Warriors

A considerable length of this chapter has been spent discussing the appearance and organization of the Roman military during this time. In contrast with all of this, the Germanic barbarians that the Romans faced at Teutoburg were nowhere near as well-equipped or organized as the Romans were. They were tribal warriors, ordinary men who were called upon in defence of their homelands, putting down their farming and hunting tools and picking up their weapons. In this case the Germans bear resemblance to the Greek hoplites or to the very early Roman military, in which all males had to serve as citizen soldiers, purchase or fabricate their own military gear, were probably grouped based upon their equipment status (light versus heavy infantry), and assemble for battle when it was called for.

In terms of their physical appearance, all of the ancient sources describe the Germans as tall. Tacitus and Plutarch state that they have blue eyes, and Tacitus further states that they have red hair. Strabo, writing a few years after the Battle of Teutoburg, states that in contrast to the Celts of Gaul and Britain, the Germans are fiercer, taller, and blonde. Indeed, the Roman authors make much of the Germans' ferocity and ability to inspire fear in others. Florus comments that the Germans possess 'irresistible fury and rage, which in barbarians takes the place of courage'.[62] Polyaenus states that the Germans who invaded the Republic during the second century BC were 'a people savage in their manners, of immense stature, with horrid countenances, and a language scarcely human'.[63] The terror which the Germanic barbarians instilled in others was applied not only to the Romans. Julius Caesar comments that even among other barbarians, the Germans had a fearsome reputation. According to him, the Gallic Celts 'asserted that the Germans were men of huge stature, of incredible valour and practice in arms—that often times they, on encountering them, could not bear even their countenance, and the fierceness of their eyes'.[64] When the Roman soldiers heard these reports, Caesar says that all of his soldiers were filled with terror. Some using one excuse or another asked to leave the army, and many began writing their wills. For the Germanic warriors, fear accomplished what spears could not. It was a useful advantage. Germanic warriors were notoriously ill-equipped. Several authors comment that the ancient Germans had little in the way of armour and weapons, and even in clothing.[65]

Both Caesar and Tacitus give descriptions of the appearance of the Germanic warriors in terms of clothing. Caesar claims that they only used cloaks made of deer skins, with most of their body being naked. Tacitus provides further details, stating that many Germans wear animals skins, that the poor wrap themselves in a cloak which is fastened either with a thorn or a man-made clasp, leaving the rest of the body naked, and that the wealthiest (assumed to be the ones who owned the most cattle) wear tight-fitting tunics and trousers.[66]

In terms of weaponry and armour, Tacitus again provides the most information. The Germans, he says, rarely use swords or long spears, but mostly carry small spears (he states that the Germanic word for 'spear' is *framea*) equipped with sharp short narrow heads (the small size of the metal heads is added proof of the meagre supply of iron within Germania, and metal was used sparingly), which can be used either as a javelin or a hand-to-hand weapon. Each infantryman carries several javelins, and the warriors as a whole shower their enemies from a distance with them. Very few wear body armour, and only one or two wear leather or metal helmets. They also carry large shields, which are brightly painted. The cavalry carry a shield and spear.[67]

In his *Annals*, written several years after his survey of the Germanic tribes, Tacitus reinforces his earlier description of the Germanic warriors. He paraphrases a speech given by General Germanicus, Drusus' son, to his men while conducting his campaign against Arminius' rebels in the hope of dispelling their fears about fighting the Germans. He told them about the deficiencies of the German warrior compared with the Roman soldier, how they did not have appropriate weapons or armour, how they did not use strategy to win battles, and how they could be overcome by the legions.

The barbarians' huge shields, their enormous spears, could not be so manageable among tree-trunks and springing brushwood as the *pilum*, the short sword, and close-fitting body-armour. Their policy was to strike thick and fast, and to direct the point to the face. The Germans carried neither corselet nor headpiece — not even shields with a toughening of metal or hide, but targes of wickerwork or thin, painted board. Their first line alone carried spears of a fashion: the remainder had only darts, fire-pointed or too short. Their bodies, again, while grim enough to the eye and powerful enough for a short-lived onset, lacked the stamina to support a wound. They were men who could turn and run without a thought for their leaders, faint-hearted in adversary, in success regardless of divine and human law.[68]

At first, spears were the dominant weapon among the Germanic tribes of what is now central Europe and Scandinavia. However, as time progressed, swords began to become more numerous and widely used. Just look at the ratios of spears to swords as the centuries go by. At Hjortspring, on the island of Als in southern Denmark, a ship 62 feet long made of linden wood was discovered buried in the soil, and with it was found an impressive cache of Germanic armour and weapons, dated from the mid-fourth to first century BC. Among the finds were 138 iron spearheads, an additional thirty-one spearheads made of bone, 150 shields, twenty chainmail hauberks (some of the oldest-known chainmail armour from Europe, possibly of Celtic manufacture and imported into Germania), and only six swords. In the peat bogs of Ejsbol North, Denmark which almost certainly served as sacrificial pools devoted to some Germanic war god during the third century AD and possibly earlier, archaeologists have uncovered 203 javelins, 191 spears, 160 shields, sixty-two knives, and sixty swords. The Nydam ship burials, dated from the third to mid-fourth century AD, contained 106 swords (ninety-three of them were pattern-welded, likely manufactured by Roman blacksmiths and then imported into the country), 552 spears, over forty bows, and over 170 arrowheads. Finds at Vimose, Denmark, dated to the late fourth century AD, consist of 1,000 spears, 150 knives, and sixty-seven swords, most of them being single-edged slashing weapons.[69]

I should state in fairness that most of the artifacts which are identified as 'Germanic' are dated to a much later time period than the one discussed in this book, ranging from the second to late fourth centuries AD. However, based up their quality and their number, we can make some inferences about how the Germanic tribesmen were armed in earlier years.

Both the ancient historical accounts state and archaeological evidence confirms that throughout much of ancient history, and certainly during the BC–AD transition period, the overwhelming majority of Germanic warriors were spearmen or javelineers. Even well into the Late Antique period when Rome was in its stages of decline and fall, most of the Germanic warriors were armed with spears. In some circumstances, the wooden shafts of the spears, which should have rotted away long ago, have been preserved due to the anaerobic quality of the water and soil. These spears range in size from 3-foot long javelins, to standard 8-footers, to 10-foot pikes which could only be wielded with both hands. Many of these recovered spearheads are almost Greek in appearance – flat with a raised central spine running down the middle of the spearpoint to increase its strength and rigidity, and keep it from being bent. This shows that the native Germanic iron was often of poor quality and was prone to being bent or broken.

Swords were very rare, which isn't surprising due to the scarcity of metal in Germania. These weapons were, in all likelihood, used by the tribal elite, including chiefs and high-ranking warriors. Both single-edged and double-edged swords have been found. The single-edged swords, which could be better described as large knives, are generally much shorter than the double-edged swords. This implies that the single-edged swords would have been used primarily by infantry, who needed a short weapon for close hand-to-hand combat, while the longer double-edged swords would have been used by cavalrymen who needed to have a longer reach. Based upon their appearance, all of these swords, whether single-edged or double-edged, appear to be more useful for chopping and slashing rather than thrusting.

Swords first came into use among the Germans in the seventh or sixth century BC. These weapons were of Celtic manufacture, made of either bronze or iron, and could be quite large, leading some archaeologists to wonder whether or not such large heavy weapons could have actually been wielded in battle or if they served as status symbols. These weapons soon fell out of favour, replaced by knives and daggers, although iron Celtic-style short swords and long swords continued to be imported into Germania until the first century BC.[70]

The Germans also made their own swords when they could. These natively-manufactured weapons, which first appeared during the mid-second century AD and possibly earlier, were the progenitors of what we would recognize as 'Viking-style' swords. These were double-edged weapons, with handles shaped like the letter H turned on its side, with large bar-shaped crossbars and pommels. The grips of the handles were often shaped to accommodate fingers, like the grips of Roman swords, and could be made of metal, wood, or bone. These handles were often decorated with bronze or silver, and the scabbards sometimes had decorative embellishments.[71]

By the late third century BC, a single-edged fighting weapon called the *sax* or *seax* (Anglo-Saxon for 'knife'; the name *Saxon* likely means 'knife-wielders') was introduced. These weapons varied widely in size, from being small knife-sized weapons to being sword-sized. These were large single-edged weapons and could be referred to as 'straight sabres'. While it seems that their primary functions were for hacking and slashing, some examples came to a sharpened point and could be used for thrusting as well. The sword-sized versions have handles which are usually C-shaped, sometimes terminating in carved animal heads. Swords of this design have been found at Hjortspring (measuring about 18 inches long) and Vimose (23 inches long), indicating that weapons of this design were in use for several centuries.[72]

Axes, the weapon long associated in the popular consciousness with northern barbarians, especially the Germans, are surprisingly rare. Axe heads dated to the seventh and sixth centuries BC have been found, but few examples have been found in western Germania, where the Romans were. Axes appear to be more common among the eastern Germanic tribes, who would have been in contact with the Illyrians and Dacians, and possibly the ancestors of the Baltic and Slavic tribes. After the sixth century BC, the battle axe apparently dropped out of use, and didn't re-appear until the mid to late second century AD in the form of small throwing axes, like the *francisca*.[73]

Bows have also been discovered, although these appear to be more common in northern Germania than elsewhere. Archery, therefore, seems to have been practised to a rather limited extent, with the majority of Germans favouring javelins as the preferred missile weapons. These were

6-foot longbows made of yew wood with a D-shaped cross-section, with the hand-grips bound with cord, and the tips capped with iron or horn siyahs. Over forty bows of this type have been discovered in Denmark, dated to 200–350 AD. These bows would have been exactly identical to English and Welsh longbows from the Medieval period. Other bows made of this time were composites, made of yew and fir wood. As far as I am aware, no bows or arrows have been found in Germanic lands dating to before 100 AD.[74]

So much for weapons. Now let's talk about body protection. The shields used by the Germanic warriors came in a variety of shapes. They could be circular, oval, rectangular, hexagonal, or shaped like an elongated octagon. Many times, these wooden shields would be constructed of thin boards which were then braced with a leather or metal outer frame, and possibly covered with a layer of leather. Among the finds at Hjortspring were large rectangular or semi-rectangular shields (each edge was slightly curved). Unlike Roman shields, which were made of multiple layers of thin wooden strips glued atop each other in an overlapping pattern, or like other wooden shields in which several thick boards were aligned adjacent to one another and were then bound with a leather or metal frame, these shields were made of single large flat pieces of wood which had been cut and carved into the shape of shields. The size and dimensions of these shields mean that only large trees of a substantial girth could be suitable to make them, but Roman authors claim that Germania was filled with large trees, so finding the properly-sized trees necessary to make shields of this design might not have been as tricky as we might think. Interestingly, the oval-shaped shield bosses, always made of metal in other cultures, are here made of carved wood, which serves to only further justify the comment made by Tacitus that iron was incredibly scarce within Germania, and was in such short supply that objects traditionally made of metal had to be manufactured out of wood.[75]

In terms of the structure of the Germanic armies, Tacitus says that the majority of warriors were infantry, and certain elite warriors were placed in the front in units of a hundred men each, with each company-sized unit numbered and named after the tribe they came from.[76] Examples could be the 1st Batavian Elite Company, or 7th Cherusci Elite Company. It's a more easily-understood way of distinguishing different units than the Romans' way, since German units were named after specific tribes and were numbered, presumably in the order that they were created; as such, no two Germanic units could have the same identity. In the Roman Army, there were several legions which had the same number (for example, by this time, there were already three 1st Legions), and had to rely on their nicknames, if they had any, for distinction.

This practice of grouping elite warriors among a tribe into company-sized units and giving these units numbers and names might be an example of the Germans copying Roman military practices. It isn't the only example. During the Battle of Teutoburg, the German warriors bombarded the Romans with a barrage of javelins before closing with them in hand-to-hand combat. This was a standard battle procedure for the Roman legionaries, who hurled their *pilum* javelins at the enemy force to cause casualties, to disrupt the cohesion of the formation, and to decrease their morale, and after they had thrown their *pila*, the Roman soldiers would advance with their swords drawn. If the Germanic warriors didn't already conduct their battles in this fashion, then they certainly copied it from the Romans, either from their experience in fighting the Romans or because Arminius instructed them in this manner of fighting.

It is often believed that barbarians of any sort, when attacking an enemy, simply charged in one massive horde. However, the historical records tell a different story. Julius Caesar states that the Germans, according to custom, formed into a 'phalanx' in battle. The phalanx was a formation used by the ancient Greeks and by the early Romans, in which men would form up in a dense square-shaped block with long spears and overlapping shields. The sources already state that the Germans were armed with spears (albeit small ones) and large shields, and therefore could have formed themselves up in such a manner as Caesar describes. This indicates a higher level of organization and coordination than often supposed. In battle, the Germans commonly formed into a wedge-shaped formation. Falling back was not seen as an act of cowardice, but viewed as a practical decision given the circumstances. However, to throw away one's shield was considered a serious offence. Any man who did so was barred from attending religious rituals or being in government. Tacitus adds that many of those who had shown cowardice in battle later committed suicide out of shame by hanging themselves.[77]

Tacitus also goes into certain detail on the cavalry tactics, or rather the lack of them, stating that their horses are neither handsome nor swift, and the German cavalry are not skilled in fancy maneuvers but simply charge forward.[78] This seems to imply blunt shock tactics, but the horses dating to this time were not particularly large. It isn't until the Middle Ages that we have the gargantuan knightly chargers, the *destriers*. Ancient horses were bred for speed and maneuverability rather than impact force. Plutarch states that the German cavalry was far more dashing and impressive than commonly believed. According to him, they were not merely shabbily-garbed warriors on horseback. In his biography of Gaius Marius, the famous Roman commander who fought against the Teutons and Cimbri in the late second century BC, Plutarch describes the Germanic cavalry as riding forward 'in splendid style, with helmets made to resemble the maws of frightful wild beasts or the heads of strange animals, which, with their towering crests of feathers, made their wearers appear taller than they really were; they were also equipped with breastplates of iron, and carried gleaming white shields. For hurling, each man had two lances; and at close quarters they used large, heavy swords.'[79] It must be stated that Plutarch was writing over two centuries after the events in question, and one wonders where he obtained this information from. Perhaps, like many classical authors, he embellished and exaggerated aspects dealing with barbarians in order to make them more sensational to his readers. Although this description raises eyebrows since it sharply contrasts with the popular image of the Germanic barbarian, it's filled with enough detail to make readers question if Plutarch's description of the German cavalry is pure literary fantasy or if it's indeed an accurate albeit exaggerated description. It's possible to see the German cavalry wearing bear or wolf pelts on their heads like the Roman standard-bearers did, or wearing Roman or Celtic-style helmets decorated with feather crests. Their iron breastplates might be copies of armour worn by neighbouring Celts and Illyrians. The 'gleaming white shields' which Plutarch writes of might be a reference to wooden shields painted all white, which would have created a sharp contrast against the natural greens and browns of the landscape, or, more improbably, shields faced with a thin layer of polished iron and which would have created a shimmering blinding glare in the Mediterranean sun. 'White armour' was the name given to the well-polished plate armour worn by knights in Late Medieval Europe.

The description of each cavalryman carrying two javelins and a long sword for hand-to-hand combat sounds perfectly believable. Swords are traditionally believed to have been the exclusive property of the tribal elite due to their expense and their prestige status, and considering only the wealthy would have owned horses, we must view the German cavalry as the *equestrians* of ancient Germania – the mounted aristocrats rich enough to own horses and take them to battle. Plutarch's description of the German cavalry, which may or may not be accurate, illustrates that the Germanic warriors were not the poorly-clothed poorly-armed poorly-equipped forest-dwelling savages that the Romans claimed them to be. Considering that some tribes, such as the Cherusci and the Tencteri, placed great social importance on horses and consequently cavalry warfare, one is forced to confront the idea that in these societies the cavalry was not the exclusive domain of the tribal elites but was much more common. In this case, then wealth itself need not be confined to the chiefs and ruling class, and as such prestige weapons and armour need not be confined to the elites, despite the assertions made by Caesar and Tacitus. In the case of the Cherusci, it might have been relatively common to see Germanic warriors riding horses, dressed in leather or possibly metal body armour, and wielding long swords, as Plutarch describes. However, since the prevailing image of the Germanic warrior is of a man with little or no body armour and minimal weaponry, we have to assume that for the majority of the Germanic tribes, this was the prevailing image of the Germanic warrior.

What the Germans lacked in weapons, armour, and strategy, they made up for in fighting spirit, and this perhaps above all made them dangerous. When writing about Rome's first contact with the Germans at the end of the second century BC, Plutarch wrote, 'Their courage and daring made them irresistible, and when they engaged in battle they came on with the swiftness and force of fire, so that no one could withstand their onset.'[80]

Another aspect of Germanic fighting style and capabilities is the ominous passage in Frontinus' *Stratagems* when it says that the Germans were experts at guerilla warfare...

> The Germans, in accordance with their usual custom, kept emerging from woodland-pastures and unsuspected hiding-places to attack our men, and then finding a safe refuge in the depths of the forest.[81]

The First Day

All of the pieces were in motion, and the stage was now set for the actual battle to begin. Varus and his men had crossed the southern ridge of Teutoburg and had marched deep into the mountains, trying to get towards the Porta Westfalica Pass. Cassius Dio describes the terrain as rough jagged peaks with deep ravines, and covered in thick forests with massive trees. Even before the attack began, the Romans were wearing themselves out by carving their own path through the wilderness.

> The mountains had an uneven surface broken by ravines, and the trees grew close together and very high. Hence the Romans, even before the enemy assailed them, were having a hard time of it felling trees, building roads, and bridging places that required it.[82]

One assumes that the Romans were moving at a snail's pace. As the Romans slowly progressed through the forest, the Germans were quickly and secretly moving into their attack positions, hiding themselves in the thick undergrowth, waiting for the perfect moment to strike.

In other translations of this passage, it states that the Romans were 'clearing the tracks' instead of 'building roads'. I found this rather puzzling because the wording of this statement implies that there were tracks which already existed in Germania, as opposed to the common perception that the Romans had to hack their own way through the forest themselves. Moreover, the act of clearing the tracks implies, or rather states outright that these pathways were blocked off. Blocked off by what, or by whom? 'Clearing the tracks' means that obstacles were placed, perhaps deliberately, in the path of the Roman advance. An immediate historical parallel which popped into my mind when I read this translation was General John Burgoyne's Hudson River campaign of 1777, culminating in the Battle of Saratoga. During his campaign, he endeavoured to invade New York from the north in Canada, travelling down the Hudson River towards Albany and seize the state capital. However, instead of taking the longer but more established route, he chose a more direct path, but although it was shorter, there were no roads, and Burgoyne and his British regulars would have to hack their own way through the northern New York wilderness. It was a slow laborious process, and to further add to their frustration, the American rebels, led by General Philip Schuyler, routinely hampered their progress by placing large fallen trees in their path and flooding areas by damming up streams, forcing the British army to advance at a snail's pace.[83] All that being said, perhaps the Germans undertook the same actions, placing large fallen trees across the paths which Varus and his men wished to travel upon, thereby slowing their progress and buying more time for the Germans to gather their forces.

However, I wish to dispel this idea. If indeed the Germans were deliberately placing obstacles in the Romans' path, the Romans would have caught onto it eventually. The Romans would have soon realized that their expedition was being deliberately sabotaged, and would have come to the inevitable conclusion that enemy warriors were in the area, trying to hamper the column's advance. Once they realized this, they would have gone on full alert and would have been prepared for battle at any second. But this is not what Cassius Dio states. He states that the Roman column was very much at ease. They took no preparation against coming under attack because they did not believe that they had entered hostile territory. It is completely contradictory to one's thinking that the Romans could be so slack if they were fully aware that the enemy was nearby and deliberately trying to stall the advance of the Roman column. They would have surely readied themselves for battle at any moment. Therefore, the idea that the Romans were 'clearing the tracks' is completely inaccurate, and should not be taken into consideration.

While the Romans were busily chopping down trees and making their own road through the wilderness, Arminius and his Cherusci friends left the Roman column.

> They [Arminius and his companions] escorted him [Varus] as he set out, and then begged to be excused from further attendance, in order, as they claimed, to assemble their allied forces, after which they would quietly come to his aid. Then they took charge of their troops, which were already in waiting somewhere.[84]

Elsewhere, I have seen translations of this passage begin with 'The leaders' rather than 'They'. If this is the correct translation, then the 'leaders' in question meant the leaders of the revolt, but it also probably meant the leaders of the column, which in this circumstance would be the auxiliary cavalry. Auxiliary cavalry often scouted ahead of the main army. One may wonder why the auxiliary cavalry were specifically entrusted with this duty, and not the regular Roman cavalry. Moreover, the auxiliaries always marched in the vanguard, leading the advance. I am tempted to think that the reason why the Romans did this was to minimize the risk to their own men. As the men in the first line of advance, the auxiliaries would be the ones to come into contact with an enemy first, and as such would be the first to take casualties, possibly heavy casualties. If this is true, then the Romans would send out the auxiliary cavalry because they didn't want to risk sending their own horsemen in case they were unknowingly riding into danger. Roman cavalry were few in number, precious, and not to be wasted. By contrast, the auxiliaries, despite their skills and their value, were expendable, a point that Arminius must have bristled under. Since Arminius was an auxiliary commander, and possibly a cavalry commander, it's highly likely that Arminius and his fellow Cherusci horsemen would have led the Roman column.

When Cassius Dio states that the rebel leaders wished to 'assemble their allied forces, after which they would quietly come to his aid', what he means is that Arminius and the other secret conspirators stated that they were leaving in order to round up Rome's tribal allies and to have them assemble in a certain place, and then to join the Roman column in support of Varus. Rome had alliances with several tribes, among them the Chauci and the Batavians. Sending out riders to inform various villages to send contingents of warriors in support of Rome's military must have been a standard practice. Since the Romans were travelling through Cherusci territory, and since Arminius was a member of the Cherusci tribe, and since the Cherusci had been subdued by Rome and established peaceful relations with them (at least on paper), Varus would have understood that Arminius was going off to rally his fellow Cherusci warriors and have them join the ranks of the Roman column. Varus believed that the Cherusci were Roman allies, and he felt that they would surely come to his aid when aid was required.

But a point must be made here – Arminius didn't have to leave with the auxiliary cavalry. In fact, he shouldn't have even been with the auxiliary cavalry by this stage. Since Arminius had been awarded Roman citizenship and knighted into the Equestrian Order, he would have been made a member of the regular Roman cavalry, and was no longer obligated to remain among the auxiliaries. However, it seems that Arminius chose to remain among his fellow Cherusci horsemen, even though he was perfectly capable of joining the regular cavalry if he wished; the bonds of tribal and clan loyalties were very prevalent. It is not known if Arminius had at any time in the past expressed his wishes to Varus to remain with his German friends. I can only assume that he had done so in order to stay with the auxiliary cavalry.

It was a good thing, too, that he was still among the auxiliaries, since it now fell on him to arrange the final preparations for the ambush. The auxiliary cavalry were the eyes and ears of the army. It was their job to make sure that the path of advance was clear. Surely, Arminius would have known his duty. If he didn't leave the column on his own to scout ahead, Varus would have *ordered* him to leave. Arminius and his scouts rode ahead to inform the Germanic warriors waiting in the cover of the undergrowth of the approaching Romans, and to get everything ready. Then, they rode back, and told Varus that all was clear up ahead.

Why didn't Arminius stay with the warriors who were hiding in the forest? If Arminius and his companions didn't return, the Romans would know that something had happened, and they'd be on alert. The last thing that Arminius wanted was for this grand enterprise to be put at jeopardy. Everything had to go according to plan.

So, if we were to re-create the whole situation up to this point, I imagine that several of Arminius' companions who were knowledgeable about the rebellion stated to Varus that they were going forward to rally Rome's tribal allies – in other words, gather up some more Cherusci warriors to come to Varus' aid. After all, the Cherusci were supposed to be loyal Roman allies. They were lying, of course, and raced off to the rebel villages telling them to bring their warriors to the planned ambush location. Some time later, Arminius must have excused himself to go scouting along with a few other Cherusci cavalrymen acting as guards (as a vital member of Varus' inner circle, it would have been standard procedure for him to travel with an armed escort due to safety reasons). They came upon the warriors hiding in the forest, told them that the Romans were coming and to get everything ready, and then returned to the column and told Varus that everything was safe up ahead.

On top of the miserable situation that the Romans were in, tiring themselves out by having to cut down trees so the wagons could pass, and bridging over the ravines and rivers, another bit of misfortune was added to their misery – it began to rain. In fact, Cassius Dio says that the rain turned into a violent thunderstorm, and that this caused the column to be spread out even further.[85]

A violent rain and wind came up that separated them still further, while the ground, that had become slippery around the roots and logs, made walking very treacherous for them, and the tops of the trees kept breaking off and falling down, causing much confusion.[86]

History does not record the precise location of where the first strike by the Germans against Varus' troops took place, and archaeology has not been able to yield up any results that I've heard of. So, is there any way for us to determine the exact location of where the first day of the Battle of Teutoburg began? I believe that there is, and to do that, we have to look at battlefield strategy.

As stated earlier, Varus was almost surely heading in a more-or-less northeastern direction from the Bielefeld Pass to the Porta Westfalica Pass. These two passes marked the major entrance and exit points out of the Teutoburg region, which, as I've mentioned before, were dominated by two high ridges. If I were Arminius, where would I attack? I would attack *exactly* in the middle. If the attack came too early along the Romans' path of advance, then the Romans could simply turn around and escape back out of the Bielefeld Pass where they came from. Attack too late, and the Romans would push on through the Porta Westfalica Pass and destroy the Angrivarian capital of Minden, as they intended. Attacking the Romans exactly at the half-way point between the two esker ridges makes the only logical sense.

By now, the Germans had surrounded the Roman column, and were lying in wait in the undergrowth, waiting for the best moment to strike. The storm had only served to further conceal them by masking over the noise of them creeping through the vegetation closer towards their intended victims. It isn't stated in any ancient source when or how the attack was begun, no mention of a signal or a massed battle cry. While the Germans crouched in the wet undergrowth with their weapons, the Romans, oblivious to the danger, continued working through the rumble of thunder and the pounding rain.

Suddenly the entire Roman column was showered with javelins from all directions. Cassius Dio says that the Germans began the attack by hurling javelins because they wanted to attack from a distance, since they were afraid that if they attacked hand-to-hand, the Romans would overpower them. There's no reason to discredit this. I would also like to contribute that since Arminius was a member of the Roman Army, he would have been familiar with Roman battle tactics, and a preliminary shower of *pilum* javelins almost always preceded the main infantry attack. It's very likely that Arminius taught the warriors this tactic, to hurl javelins *en masse* at the Roman column to disrupt them and cause panic. It evidently had the desired effect – many Romans were wounded in this initial barrage.[87]

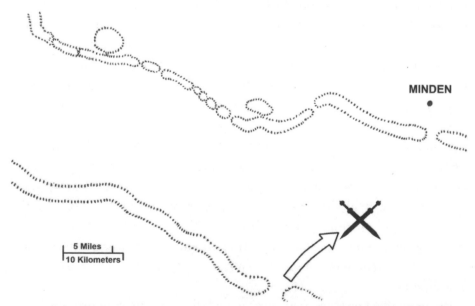

Map 4. The Battle of Teutoburg, Day 1. Varus and his men are ambushed along their route. They were probably attacked halfway between the Bielefeld Pass and the Porta Westfalica Pass. (*Illustration by Jason R. Abdale*)

When the legionaries didn't counter-attack after the first volley of javelins, the Germans became bold and charged the column.

The Romans were not proceeding in any regular order, but were mixed in helter-skelter with the wagons and the unarmed, and so, being unable to form readily anywhere in a body, and being fewer at every point than their assailants, they suffered greatly and could offer no resistance at all.[88]

The Roman cavalry might have been especially targeted.[89] As stated earlier in this book, the Cherusci were primarily horsemen, and they knew the value of cavalry. During his Germanic campaign, Drusus had confiscated the Cherusci's horses, though it is unknown if Varus did or didn't give the Cherusci new ones as a sign of his good will as Governor. If the attacking German warriors, especially the Cherusci, deliberately went out of their way to go after the Roman cavalry, it would deprive the Romans of their eyes and ears, and would prevent messengers escaping, warning others of the battle and asking for reinforcements. It would have also been a poetic act of revenge for when the Romans had taken away the Cherusci's precious horses so many years ago. Doubtless, some horses must have been killed in the initial javelin barrage, but the main target was not the horse, but the horseman. True, in cavalry warfare, the horse was usually seen as a large soft target, but the Cherusci prized horses, and would have wanted to capture as many as possible. It's likely, therefore, that the German warriors were trying to kill the riders rather than the horses, hoping to use the horses themselves.

Cassius Dio states later on 'They [the Romans] encamped on the spot, after securing a suitable place, so far as that was possible on a wooded mountain.'[90] This must mean that the Romans were able either to break free from the ambush and retreat to a different location, or somehow managed to fight the Germans off. I wish to discredit the first of the two options, because if the Romans had somehow managed to break free and escape, retreating perhaps to the rear, the Germanic warriors would have pursued them and cut them down as they fled. The Romans, therefore, would not have had the security to establish a camp for the night, because that could only be done if they were not under attack. Therefore, it has to be the second option – the Romans somehow managed to gain the upper hand and drive the Germans away. There's only one way that this could have been done – Varus, initially surprised at the ambush and after suffering many casualties among his men, organized a counter-attack, and the Germans fled back into the forest. This shows that Varus was not entirely incompetent. He was able to turn a bad situation around, and his attackers were forced to retreat. Once that was done, Varus and his army moved to a safer location and set up camp for the night.

It isn't stated whether or not Varus was aware of Arminius' deception by this point. We'll never know. Perhaps he knew that Arminius had betrayed him the moment that the attack started. Perhaps he knew but was in denial – they had, after all, been very close and it may have been hard for him to believe that his trusted friend had led him into a trap. Perhaps he still firmly believed that Arminius was faithful, and believed that the Germans had been hiding in the forest, and that Arminius and his scouts hadn't seen them. Well, any of these views depend solely on where Arminius was during the first day's fighting, and what he was doing once the fighting started. It's certain that he was with the Roman column when the attack began. He had to be, because if he didn't return from his scouting mission, the Romans would have guessed that something evil was brewing. But once the attack began, what would Arminius have done? If we answer that question, then we can guess what Varus' thoughts were about his friend.

Obviously, Arminius couldn't stand and fight with the Romans, because then he would be betraying his countrymen, which was against the whole purpose of the rebellion. Was Arminius fighting with the Germans in plain view of every Roman on the battlefield? If that was the case, then Varus would have immediately known that he was betrayed because everyone there would have seen Arminius killing the legionaries. There's no reason to discard this hypothesis, but I want to add that if he had acted in this manner, he would instantly have become a target. The Romans would have gone after him, rightly thinking that he was the ringleader, and try to kill him. Only with a suitable amount of protection could Arminius afford to make his true loyalties known with minimal risk to his own life. But Arminius had a big following among the warriors, and it's very likely that they would have fought ferociously to keep him safe. Still, although this scenario is plausible, it just seems too risky to me.

My best guess (and I am only guessing) is that Arminius mysteriously and conveniently disappeared when the actual fighting began. He couldn't have taken part in the battle since he would have been spotted, and therefore, targeted. So, he must have left the Romans when the battle started. How? Did he and his fellow Cherusci auxiliaries suddenly charge off into the woods when the first javelins began to fall onto the Roman lines, abandoning Varus and his men to their fates? This scenario was portrayed in the four-part German documentary *Die Germannen*, released as *The Germanic Tribes* in English; the second episode deals with this battle. If this happened, then the Romans surely would have known that Arminius had betrayed them, but would have had little time to react.

Perhaps the attacking German warriors acted like a screen, and Arminius managed to quietly creep away un noticed. When in combat, especially hand-to-hand combat, people tend to be aware of only their immediate surroundings, and don't notice things happening some distance away. Arminius could very well have managed to sneak away and no one would have noticed. But there is always the risk that someone *would* have noticed, and therefore, I believe this hypothesis is not suitable.

Perhaps Arminius staged a scene to make it look like he had been taken captive by the attacking Germans and was dragged off into the forest, making him look like a prisoner to the on-looking Romans who may have witnessed it. If so, he would have had to rehearse this with his fellow Germanic tribesmen like a theatrical performance. But then again, he would have had plenty of time to do this beforehand, so this hypothesis is plausible.

Arminius and his comrades-in-arms had achieved something that few pre-gunpowder armies had achieved – total surprise. The Romans had been caught with their pants (or should I say their tunics, since they didn't wear pants) down, and they suffered for it. Casualty estimates are unknown, but they must have been in the hundreds.

After driving the Germans back into the forest, Varus and his men re-located and set up camp in a flat clearing, which Cassius Dio says was fortunate that they found, considering that the landscape was rugged forested mountains. Despite the fact that Varus had somehow gained the upper hand and had driven the barbarians off, he knew that the situation was much more serious and dangerous than he previously thought. He had possibly anticipated that something like this would happen (after all, that may have been the reason why he brought so many troops along in the first place), but he was not expecting to be caught in 'friendly' territory. Clearly, the Cherusci were not Roman allies. It must have dawned on him that his force was now cut off and surrounded in enemy territory. Although he had three legions under his command and a large number of auxiliaries, the total number of all of these men combined probably amounted to only around 10,000 men. It would not be enough. Varus realized that he needed to get his army out of Teutoburg as quickly as possible. He couldn't afford to have his army burdened down with extraneous supplies and equipment. Cassius Dio states that after Varus set up camp for the night, he ordered the baggage train and all things deemed unnecessary to be burned or abandoned. It's likely that everything was set on fire and that nothing was merely abandoned – no commander would be foolish enough to allow the enemy to procure your supplies, regardless of how unnecessary they may have been to you, since a resourceful opponent can always find a use for everything.[91]

It's clear from the archaeology of the area and the recovery of various artifacts that once hostilities began, the Romans certainly began travelling in a westward direction from then on. Why go west? Why not retrace their steps and march back from whence they came, travelling southwards until they got to Paderborn and the Lippe River, and *then* marching west along the river until they got to Fort Aliso?

I have two hypotheses which may answer this crucial question. First, Varus was prevented from going backwards because he couldn't. Arminius wasn't stupid. He knew that if the Romans managed to turn around and exit through the southern Bielefeld Pass, they had a very good chance of escaping with a large amount of their force. Arminius did not want a single Roman alive – he wanted to destroy the Romans completely. The Romans had to be prevented from returning to their base camp, and that meant sucking them further and further into the Germanic interior. So, I believe that Arminius stationed a very large body of Germanic warriors in the rear of Varus' position, blocking his path. Varus couldn't go back south. He could only go north and west.

Second, I believe that Varus was so shaken up by recent events and the realization that his Germanic allies were actually his enemies that he might have gotten the idea that nowhere in Germania was safe. Fort Aliso was within the province, and as such, it could come under attack, if it wasn't under attack already (he may have been thinking about this). Fort Vetera, by contrast, was located *outside* the province of Germania Magna, protected by the wide expanse of the Rhine River. If he and his army could somehow get to the Rhine, they could round up reinforcements, or at least get across the Rhine to a safe position. That may or may not be true, but it seems certain that he realized after this short but terrifying battle that this expedition was doomed to failure if he proceeded on his previous course, and he just wanted to get out of the territory as quickly as possible.

The Second Day

Varus and his men were now eager to get out of Teutoburg as quickly as they could. Varus realized that his men had been cut off and surrounded by enemy forces; they would have to fight their way out. The previous night, after the Romans had made camp, Varus had ordered that everything which was unnecessary or which would slow the men down should be destroyed. Speed was now of the essence.

Cassius Dio states 'The next day they advanced in a little better order, and even reached open country, though they did not get off without loss.'[92] This statement shows that Varus was now not as careless as he had been the previous day. His men were now marching in formation and were on guard for another attack.

I assume, albeit with no proof, that the Romans left camp as early as possible, probably dawn or before dawn. They needed to travel as much as they could during the course of the day, and starting early would get them to their destination sooner. It might have also put some distance between them and the Germans. However, since the Germans caught up with them, that must have meant that they had kept their eyes on the Romans in their camp. This makes sense. Based on his experience in the Roman Army, Arminius must have known that attacking the Romans while they were in a defensive position was suicide. So, we can imagine that while the Romans stayed in their camp in the forest clearing following the first day of the battle, the

Germans kept a careful watch on them all night long from the cover of the nearby trees. When the Romans left camp, the Germans followed.

It also seems clear that the Romans wanted to leave camp without making too much noise. Destroying or leaving behind everything unnecessary would certainly help, but one small snapshot in time shows just how terrified the Romans were. During the archaeological excavations of the battlefield, the skeleton of a mule was found with a bell hanging around his neck. The bell was stuffed with straw, probably collected from the field where the Romans were encamped during the previous night, to keep it from ringing.

The aforementioned passage from Cassius Dio's writings also corroborates the idea that Germania was not the endless forest which Victorian-era literature imagined it to be – there were areas that were clear of trees. Whether these were grassy fields or muddy marshes, Cassius Dio doesn't say. But there may be more information implied within the passage than at first glance, because Cassius Dio gives us a clue as to Varus' new route, the route of retreat that he and his army were now proceeding on. He clearly states that the men reached open country, as opposed to the confining mountainous and forested territory that they had seen so far. The Romans had discovered only one small open area within the mountains which afforded the building of a camp, which Cassius Dio says was rare and fortunate. This can only mean that Varus and his men had crossed out of Teutoburg into open territory, meaning the North German Plain.

Earlier, I said that it might be impossible to determine the exact sequence of locations in which this battle took place, but I would like of offer my own hypothesis, one which I believe is highly likely. On the first day of the fighting, Varus and his men were in the mountains of Teutoburg, travelling in a northeastern direction towards the Porta Westfalica Pass in order to get to the Angrivarian capital of Minden. Somewhere along their route, almost certainly exactly in the middle spot between the two esker ridges, the German warriors attacked them. After they had been repulsed, Varus needed to get himself and his men out of there as fast as they could. They couldn't continue travelling towards the Porta Westfalica because the Germans would surely attack them along the way, and they couldn't backtrack because they were cut off. So, Varus decided to change direction. He would march his men northwest instead of northeast, and try to break out of Teutoburg by crossing the northern ridge and getting out onto the North German Plain, where his army might stand a better chance. But in order to do that, he couldn't afford to waste time hacking his way through the wilderness so that wagons and other encumbrances could more easily pass through. He had no intention of having his men carry the luggage because they would be slowed down. So he gave the order to destroy everything that was unnecessary so that the army could move faster. Then, marching in a northwest direction, he hurriedly tried to get out of Teutoburg. The esker ridges which formed the northern and southern boundaries of the Teutoburg region were not continuous; the Porta Westfalica Pass was the largest pass out of Teutoburg, and was probably the main one used when travelling through the area, but there were smaller narrower breaks in the ridgeline here and there, and Varus and his men were lucky enough to find one of these narrow gaps in the northern esker. Then again, luck might not have had anything to do with it. I think that it's highly unlikely and unrealistic that Varus and his men travelled blindly through enemy territory until they just happened to come across a pass through the mountains. Remember, Varus had been the governor of Germania Magna for three years, and during that time, Arminius acted as one of his top officials. Varus might very well have had knowledge of the terrain reported to him by Romans or by Arminius and other Germans, and he might have had access to maps. If he did order his army to suddenly change course from a northeastern to a northwestern trajectory, it is almost certainly because he already knew of the existence of other passes which were smaller and narrower, but still serviceable. Perhaps the Roman force used the pass near the modern-day town of Lübbecke, where Federal Road 239 crosses through today.

Now they were out of the Tribal Stronghold, and the vast swamplands to the north spread out before them. From here on, they hurriedly travelled westward along the northern edge of the northern esker ridge, possibly using it as a guide towards getting to the Rhine River. If this is true, then Varus and the surviving Romans likely travelled along the route of what are now Federal Roads 65 and 218.

The distance between where Varus and his men were supposedly attacked on the first day (somewhere along the northeastern trajectory between Bielefeld and the Porta Westfalica Pass) and where they were eventually

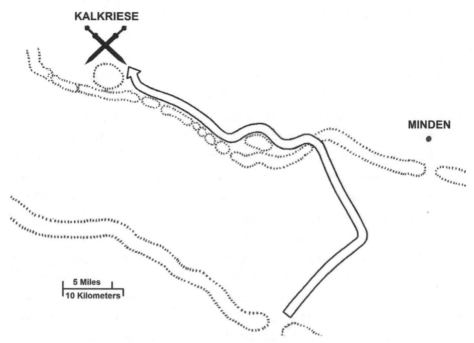

Map 5. The Battle of Teutoburg, day 2. The path of Varus' escape route on the second day of the battle. After emerging from the hill country, his army travelled westward along the northern edge of the Wiehen Ridge, being harried by German warriors the whole way, until much of the Roman army was destroyed in an ambush located at Kalkriese Hill, located on the far western point of Wiehen Ridge. (*Illustration by Jason R. Abdale*)

attacked on the second day (the base of Kalkriese Hill) is an incredibly long distance. The idea that Varus' army could cover so much ground in less than twenty-four hours is impressive, almost unbelievable. It does, though, give further vindication to Varus' decision to destroy the wagons and the unnecessary baggage in order to travel as quickly as possible. It also shows the level of panic and the sense of emergency that Varus and his men must have felt. Moreover, there are parallels to such a fast-paced march. In 1066, when King Harold Godwinson of Anglo-Saxon England heard that the Vikings had landed on the Yorkshire coast, he hurriedly marched north from London to meet them, gathering up his *fyrd* militia along the way. It took him just four days to cover the 185 miles from London to Stamford Bridge. That means that his army must have been travelling between 46 to 47 miles per day, more than double the standard marching pace of 20 miles per day, fully showing that these men were literally racing towards the battlefield.[93] Varus' army, no doubt, was travelling at an equally speedy pace. Cassius Dio states that the Germans were in hot pursuit of Varus' men, killing them as they went. The Romans continued their hurried retreat westwards towards Kalkriese Hill, where Arminius and his warriors were waiting to carry out 'stage two' of their grand strategy.

The Romans were advancing westward, travelling along the northern side of the northern esker ridge, and soon they would encounter the second part of Arminius' plan. It involved trapping the Roman column between two large obstacles, and it just so happened that there was a location nearby which suited Arminius' needs perfectly. To the south was a small but steep tree-covered hill now known as Kalkriese Hill. To the north was a vast swampland known as the Great Moor. In between these two obstacles was a narrow belt of firm flat ground. Only this path had enough solid ground to traverse upon, and was approximately two hundred yards wide at its widest point, but Cassius Dio remarks that during this day's fighting, the Romans frequently collided with trees,[94] which means that this route was not clear open space but was forested, and that there was only a narrow forest path to walk down. Arminius must have spotted this site some time ago, and like Wellington observing the terrain at Waterloo, had kept this location in his mind, knowing he would put it to use. When the time came, he incorporated this location into his grand strategy. It would be hard to find a more perfect location for an ambush.

But there is one other location that exists which seems absolutely perfect for an ambush site. West of the town of Lübbecke, there is a large mountain which lies just north of the northern esker ridge. The space between this mountain and the esker ridge forms a tight bottleneck, and speaking from a barbarian perspective, it would have been an absolutely ideal place to hit Varus hard. If his army passed through this narrow valley, it would have been cut to pieces. However, I am not yet aware of large quantities of artifacts found within this tight space, nor am I aware of any large amounts of human remains found here. So it seems that Varus recognized that the narrow space between this mountain and the ridge was dangerous, and instead of squeezing his large army between the mountain and the ridge, he instead decided to march *around* the mountain. Again, Varus was not the fool that many historians claim him to be.

However, Varus' presumed prudence in making this decision would not be enough to keep his men entirely out of danger. The Germans were harrying Varus' column the whole way. That being said, it's possible that the Germans were herding the Romans into the ambush that Arminius had arranged. Some have dismissed this idea outright, claiming that Arminius had anticipated that Varus would come this way and that there was no need to herd him into the trap, citing that this pathway was the only route that could have been used.[95] This hypothesis may or may not be true, but the fact that the Germans were in hot pursuit of Varus' column, killing men as they marched, must have had some effect on which way Varus' men went. Eager to get away from their pursuers, they might have chosen to march via the straightest and most easily-accessible path. In many people's experience, when something dangerous is chasing after you or if you come under attack, you usually don't think about dodging and out-maneuvering. Most of the time, you run in a straight line, hoping merely to outrun your pursuer or attacker. That being said, given that the Germans were hot on the Romans' heels, killing men as they went, perhaps showering the column with arrows from the cover of the woods, the Romans might not have done anything more than to try to make a beeline for some safe zone. If the only thing that they were thinking about was to simply get the hell out of there as fast as they could, then it's not likely that they were thinking much about tactics and manoeuvres.

In a way, it made sense that Varus' men went this way since it was the only way in or out. But it should have been immediately noticed that such ground could become a deadly spot for an ambush for the very same reason. Any piece of ground that an army is forced to march through or towards due to one impediment or another which prevents it from acting otherwise should be seen as a red flag to any experienced commander. But the problem was that Varus wasn't an experienced commander, despite his brief stint as a legate; he was an experienced administrator. Varus knew he was in hostile territory surrounded by enemies. Pressured to keep his men safe, he perhaps was only concerned with quickly getting his soldiers out of harm's way. Ironically, he would lead them into it.

Arminius and his comrades were waiting. Varus and his men were coming straight into his trap. The Germans had prepared defensive positions along the base of the hill – massive earthen-and-wickerwork zig-zag shaped walls. The base of the wall was approximately 15 feet wide and estimated to be 5 feet high, and ran in an east-west direction at the bottom of Kalkriese Hill. This wall may have had a wooden or wickerwork fence built atop it. In front of the wall was a ditch.[96] These defences must have taken considerable time and manpower to construct, which shows both the capabilities of the Germans as well as the false security Varus felt in his position as the governor of a supposedly pacified province.

There's an interesting point about this battle. In all of the ancient sources, there is no direct mention whatsoever of the walls built by the Germans which were employed on the second day of the battle. This is hard to believe, since these earthen walls were important in shaping the battle's dynamics. Tacitus is the only source that describes what could be the Germans' fortifications, but this could also be construed as part of Varus' camp that was constructed at the end of the first day of the battle.

First, there was Varus' camp, with its wide perimeter and headquarters measured out, demonstrating the handiwork of the three legions; then, in a half-destroyed rampart, in a shallow ditch, their remains, now cut to pieces, had evidently huddled together.[97]

Why would there be no direct mention of the Germans' walls? As one of my college professors bluntly stated, the Romans were more willing to say that one of their commanders was an idiot than to acknowledge that the barbarians had outsmarted them. Understandably, the presence of the Germanic fortifications would give credence to the latter, and therefore the topic of the walls was omitted. This would also explain why the ancient writers spared no venom in their criticisms of Varus, even Gaius Paterculus who knew the man personally. Calling the commander a fool was better than acknowledging that you had been bested by supposed inferiors.

Regardless of whether the Romans were being pushed towards Arminius' defensive position by the Germans or not, they were heading straight into

Arminius' trap. Cassius Dio gives a description of the chaotic nature of the second day's fighting...

> Upon setting out from there [the camp] they plunged into the woods again, where they defended themselves against their assailants... Since they had to form their lines in a narrow space, in order that the cavalry and infantry together might run down the enemy, they collided frequently with one another and with the trees.[98]

There are no further descriptions in the ancient accounts of the second day's fighting. One particular glimpse of the chaos is the story of what happened to two Roman mules during the battle. One mule had a bell that was stuffed with straw, as stated earlier. The fighting had grown so intense that a large segment of the wall broke apart and collapsed on top of the poor animal, crushing or suffocating it. Another skeleton of a mule was found with a broken neck, and it has been hypothesized that the animal, in its panic, may have tried to climb over the wall and fell down.[99]

There's an interesting thing to take note of. Artifacts discovered at the Kalkriese site are spread out in a distinctive Y-shaped formation. It looks as if the Romans were split in half, with some skirting around the base of the hill while others were making a break for it out into the open marshland of the Great Moor.[100] Although they may have tried to escape, the Romans, outfitted in heavy body armour, may have become trapped in the mud and slaughtered by the lighter Germanic tribesmen. Or perhaps this was the main body that *did* escape, with the Germans preoccupied with plundering the bodies piled up by the wall. This is the more likely scenario, as I will explain in detail later.

In all likelihood, Arminius had originally planned to completely obliterate the Roman force near Kalkriese, and he very nearly succeeded. Cassius Dio says that it was on the second day that the Romans suffered their highest casualties of the battle.[101] This implies that over half of the Roman force would have been killed, somewhere in the realm of 5,000 men out of a total 10,000 man force. The ground must have been covered with dead bodies, the grass and the fallen early autumn leaves slippery with blood. However, a large number of Romans, including Varus and other

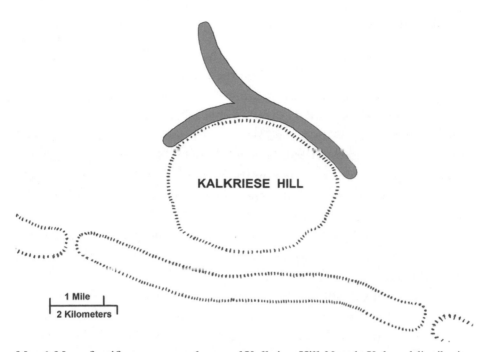

Map 6. Map of artifacts uncovered around Kalkriese Hill. Note the Y-shaped distribution of Roman artifacts. The southern arm indicates where the Roman soldiers were killed, while the northern arm indicates the group of Romans, including Varus, who escaped into the northern marshes, only to be massacred on the fourth day. (*Illustration by Jason R Abdale*)

high-ranking officers, had managed to escape northwards into the marshes. They were not pursued because the Germans were almost certainly pre-occupied with plundering the bodies of the fallen. It would not be the first time that Arminius let victory escape due to the behaviour of the warriors that he commanded.

Presumably, Arminius was not expecting this to happen – he had anticipated that his fellow Germans would completely wipe out the Romans, and not be distracted by the lure of plunder. Unfortunately for him, although most of the Roman force was destroyed, many had still managed to get away. One wonders if Arminius had a back-up plan. I believe that he did not. He needed time to formulate a new strategy as to how to deal with this new situation. This scenario explains what happened, or should I say what *didn't* happen, on the third day of the battle.

The Third Day

Cassius Dio skips from the second to the fourth day. Maddeningly, he mentions *nothing* of what happened on the third day of the battle. In fact, it is only through his account that we know that the battle lasted for four days. So, the conduct of the third day's fighting is entirely guesswork.

At the beginning of the second day, the Romans broke camp, marching in formation, and were harried the whole way by German guerilla fighters. Perhaps the same thing occurred on the beginning of the third day as well. It's not unreasonable to think that the Germans would keep stabbing at the column as it made its frantic way back to the Rhine. If Arminius slackened, the Romans might be able to send word of the ambush, and reinforcements would be sent. In order to keep the Romans isolated, Arminius had to keep up the pressure.

But I think it's doubtful that any messengers would be sent out. Varus couldn't send out messengers because it's highly likely that they would have been killed or captured as they made their way through the German countryside. So, the Romans had to stick together, and being concentrated in one place might have protected them from large scale attacks, but it also hindered them since no word of their situation could be sent out without risking lives.

Perhaps something else entirely occurred – maybe there was no actual fighting. If any fighting *had* taken place on the third day, surely Cassius Dio would have recorded it, so maybe a respite occurred on this day. As I wrote earlier, Arminius probably wanted to destroy the entire Roman force in a single engagement at the base of Kalkriese Hill. Unfortunately for him and his well-laid plans, his warriors were more interested in gathering loot than with polishing off the Romans, and many of them, including Varus and other high-ranking officers, were able to escape northwards into the swamps. Arminius probably didn't have a plan B. He now needed time to revise his strategy. This meant that he couldn't spend time harassing the Romans. A temporary reprieve in the fighting would have allowed Arminius to take his wounded away for medical treatment, to further organize his men, and to give him plenty of time to plan his final *coup de grâce* attack.

A sudden lack of hostility might also have had an important psychological effect on Varus. The landscape may have been eerily silent on the third day.

Varus might have thought that the Germans were not going to attack him, now that he was better organized and was not going to send out scouts or messengers that could be easily picked off. With everyone present and ready for battle, no wonder the Germans weren't attacking, he might have thought. Maybe with no one attacking them on this day, Varus and his surviving men might have thought that the worst was behind them, that it was all over and that they were going to get back home safely. If this was the case, then perhaps they became more relaxed and less alert, if not on this day, then almost certainly the following day. Perhaps Arminius was banking on this. A return to complacency and calm among the Roman ranks would create a vicious *déjà vu* of what had happened on the first day of fighting, when he and his men had taken the Romans completely by surprise. If Arminius was able to pull that off not just once but *twice*, it would be magnificent.

The Fourth Day

Varus and his men had turned away from Teutoburg altogether and were now marching north, possibly towards the territory of the Chauci, who were Roman allies, or at least were believed to be. Personally, I doubt that this was the intended goal. After all, Varus had believed that the Cherusci were staunch Roman allies, and look where that got him! In his mind, why should the Chauci have been any different? What was to prevent them from cutting his throat as well? More likely, he had, in a moment of panic during the second day of the battle, chosen to march north or northwest just to get away from the forested mountains that had caused him so much trouble and had cost him so many lives. At least out in the open, they were safe from ambush attacks. The terrain here would have been open or sparsely-wooded swamps, meadows, and farmland.

Now was the time for the final attack, the attack that would finish off the Romans for good. Cassius Dio states that Arminius' ranks were swelled by last-minute volunteers, eager to claim their share of the captured loot: 'The enemy's forces had greatly increased, as many of those who had at first wavered joined them, largely in the hope of [gaining] plunder.'[102]

Where did all of these people come from, and how did they learn of the battle? It's clear that many in Germania were aware of Arminius' plans, but a large portion of the population had refused to join him. What changed their minds? The answer to this question lies in the practice of trophy gathering. Warriors in many tribal societies need physical proof of their battlefield prowess. This means that you need to bring back items from the battlefield, either severed body parts (especially decapitated heads), weapons, or equipment. This would mean that Arminius' Germanic warriors had taken plunder and had left, presumably going to local villages and telling the inhabitants of what had happened and how there could be a great deal of plunder for those who participated in the battle. Many young lions, eager to prove their worth, joined up at the last minute in the hope of getting in on the action. This also corroborates the idea that the Germans were preoccupied on the second day, plundering the bodies of the slain Romans, and therefore allowing Varus and the remaining survivors to escape.

If indeed there was no fighting on the third day with Arminius hoping among other things to re-create the situation that had occurred on the first day, it was re-created in more ways than Arminius could have hoped, because just like on the first day of fighting, a torrential thunderstorm occurred. The ground turned into a thick sucking mud. The Romans slipped and fell as they tried to advance through the terrain. Due to the saturating rains, and with little or no shade or shelter, the Romans' large *scutum* shields, which weighed 12lbs when dry, became so saturated with water that they became too heavy to carry. The ground, already swampy bogland, would have turned into a slippery sucking mire.

The sudden surge in his numbers would have allowed Arminius to completely surround the Romans with his warriors, eliminating almost all hope of escape. With the Romans once again molested by the abominable weather, and perhaps once again at ease, believing that their troubles with the Germans were over, Arminius hit the Romans with everything that he had. What happened next was sheer slaughter.

They were still advancing when the fourth day dawned, and again a heavy downpour and violent wind assailed them, preventing them from going forward and even from standing securely, and moreover depriving them of the use of their weapons. For they could not handle their bows or their javelins with any success, nor, for that matter, their shields, which were thoroughly soaked. Their opponents, on the other hand, being for the most part lightly equipped, and able to approach and retire freely, suffered less from the storm.[103]

The location of the battle's climax is debatable. Tacitus uses the words *in medio campo*, which can mean either of two things: in the middle of a field, or in the middle of the *campus*, the open parade ground in the centre of a military camp.[104] If it was the first option, in the middle of a field, it would corroborate Tacitus' writings when, describing Germanicus' discovery of the battlefield, that 'in the middle of the plain there were whitening bones, scattered or piled up, exactly as men had fled or resisted. Nearby lay fragments of weapons and horses' limbs.'[105] If it was the second option, in the middle of a military camp's parade ground, this would give some credence to the writings of both Tacitus and Florus. Tacitus states that when Germanicus and his men returned to the battlefield six years later, they had found Varus' camp, and then 'in a half-destroyed rampart, in a shallow ditch, their remains, now cut to pieces'[106] – this passage could be interpreted as pertaining either to Varus' camp or to the walls that the Germans had erected at the base of Kalkriese Hill. Florus states 'His camp was seized and three legions were overwhelmed'.[107] Understandably, this is confusing since Tacitus gives evidence to support both hypotheses, so let's see if we can clear this matter up.

It would be best to place a camp in an area with plenty of open space around it for obvious reasons – to see your enemy, and to deprive your enemy of cover. The middle of a field would be an ideal location to place a camp. Therefore, the controversy of whether the fighting took place in a field or at a camp may be a moot point. However Cassius Dio, who gives the most detailed account of the battle, makes no mention of the Germans assaulting a legionary camp, stating instead that Arminius and his warriors had attacked the Romans while they were on the march. Besides, Arminius had spent too much time in the Roman Army to know that attacking a legion that was stationed behind defensive fortifications was risky at best and utter suicide at worst, and therefore presumably would never have attacked a camp unless absolutely certain of victory. To prove this, he and his men had not attacked

Varus and his legions when they established their camp following the first day's fighting. Arminius was a very careful commander, and knew that the tide could turn against him at any moment. As proof of this, the Romans had managed to rally and force the Germans to flee back into the forest on the first day to avoid high casualties among their warriors, and on the second day the Germans had attacked the Romans only when behind extensive fortifications. Both of these instances show the Germans not wanting to experience too many losses among their own ranks. There's no reason to think, even with the plunder-hungry rabble that was now following him, that Arminius would abandon his caution for boldness. Therefore, it's likely that the fighting took place in an open field and not an assault upon the camp. This can only mean that the final battle took place somewhere north of the northern esker ridge, out in the open boglands. This is important because, as we'll see later, Publius Florus states that when the battle was over, one of the eagle-bearers deliberately drowned himself in a bog, taking the precious eagle with him. This is confirmation that the last day's fighting took place somewhere north of the northern esker ridge in the open marshland, and this also justifies the idea that the Y-shaped deposition of artifacts indicates that the Romans chose to take their chances by venturing northwards out into the open swamps and bogs rather than continuing to march along the edge of the esker ridge. The northern arm of the Y shows the panicked path of the retreat of the main Roman body across the northern marshlands, while the southern arm of the Y, which curls around the base of Kalkriese Hill, indicates where the Roman soldiers were being massacred.

When Tacitus speaks about the skeletons piled up in a ditch next to a half-destroyed rampart, he might not be referring to a ditch surrounding Varus' camp and the collapsed walls of that camp, but he may actually be referring to the ditch that was dug near the Germans' earthen walls, which served their deadly purpose on the second day of the battle. Many bones and Roman artifacts were found in this ditch, which could mean that it was open during the battle.[108] Moreover, according to archaeological evidence, the wall does appear to have collapsed in at least one spot. This, therefore, seems the more likely explanation for Tacitus' comment about bones piled up in a ditch near a half-destroyed wall, and this would add further verification to the theory that the battle's end took place in an open field or some other open terrain, and not at a military camp, or even near Arminius' famous earthen walls, which he employed to great use on the second day.

Regardless of where precisely the fourth day's fighting took place, all of the accounts give the air of chaos, panic, and confusion among the Roman column. Paterculus gives some detail on the conduct of Varus' subordinates on this day...

Of the two prefects of the camp [that were present with Varus], Lucius Eggius furnished a precedent as noble as that of Ceionius was base, who, after the greater part of the army had perished, proposed its surrender, preferring to die by torture at the hands of the enemy than in battle. Numonius Vala, lieutenant of Varus, who, in the rest of his life, had been an inoffensive and an honourable man, also set a fearful example in that he left the infantry unprotected by the cavalry and in flight tried to reach the Rhine with his squadrons of horse. But fortune avenged his act, for he did not survive those whom he had abandoned, but died in the act of deserting them.[109]

It seems obvious that Lucius Eggius died fighting while Ceionius surrendered, anticipating mercy, only to be killed; whether Ceionius was killed during the battle or later during the execution of prisoners isn't clear.

Paterculus shows General Gaius Numonius Vala, one of Varus' two deputy governors, and who would have served as Varus' second-in-command during this battle, fleeing for his life, taking a majority of the cavalry with him, and being repaid for his cowardice by being killed while on the run, presumably by Germanic warriors. However, Murdoch suspects that Vala may have been *ordered* to leave with the remaining cavalry, stating that the horsemen may have proven a hindrance in the crowded conditions of the battle.[110] However, I believe that there was a more important reason than the fact that the cavalry was getting in the way of everyone else. As stated before, the cavalry were the army's eyes and ears. Not only were they essential for scouting and patrols, but also for carrying messages. Varus may have dispatched Vala and his remaining horsemen to get to the nearest Roman fort as fast as they could to warn the garrison of the danger, telling whomever that they found that Varus and his men had been under attack for four days and weren't likely to make it out alive, and that the Germans were probably going to attack the forts next. After delivering their message to the fort's commander, the horsemen, possibly after changing their tired mounts, would be dispatched to various other Roman outposts throughout Germania Magna, each delivering the same message: 'Beware! The barbarians are coming!'

If this was what Varus had done, to send the cavalry out in a desperate attempt to warn others of the danger, then it's likely that he thought that the battle was going to end in defeat, and this was his last act to try to save others in the province from meeting the same fate that he and his men had. Of course, to most Romans on the battlefield who saw it, they would not have known about Varus' orders, but merely would have seen the cavalry dashing off, and naturally would have assumed that the horsemen were running away, saving their own skins. Regrettably, General Vala was never able to complete his assignment, if indeed he was sent on one. But I must state that Vala's actions may very well have been a genuine act of cowardice. We'll never know the real answer.

By now, it was clear to Varus that the battle was lost. Faced with defeat, and with the possibility of being tortured and executed by the Germans, Varus and his staff officers knew that there was only one thing left to do.

Varus, therefore, and all the more prominent officers, fearing that they should either be captured alive or be killed by their bitterest foes (for they had already been wounded), made bold to do a thing that was terrible yet unavoidable: they took their own lives.[111]

The general had more courage to die than to fight, for, following the example of his father and grandfather, he ran himself through with his sword.[112]

Cassius Dio states that Varus and his subordinates killed themselves because they feared that they would be either captured or killed by the Germans. Well, it's not as straightforward as that. It was expected that a Roman commander would kill himself if he lost a battle, and for two reasons. Firstly, he would rather die than allow himself to be captured by his enemies, who would probably execute him anyway. Secondly, it was felt that he had brought shame to Rome and could only alleviate it by taking his own life, which would both wipe away Rome's shame and restore something of his own honour and dignity. This second reason would be familiar to the Japanese samurai and their code of *bushido*.

With Varus and his subordinate commanders dead, many of the soldiers began to give up. Some killed themselves, but others threw down their weapons, hoping to get some measure of mercy from their victors. But it was not to be, as Cassius Dio states…

> When news of this had spread, none of the rest, even if he had any strength left, defended himself any longer. Some imitated their leader, and others, casting aside their arms, allowed anybody who pleased to slay them; for to flee was impossible, however much one might desire to do so. Every man, therefore, and every horse was cut down without fear of resistance.[113]

Contrary to what Cassius Dio states, some men *did* escape and prisoners *were* taken. But what were prized above all else in terms of captured spoils were not prisoners but the legionary eagles. Florus states that the Germans had managed to capture two of the legionary eagles during the battle – we don't know which two. As for the third, rather than have the eagle fall into the Germans' hands, the *aquilifer* pulled the eagle off from its staff and, using it as a weight, jumped into the bog, where he sank down into the murk with it. However, it was eventually found. In the end, the three eagles were sent to various tribes. One was sent to the Bructeri, another to the Marsi, and the third to the Chauci.[114]

I find it very odd that an eagle was given to the Chauci, since this tribe had been staunchly pro-Roman. If anything, I would have assumed that the third eagle would have been given to the Angrivarians, who were one of the instrumental tribes involved in this rebellion, or maybe the Cherusci, who had been the ringleaders of this revolt, would have kept one of the eagles for themselves. The fact that Arminius gave an eagle to the Chauci strongly suggests that this tribe was one of those who joined Arminius at the last minute. Apparently, they realized on which side their bread was buttered, and they acted accordingly. For Varus and the other Romans, who might have been pushing northwards in order to find refuge within Chauci territory, seeing their Germanic allies arrayed against them would have confirmed that no one's loyalty is 100 per cent guaranteed.

In the end, those Romans who were not killed either surrendered or were forcibly taken prisoner. As improbable as it was, the young Cherusci prince Arminius, who was only 25 years old, had managed to defeat an army estimated at 10,000 men, all of them experienced and battle-hardened veterans. The Germanic barbarians at last had their revenge.

Chapter Seven

The Aftermath

Casualties

How many died in the battle? Paterculus says that the casualties of the Battle of Teutoburg were the heaviest incurred by the Roman military in a single battle since the Battle of Carrhae, which was fought in 53 BC between the Romans and the Parthians. During that battle, 20,000 Romans were killed and 10,000 were captured.[1] If there were around 10,000 Romans who marched with Varus, and possibly more, then this statement by Paterculus is true. Casualty estimates for the Battle of Teutoburg are unknown, but both sides' might have been more or less equal to each other. One thing that we do know for certain is that this battle had a severe social impact. Several up-and-coming members of the Roman aristocracy, seeking to establish their reputations, had met their ends too early. Seneca the Younger makes a reference to the battle in his *Moral Letters to Lucilius*, written during the reign of Emperor Nero. In letter 47, he states, 'In the disaster of Varus, many of most distinguished birth who were obtaining the senatorial rank by service in the military were sunk by fortune.'[2]

Many secondary authors have stated that the Germanic barbarians completely destroyed the Roman force, and that not a single Roman escaped. This idea likely comes from the writings of the Roman poet Marcus Manlius. In his work *Astronomicon*, which was written shortly after the Battle of Teutoburg, he makes a brief reference to the battle, stating loftily that the Germans 'washed the field with the blood of three legions, burning everything everywhere'.[3] It's a rather over-the-top statement, and was likely put in for dramatic effect. The historian Florus, writing many years later, makes a similar claim.

To this day, many people – both professional historians and history buffs – state that the Germans managed to destroy three whole legions. This has become the enduring popular story behind this battle. However, the popular legend is wrong. Considering that many Romans were held prisoner for years, and some managed to escape during the fighting, it's clear that the Roman force was not wiped out entirely as many have suggested. The proportion of the Romans killed versus those who were kept as slaves or who escaped from the fighting is not recorded. In one episode of a television show dealing with military matters, it was stated that out of the thousands of Roman soldiers who fought at Teutoburg, only 300 escaped. This number is pure invention. No ancient source states the number of men who managed to escape, and it is my belief that the writers of this show attempted to connect this battle with another important battle, that at Thermopylae, by giving it an instantly-recognizable number in order to increase the battle's popular credibility. Who *hasn't* heard of the 300 Spartans? This is also the case with the arbitrary dating of the battle to early September, in which the battle has been commonly and erroneously stated to encompass only three days instead of four (which in itself is an inaccuracy), and to have taken place from September 9 to 11. This also appears to be a deliberate act of connecting this battle with another important historical event, in this case the terrorist attacks of 11 September 2001, in order to give the battle increased socio-cultural standing. Such actions are incredibly dangerous because they deliberately mislead those who are ignorant of the battle's history into believing that circumstances which are fictional are factual.

But something must be stated here. When these people, whoever they are, attempt to connect this battle with other important historical events in order to increase the battle's credibility, it implies that the Battle of Teutoburg is *not* the epic clash that many people think it was, and therefore it needs to have its importance built up. Indeed, if we look at the military defeats that Rome suffered during its history, which lasted for over 1,000 years, the Battle of Teutoburg appears to have been relatively minor by comparison with some disasters. The Battle of Teutoburg has been commonly regarded as the greatest defeat ever inflicted upon the Romans by northern barbarians. This statement is also incorrect. The Battle of Arausio, also fought between the Romans and Germans over two hundred years earlier during the late second century BC, resulted in far more casualties. According to the sources, 80,000 Roman soldiers perished upon the battlefield, which makes the Battle of Arausio the worst defeat ever inflicted upon the Roman military by the Germanic barbarians, and one of the worst defeats for the Roman military in general, far greater than Teutoburg. Casualties at Teutoburg were also far fewer than the 15,000 or 16,000 Romans killed at the Battle of Hadrianopolis (commonly referred to by the Anglicized name of Adrianople) in 378 AD, another epic battle which was fought between the Romans and the Germans, in this case the Goths. The Battle of Teutoburg lasted for four days and resulted in fewer than 10,000 killed. By contrast, the Battle of Arausio lasted for only a few hours, and resulted in over eight times as many casualties.

The Fate of the Prisoners

What was preferable: a painful death on the battlefield, or the unknown and terrifying ordeals of being a prisoner of the Germans, eager to exact revenge for twenty years of Roman oppression? Heaven knows the things they'd do to you.

Cassius Dio says that all of the remaining Romans were massacred at the end of the fighting on the fourth day. Well, that didn't happen. There *were* survivors, as Tacitus clearly states, who had somehow managed to escape from the battle. Others were not so fortunate. The Germans took prisoners, and in certain ways, their fates were worse than being killed on the battlefield. You definitely know what will happen to you on the battlefield if you make a mistake – you'll die. Although morbid, there's a certain comfort in knowing your life is more or less in your own hands, and if you keep your wits about you, you might survive. Now, can you imagine what it's like when you are a prisoner and you have no control over your fate at all? All sorts of horrible scenarios race through your mind. Both Florus and Tacitus relate the grisly fates of the Roman prisoners.

> They put out the eyes of some of them and cut off the hands of others; they sewed up the mouth of one of them after first cutting out his tongue, exclaiming, 'At last, you viper, you have ceased to hiss.' The body too of the consul himself, which the dutiful affection of the soldiers had buried, was disinterred.[4]

Varus' grave was dug up and his head was cut off;[5] Arminius might have done the honours himself, or possibly it was Sesithacus, whom Strabo records had defiled Varus' corpse. The decapitation of Varus might have served several functions. First, his severed head was conclusive proof that the man was dead. Second, the head was believed by many people to be the seat of the soul, not the heart. Possessing the head meant that you were possessing the soul as well, granting you his spiritual power and denying that person a chance to go to the afterlife. Third, even if the soul could go to the afterlife, many cultures believed that the body had to be intact in the mortal world in order to be intact in the spirit world. Mutilating a body would mean that the soul would be headless for all eternity.

Varus wasn't the only one who lost his head. Tacitus writes that when Germanicus and his men discovered the battlefield six years later, he saw with his own eyes what had been the fate of the unfortunate captives, and the survivors of the battle who had managed to flee relayed their tales of the prisoners' fates…

> On the trunks of trees, skulls were impaled. In the neighbouring groves were barbarian altars, at which they had sacrificed the tribunes and first-rank centurions. And survivors of the disaster who had slipped away from the fight or their bonds reported…how many gibbets there had been for the captives and which were the pits; and how in his haughtiness he [Arminius] had mocked the standards and eagles.[6]

Why did the Germans do all of this? To scare the Romans? Just for the hell of it? One answer that's been forward by some historians is that the site was a battle shrine, possibly consecrated to the Germanic war god Tiwaz, or possibly to Donar who had a strong cult presence in the area.[7]

To get a better understanding of the significance of what the Germans did to their Roman prisoners, we need to look at places where similar rituals were enacted, and thankfully, one such location was discovered recently near Ribemont-sur-Ancre, France. The site, dated to the third century BC, had a large deposit of bones from an estimated 200 to 250 individuals north of the enclosure, and a second deposit contained not only bones but also weapons and shields. Gerard Fercoq du Lesley of the Ribemont-sur-Ancre

Archeological Centre believes that this is an example of a trophy site, where the bodies and panoply of a defeated enemy were gathered together and put on display as a warning to would-be adversaries. Fascinatingly, all of the bodies had their heads cut off. This description corroborates many features of the Teutoburg battle site as well as accounts from ancient authors. Tacitus claims that the bodies were left out in the open, unburied, and if other historians are right that this place was sanctified by the spilling of enemy blood, if it wasn't already holy, then the discovery of the Celtic 'battle shrine' at Ribemont-sur-Ancre is a perfect illustration of this belief.[8]

Perhaps the one thing in Tacitus' account which grabs the most attention is his statement that the Romans' skulls were nailed to trees. The discoveries at Ribemont-sur-Ancre show that all of the bodies had been decapitated, so there must have been some common practice involved here, but why would they do it? What significance would it serve? Well, if the forest of Teutoburg was sacred, a sort of natural temple, then the placement of skulls within this sacred forest had a definite spiritual significance. Ancient accounts state that people would decapitate their enemies and bring the severed heads home to be either put on display in the house or in their temples. Heads were believed to be the seat of the soul and had great spiritual power, and putting heads in temples would give greater spiritual power to that temple. If Teutoburg was a sacred site, then it would make sense to have heads on display in this natural temple, where the columns and arches were formed not out of stone, but out of the trunks and boughs of the oaks and pines that grew here.[9]

There's one problem, however, with all of this comparison between Teutoburg and Ribemont-sur-Ancre: the relatively few weapons found at Teutoburg. If this was a true battle shrine, then surely there would have been piles of weapons and armour laid about, but there were only a handful of weapons and pieces of armour that were discovered. Perhaps the Germanic tribes were more pragmatic about things and realized that they needed the weapons and equipment themselves, preparing for the inevitable revenge campaign that Rome was certain to launch once they heard about the disaster. Or, the Romans could have taken away all of the things themselves when they returned to this site six years later and buried the bodies – either of the two hypotheses is plausible. But it seems clear that the Germans did indeed construct some sort of battle shrine here at Teutoburg using items taken from the dead Romans.

When the Roman officers, presumably after witnessing the painful fates of other fellow captives, saw what was in store for them, some chose to quickly put themselves out of their misery rather than face the agonies of torture followed by a ritual sacrifice. One of them, Caldus Caelius, took the chains that bound him (I'm assuming on his wrists) and brought the chains with full force onto his head and cracked open his own skull.[10] Was Caldus Caelius a relative of the 18th Legion's chief centurion Marcus Caelius? We'll never know definitely, but it's probable, considering that sometimes brothers and even all the males of an entire family were enlisted in the Army at a certain time, sometimes in the same unit.

Many prisoners were held in captivity as trophies of war. One group was ransomed a few years after the battle, but they were not allowed to enter Italy, presumably due to the shame that came with them from being taken prisoner instead of dying bravely on the battlefield. Another group remained as slaves for over forty years until they were ransomed during the reign of Emperor Claudius. By that time, most of them would have been in their 60s, and might have forgotten how to speak Latin.[11]

Arminius sent Varus' head to King Maroboduus of the Marcomanni, asking him to join his side in his great war against the Romans. Surprisingly, Maroboduus refused, and sent Varus' head back to Rome for proper burial.[12] Why did he refuse? Knowing that if he joined the rebels, it would invite the wrath of Rome, and knowing that eight legions had already amassed on his borders a few years prior, Maroboduus decided that favour shown to Rome might spare him and his people, so he sent the head back to Rome so that it could be properly buried.

The Germans Push the Offensive

Varus and most of his men had been killed or captured. Flushed with victory, the Germans looked for their next target, eager to drive the Romans from their lands once and for all.

In the town of Waldgirmes, a Roman town which had been established within Germania Magna, evidence for habitation abruptly ends in 9 AD. No coins found at the site are dated afterwards. This means that the town must have been either abandoned, or that the settlers were killed. At the excavation site, there is a heavy layer of ash, and therefore it seems clear that the town was set on fire. It isn't known if it was done by the Roman settlers as they were evacuating the town in order to deprive the Germans of it, or if it was done by the Germans as an act of revenge and anti-Roman fervour. Personally, I believe that it was the second option – the Germans burned the town after ransacking it. Evidence for this is based on the opinion that the large bronze statue of Augustus, which had hitherto stood in the forum, appears to have been intentionally smashed to bits. If the statue had simply collapsed, the pieces would have been found in a pile, but the pieces were found spread out over the entire site, indicating that it had been broken apart and kicked around. An image that comes to mind is of the Germans using ropes to pull down the statue of the emperor, cheering as it hit the ground with a sharp metallic thud, reminiscent of when New Yorkers pulled down the statue of King George III in 1776. Other Roman bases in the area were quickly abandoned as well.[13]

The whole province of Germania Magna must have exploded in anti-Roman rage, since Waldgirmes is located nowhere near the battlefield, about 220 miles south of Kalkriese. As to the precise date of Waldgirmes' abandonment, nobody knows. It would have taken eleven or more days of constant marching from dawn to dusk if Arminius' men were to advance from the battlefield to Waldgirmes. It's more likely that Waldgirmes was attacked and overwhelmed by local tribesmen. The town was located within the territory of the powerful Chatti tribe. The Chatti, led by Chief Ucromir, had originally been reluctant to join Arminius in his revolt against the Romans. They had long been a target of Roman aggression, and they knew that if the rebellion failed, they would once again be on the receiving end of Roman military power. However, with the great success that Arminius had achieved further north, the Chatti became bold, and attacked.

Another Germanic tribe which might have suddenly joined sides with Arminius was the Sicambri. They were a small but powerful tribe living along the Rhine River, and had frequently engaged in hostilities with the Romans. In 17 BC, the Sicambri were one of three Germanic tribes who crossed the Rhine and invaded Gallic territory, defeating Marcus Lollius and capturing the 5th Legion's eagle.

During Drusus' campaigns against them in the last years of the first century BC, the Sicambri had intensely felt his wrath. Although there's no record of it, they might have also engaged in the Germanic revolt of 1–4 AD. However, among the roster of tribes who participated in the Battle of Teutoburg, the Sicambri do not appear. Perhaps they were hesitant about engaging in yet another war against the Romans. However, after Arminius's victory, they decided to take a chance and they joined his side.

Tacitus makes reference to the Sicambri participating in Arminius' revolt. Tacitus states that during Germanicus' triumph celebration for his coming victory against the Germans, one of the captive German prisoners was Prince Deodorix, the nephew of Chief Melo of the Sicambri. This implies that the Sicambri tribe, or at least a certain portion of its population, had sided with Arminius, but was defeated.[14]

Arminius and his warriors overwhelmed all of the Roman outposts except one – Fort Aliso. The man in charge there was Lucius Caedicius, the commandant of Fort Aliso, chief centurion, and the third-in-command of the 19th Legion. He had presumably been ordered to stay behind for reasons unknown. It isn't known when Caedicius heard about the unfortunate fate of Varus and his men – perhaps when the first blood-covered soldiers scrambled into the fort, or perhaps when he saw the Germanic warriors amassing beyond the walls. The events that follow couldn't have happened soon after the battle, for Haltern, the probable site of Fort Aliso, lies about 120 miles southwest of Kalkriese, and it would have taken Arminius and his men a considerable amount of time to get there, at least six days if they travelled the standard marching pace of 20 miles per day.

> The barbarians occupied all the strongholds save one, their delay at which prevented them from either crossing the Rhine or invading Gaul. Yet they found themselves unable to reduce this fort, because they did not understand the conduct of sieges, and because the Romans employed numerous archers, who repeatedly repulsed them and destroyed large numbers of them.[15]

> Caedicius, a centurion of the first rank, who acted as leader in Germany, when, after the Varian disaster, our men were beleaguered, was afraid

that the barbarians would bring up to the fortifications the wood which they had gathered, and would set fire to his camp. He therefore pretended to be in need of fuel, and sent out men in every direction to steal it. In this way he caused the Germans to remove the whole supply of felled trees.[16]

Frontinus clearly states that Caedicius was 'leader in Germany'. This could only mean that he was now the highest-ranking Roman officer within the province itself – everyone else of higher rank had been killed. Lucius Caedicius, a man who would have held the rank of either Chief Captain or Major in a modern army, was now *de facto praeesse* of Germania Magna. The revelation must have weighed heavily upon him.

Fort Aliso was now under siege by the Germans. However, their repeated assaults were repulsed, and the barbarians suffered heavy casualties. Faced with such losses, and realizing the futility of attacking a fortified position without siege weapons, many of the Germans left, leaving only a small detachment to keep watch on the roads, hoping to intercept supply wagons or catch the garrison if it came out from behind the protection of the fort's walls. Meanwhile, those inside the fort, as long as they were supplied, stayed where they were, waiting for reinforcements to come and push the Germans back. But no one came, and their food began to run out.[17]

Sextus Frontinus says that with food running short, Caedicius assembled all of the German prisoners that he and his men had taken, cut off their hands (so they were not able to carry weapons anymore), and then sent them out of the fort. When they made their way back to their lines, the mutilated ex-captives told their chiefs that the Roman garrison had plenty of food and could withstand a long siege.[18] The purpose here was that the Germans who were now holding the areas around the fort were just as much prisoners as the besieged Romans, forced to stay in the same location in order to keep close watch on their enemies. In circumstances like this, besiegers were just as likely to be defeated as the besieged, not from enemy attacks, but from hunger, thirst, and the greatest killer of besieging armies, disease. Being told that the surrounded Romans had enough food, water, and supplies to last for a long time, Arminius may have begun to seriously consider if his efforts were going to pay off, or if sickness was going to wear his men out one-by-one.

But this was not an invading army forced to live off the land as it besieged an enemy castle. This was Germania, and these were Germans, and *they* were besieging the invaders who had come into *their* homeland. Moreover, this would have been around harvest-time, and food should have been abundant. One would naturally think that the Germans were in no danger of becoming damned themselves because cartloads of supplies could be brought to them whenever they wished.

Caedicius was lying, of course, when he told them about his abundant rations, but the Germans didn't know that. Knowing that his own men could never hold their positions unless they too were amply supplied, Arminius tried to speed up the siege before the bite of winter set in. If military force could not compel the Romans to surrender, maybe intimidation would.

> When Lucius Sulla was besieging Praeneste, he fastened on spears the heads of Praenestine generals who had been slain in battle, and exhibited them to the besieged inhabitants, thus breaking their stubborn resistance. Arminius, leader of the Germans, likewise fastened on spears the heads of those he had slain, and ordered them to be brought up to the fortifications of the enemy.[19]

The sight was a clear warning to the defending garrison of their fates if they did not immediately surrender to him. Arminius wanted to get the siege over and done with as quickly as possible. The longer he delayed, the more time would be lost to take control of the Rhine bridges and prevent the Romans from launching retaliatory attacks. He needed to wipe out this stubborn thorn in his side and reach the river before winter. He could use the winter months to further prepare his men, for surely, the Romans would attack – it was just a matter of when. The longer this siege dragged on, the less the odds were in his favour of forming an adequate defence against the inevitable revenge campaign.

But Caedicius wasn't intimidated by this grisly display, or if he was, then he didn't show it, because he stubbornly refused to surrender. Perhaps it was bravado, perhaps it was a calculated decision out of the belief that reinforcements would arrive sooner or later and he needed to hold on just a little while longer. If it was the second option, then he must have been disappointed, because with each day that passed, there was still no sign of help. By this time, Caedicius must have known that reinforcements weren't coming. He and his men were on their own.

Then, on a stormy night, those inside Fort Aliso saw an opportunity to make their getaway. Using the cover of both darkness and the storm, the soldiers and their civilian charges crept away silently.[20]

Archaeological evidence from Haltern, the probable site of Fort Aliso, is haunting. The inhabitants of Haltern left in a hurry, burying supplies and money to prevent them from falling into rebel hands, and possibly for themselves to retrieve if they should be fortunate enough to return. Only the bare essentials would have been taken. As an example of things which were obviously treasured but discarded in the face of this emergency, many expensive pottery vessels, with their owners' names scratched into the glaze, were left behind. One underground cellar had thirty intact pots. Perhaps the owners were trying to protect them, putting them in a safe spot just in case the barbarians began ransacking the fort. Other pits contained weaponry and tools, and others included vast amounts of coins. Almost 3,000 coins have been unearthed at Haltern, but none of them date to after 9 AD.[21]

The soldiers and civilians managed to get past both the first and second line of German sentries unnoticed, but were spotted by the third line of warriors, and the alarm was sent out. Cassius Dio states that the Romans probably would have been massacred right then and there. However, the Germans, knowing that the fort was now unoccupied and undefended, decided instead to ransack it rather than kill the Romans as they left. Since this was the whole reason the warriors had surrounded the fort in the first place – to slaughter the Romans should they be so foolish as to venture beyond the protection of the walls[22] – I imagine that Arminius was enraged, cursing his men for going after plunder rather than finishing off the Romans when they had the chance. It wasn't the first time that Arminius' men acted against his intentions – something similar happened on the second day of the Battle of Teutoburg. It also would not be the last time that this sort of thing would happen to him, that victory against the Romans would be cast aside for the sake of grabbing some loot.

It seems, however, that not everyone left the fort. There was, apparently, a small body of men which decided to stay. There's no way to know what their reasons were for remaining behind. Perhaps they did it out of fear of leaving their homes, out of some stubbornness in refusing to run away and acknowledge that they had been forced to run away by barbarians, or out of self-sacrifice, hoping to stall the Germans so that the remainder of the population could make it to safety. Unfortunately, they met their bloody ends, and not in a way that I would wish upon anyone. In the archaeological excavations at Haltern, twenty-four human skeletons were found inside a giant kiln used for firing ceramic pottery. Evidently, these twenty-four were captured by the Germans, thrown into the giant oven, and cooked alive.[23]

With the warriors preoccupied with plundering the vacant fort, the Romans had managed to escape. As if that wasn't bad enough, Fort Aliso was torched,[24] which probably further angered Arminius. Why burn down the fort when you could use it yourself? And what if there were valuable supplies, such as weapons, tools, and medicine still inside when it was burned down? Would Arminius have ordered the fort burned? I highly doubt it. Being a veteran of the Roman Army, he likely understood the value of fortifications, and probably would have liked to capture the fort intact and undamaged so that it could be used by his own men should the Romans retaliate the following year. So I believe that the fort was burned down by his warriors in a flush of anti-Roman passion. 'Fools! Idiots!' Arminius must have screamed out as he watched the flames rise higher, while his men cheered as the fort slowly crumbled into smoldering ruins.

As they left, the Romans played a trick on the Germans – the trumpeters started playing the 'double-quick march' tune. This was done to make the Germans think that reinforcements had at last arrived, and that they were preparing to charge! It had the desired effect – the Germans, thinking that a large body of Roman soldiers was about to attack them at any second, fled for the hills, and this gave the retreating Romans more latitude in terms of getting to safety without being attacked along the way.

At some unspecified time later, the swiftest of them managed to cross the Rhine into Gaul and get to General Lucius Nonius Asprenas, stationed in the city of Mainz. He was Varus' nephew who acted as one of his deputy governors; he was also the commander of the Upper Rhine Army and was the legate of the 5th Legion specifically. Asprenas was unaware of what had happened in Germania Magna. When he was informed of the battle at

Teutoburg, the death of his uncle, and of the siege of Fort Aliso, General Asprenas immediately assembled a rescue party to escort the fleeing soldiers and civilians to safety.[25]

News reaches Rome

It's hard to tell when news of Varus' defeat reached the capital. Gaius Paterculus says that news of the battle arrived in Rome five days after the rebellion in Illyricum ended.[26] Cassius Dio says that news of the disaster arrived shortly after celebrations were ordered for Tiberius' victory over the Illyrian rebels (which means that word had already reached Rome of Tiberius' victory, which would have taken considerable time from modern day Hungary), and that the victory festival had to be cancelled due to the sudden crisis.[27]

There are also different tales as to Augustus' response. Suetonius says that the Emperor declared a state of emergency, taking immediate measures to keep Gaul and Italy secure. He also reports that Augustus went a little crazy.

> When the news of this came, he ordered that watch be kept by night throughout the city, to prevent outbreak, and prolonged the terms of the governors of the provinces, that the allies might be held to their allegiance by experienced men with whom they were acquainted. He also vowed great games to Jupiter Optimus Maximus, in case the condition of the commonwealth should improve, a thing which had been done in the Cimbric and Marsic wars. In fact, they saw that he was so greatly affected that for several months in succession he cut neither his beard nor his hair, and sometimes he would dash his head against a door, crying: 'Quintilius Varus, give me back my legions!' And he observed the day of the disaster each year as one of sorrow and mourning.[28]

Cassius Dio gives a similar reaction, although nowhere near as dramatic as the mad emperor pacing about in the hallways cursing Varus.

Augustus, when he learned of the disaster to Varus, rent his garments, as some report, and mourned greatly, not only because of the soldiers who had been lost, but also because of his fear for the German and Gallic provinces, and particularly because he expected that the enemy would march against Italy and against Rome itself.[29]

Augustus feared an invasion, considering that there were no soldiers of military age left around Italy, and other military units had 'suffered severely',[30] possibly used to great extent during the Great Illyrian Revolt. When none signed up for service voluntarily, he instituted a draft, seizing every fifth man under the age of 35, and every tenth man over 35.[31]

Augustus also feared an internal uprising amongst the Germanic troops in Rome's service. Not only did he have to worry about hundreds or possibly thousands of Germanic auxiliaries serving in the Roman Army launching a revolt (after all, Arminius had been an auxiliary commander), but there were other threats that were alarmingly close to home. Augustus had two bodyguard units protecting him: the famous Praetorian Guard, and the lesser-known Germanic Bodyguard. Both of these units had been created by Augustus. The Praetorian Guard could be best described as a Roman version of the US Secret Service, with both uniformed and undercover units patrolling the palace and the city of Rome as well as the area around Rome. Their job was general security of the emperor, the imperial family, the imperial palace, and the city of Rome in general, specifically with the purposes of surveillance and intercepting and combatting threats to the emperor and his family. By contrast, the Germanic Bodyguard was much more personal. This was a small elite guard unit of just 500 men, mostly from the pro-Roman Batavian tribe who inhabited the islands of the Rhine Delta, whose only job was to protect the person of the emperor, and followed him everywhere that he went. Roman emperors trusted the *Germani Corporis Custodes*, as they were called in Latin, specifically because they were foreigners, and were believed to be unconcerned with the scheming and intriguing machinations of Roman power politics. Furthermore, Germanic warriors had a reputation for being tough fighters and very loyal to the chief they served. To them, the Roman emperor was a chief above all chiefs. Still, with the threat of a mass German uprising looming, Augustus made the cautionary decision to temporarily disband the Germanic Bodyguard following Varus' defeat.[32]

News of the battle must have been received with sadness as well as fear. An example of the sorrow felt by some can be easily seen in a gravestone to Marcus Caelius, the commanding centurion of the 18th Legion. The gravestone is currently on display in the Rheinisches Landesmuseum in Bonn, Germany, but it was found in Xanten, the supposed base camp of the 18th Legion.[33]

The gravestone bears his image, which shows that he was a highly-decorated officer. He is wearing a muscle cuirass, although whether it was made of hardened leather, steel, or bronze cannot be known. There are only a few examples in Roman art in which a centurion is portrayed wearing such armour, since they usually wore chainmail *lorica hamata* or, occasionally, the armour made of overlapping metal scales known as *lorica squamata*, 'lizard armour'. Muscle cuirasses were usually only worn by high-ranking officers, but since Marcus Caelius was a *primus pilus*, the chief centurion within a legion, I suppose that his rank and experience merited such an outfit. Poking out from underneath his armour is a jerkin with double-layered *pteruges* ending in fringes. On his head, he wears an oak-leaf crown called a *corona civilis*, the 'civic crown', an award for saving the life of a Roman citizen. On each of his shoulders is a torque, presumably of gold or bronze, decorated in teardrop designs. The torque was a rather minor military award, always bestowed in pairs. The origin of this Celtic form of decoration being awarded to Roman soldiers comes from 361 BC when the Gallic champion challenged the Romans to send forth their best soldier to defeat him, whereupon a man named Titus Manlius accepted his challenge, defeated him, and claimed the dead Gaul's neck torque as a trophy of war.[34] The exact conditions for the awarding of torques has been lost, but based upon the original context, and the fact that torques were only awarded to centurions or men of lower rank, it appears that these were awards given to individuals who had slain a prominent enemy in battle, either the enemy commander or high-ranking officers. These torques serve as the anchors for Caelius' cape, only slightly visible in the relief sculpture. On each of his wrists is a metal bracelet called an *armilla* (plural *armillae*). Like the torques, the awarding of a metal bracelet originated in defeating and then despoiling

M·CAELIO·T·F·LEM·BON
I·O·LEG·XIIX·ANN·LIII S
OCCIDIT·BELLO·VARIANO·OSSA
INFERRE·LICEBIT·P·CAELIVS·T·F
LEM·FRATER·FECIT

Marco Caelio Titi Filio Lemonia Tribu Bononia
I Ordinis Legionis XIIX Annorum LIII S
Occidit Bello Variano Ossa
Inderre Licebit Publius Caelius Titi Filius
Lemonia Tribu Frater Fecit.

Marcus Caelius, son of Titus, from the district of Lemonia and from [the city of] Bononia. First Centurion of the 18th Legion. 53½ years old. He was killed in the Varian War. May his bones be buried here. Publius Caelius, son of Titus, of the district of Lemonia, his brother [erected this monument].

Figure 5. The gravestone of Marcus Caelius, Chief Centurion of the 18th Legion. He is one of the few people that we know of by name who participated in the Battle of Teutoburg. His body was never found, or at least was never buried in its intended grave. His bones could have been among those discovered by Germanicus' soldiers, where they were laid in a single mass grave. Rheinisches Landesmuseum. Bonn, Germany. (*Photo by Jona Lendering, used with permission*)

enemies on the battlefield. The awarding of jewellery, such as torques and bracelets, to men must be seen not so much as a specific award for a specific action, but rather an act of giving a valuable object to a person in recognition for their actions. In the absence of rewarding their troops with money, as some commanders did, the commanders would portion out the captured plunder to the men, including neck torques and bracelets. Over time, this became standardized to a point, and the awarding of neck torques and bracelets became a form of commendation for their actions, and should not be seen as a parallel with modern soldiers being given medals for heroism. But like modern medals, there were various 'grades' or 'classes' of *armillae* – a gold *armilla* was the higher, and a silver *armilla* was the lesser.[35] There are also five metal discs called *phalerae* strapped onto his body armour. These were military decorations awarded to the unit as a whole, but worn by the unit's commander. This indicates that his particular century, the 1st Century of the 1st Cohort, had distinguished itself in battle five times. In his right hand he carries a *vitus*, a twisted wooden rod made from a grape vine that was used to whip disobedient or below-standard soldiers. On either side of his figure are the heads of two of his slaves, Privatus and Thiaminus

Marcus Caelius' remains were never found.

The Fate of the Three Legions

In the years following the Battle of Teutoburg, there is no mention of the 17th, 18th, and 19th Legions operating within the empire. It's as if they just disappeared. For years, it was assumed that the reason why we hear no more of these three units was because the Germans annihilated them all right down to the last man, but the historical records show that this is wrong. There were members of these three legions that were still alive. As stated earlier, only one-third of each legion had likely participated in the battle, so that leaves two-thirds possibly intact! Moreover, soldiers had survived the battle and had made it to safety, though it isn't known just how many survivors there were. It's obvious that the three legions weren't annihilated, so what happened to the members who were not killed or captured? The only logical explanation is that the three legions must have been disbanded.

Why would Augustus disband these three legions? The empire was in a state of emergency. You'd naturally think that the emperor would grab as many soldiers as he could get his hands on. Why on earth would he disband these three units of hardened professional veterans and then send out the press gangs to draft new recruits that had no discipline or experience whatsoever? It's puzzling, but one idea is that the 17th, 18th, and 19th Legions had been stained by defeat. Did this mean that the Romans believed that these three legions somehow had a cloud of bad luck hanging over them? If so, then it would make sense that the legions would be disbanded even though only one-third of each legion's strength was lost. This sentiment would make sense, considering that certain members of these legions who had surrendered were banned from setting foot on Italian soil. Their disbanding may also have to do with the shame brought about by being defeated by supposed inferiors. Either way, be it out of superstition or dishonour or both, it was believed that the men of these three legions were no longer deemed worthy of combat, and they were told to pack their bags and go back home.

Perhaps that is why Cassius Dio, who was writing in the 200s AD, stated in *The Roman History* that there were no survivors of this battle, that absolutely everyone had been killed. Maybe he was trying to erase the shame that had been brought to Rome when her invincible legionaries had been taken prisoner by the enemy. No self-respecting Roman would dare allow himself to be captured, let alone remain in bondage for decades. Unfortunately for Cassius Dio and his patriotic attempts to cover up the shame of capture, Tacitus' earlier account, dating to the late 90s to early 100s AD, clearly states that Roman soldiers *had* been taken prisoner during the battle.

If the 17th, 18th, and 19th Legions were disbanded, and there's really no reason to suspect otherwise, it would not be first time that Augustus had taken such drastic action. According to Suetonius, Augustus had on one occasion given every soldier of the 10th Legion a dishonourable discharge due to poor conduct. Yet, there are two sticky points. Suetonius' account does not specifically state if the conduct in question was poor conduct on the battlefield, or if the soldiers had participated in a mutiny. It also does not state if the soldiers who had been dishonourably discharged were replaced by new recruits or if the legion was disbanded altogether.[36]

It has long been stated and affirmed by ancient scholars that once the 17th, 18th, and 19th Legions were disbanded that they were never recreated again. That's only partially true. During the reign of Emperor Nero, probably in 66 AD, the 18th Legion was briefly recreated to participate in a grand campaign against Parthia and Ethiopia. Six of the legion's ten cohorts were stationed along the Rhine frontier, while the remaining four cohorts were stationed in Egypt. These four cohorts were transferred to Palestine and participated in Titus' siege of Jerusalem. The 18th was permenantly dissolved once Vespasian came to power.[37]

Rome's Revenge

After sufficient time had been allowed to mourn the fate of the three legions, the Romans wanted vengeance. In 10 AD, the empire's favorite warhorse,

General Tiberius Claudius Nero, was sent north. After amassing his forces along the border to prevent a Germanic invasion and providing security to an increasingly panic-stricken Gaul, he crossed the Rhine with his army the following year. His campaign was an exercise in mass destruction. It is said that his army took 40,000 prisoners, and resettled them in Gaul. After two years of killing and burning, he returned to Rome at the end of 12 AD. By this time, Augustus was very ill. Believing that Germania was more or less pacified by this stage, Tiberius was replaced by his nephew Germanicus, who would act as the commander of the 'mopping up' forces. Tiberius himself would be sent elsewhere where he was needed.[38]

The earliest known person to write about these events was not a historian, but a poet, Ovid, long in exile on the other side of the empire on the shores of the Black Sea in a small coastal village called Tomis, heard about the battle and the destruction of Varus' army in 'spring', although which year is not stated. News was slow in coming to such an isolated corner of the empire, and Ovid, who longed for the city life, eagerly sought information from any ship's captain that happened to dock at the small seaside village. It was then, amidst the welcome appearance of springtime, that Ovid heard about the battle, and the revenge campaign that Rome was in the process of undertaking, and composed a few verses on the subject.[39]

It's commonly held that Ovid heard about the battle in the spring of 10 AD, but this cannot be true since he describes the Roman revenge campaign as being well underway, hoping that the rebellious German tribes have been crushed by a Roman general, likely meaning Tiberius. This means that he's describing events which happened, at the earliest, in 11 AD, because this is when Tiberius crossed the Rhine and attacked Arminius' rebels.

In early 13 AD, Drusus Claudius Nero Germanicus became the commander of the legions operating in Germania. Suetonius writes a very glowing description of the young commander, calling him handsome, cultured, and virtuous. According to him, Germanicus 'possessed all the highest qualities of body and mind, to a degree never equalled by anyone'.[40] He was a handsome man, except his legs were too thin in proportion with the rest of his body, and he had to strengthen them through constant exercise. He was skilled in the art of public speaking, was knowledgeable in the histories of Greece and Rome, and he liked to read Greek comedies. He was brave in battle, taking his place amidst the soldiers rather than viewing the fighting from a distance. He was also kind, respectful, humble, dressed modestly, and whenever he passed by the mausoleums of distinguished men, he always offered sacrifices to their spirits.[41] Thus, we can get a view of his appearance and character. No wonder, therefore, that so many people in Rome thought highly of him.

Regrettably, no account is given of Germanicus' conduct for that year. In 14 AD, Caesar Augustus died, and Tiberius became the next Roman emperor. Not long after the emperor's death, the legions in Pannonia and Germania mutinied at roughly the same time. When news of the soldiers' uprisings reached Emperor Tiberius, he dispatched his son Drusus Castor to deal with the Pannonian legions, and his nephew Germanicus (who was away on business in Gaul) to quell the revolt in Germania. In both circumstances, the mutinies were put down with bloodshed.[42]

The mutiny had an unexpected side-effect: it stirred up the bloodlust in the legionaries. Tacitus relates that 'into their minds...there flew the desire of going against the enemy',[43] and attack they did. Germanicus led eight legions across the Rhine and began a campaign of slaughter that lasted for years, targeting the tribes that had taken part in the Germanic uprising. The first to feel his wrath were the Marsi. The Romans destroyed the Germans' temples, which of course led to the warriors retaliating, but the Romans defeated them.[44]

The next year in 15 AD, Germanicus was given a triumph, and afterwards returned to the fighting. He and his legions attacked the Chatti and the Cherusci, the latter of which had besieged Chief Segestes, along with his family and followers, in his town. Germanicus drove off the Cherusci, and found in Segestes' company Arminius' pregnant wife Thusnelda, every bit as defiant and rebellious as her husband. Of course, Arminius was enraged when he found out that his wife had been taken prisoner and the tribes swelled to his banner. The Romans countered by attacking the Bructeri, and in one of their villages discovered the 19th Legion's eagle. By this time, the Romans had reached Teutoburg. The battlefield was re-discovered, and Germanicus and his men laid the exposed bones to rest. Suetonius states that when they discovered the old battlefield, Germanicus wished to collect all of the bones and bury them all in one mass grave. It is stated that he was the first one to begin collecting their remains, gathering the bones by hand.[45]

Arminius tried to lure Germanicus and his legions into a trap as he had done with Varus. The battle, although initially in the Germans' favour, ended in a draw. Germanicus decided that the army had to fall back, and made the mistake of splitting his force. Arminius and his rebels repeatedly attacked one of the two groups, but they could make no progress until legionaries fled the safety of their camp, and the Germans attacked them while mired in swampland. It was the timely arrival of the other soldiers, as well as the Germans' interest in plunder rather than decisive victory, that saved the Romans from complete destruction.[46]

> He [Arminius] and his picked men cleft the column and inflicted wounds on the horses especially; the latter, slithering in their own blood and the slipperiness of the marshes, threw their riders, scattered everyone in their path, and trampled people as they lay. Most of the toil was around the eagles, which could be neither carried in the face of the hail of weapons nor planted in the boggy ground. While Caecina was trying to maintain the line, he tumbled from his horse, which had been pierced beneath him, and was in the process of being surrounded, had not the First Legion placed itself in the way. The greed of the enemy helped, as they neglected slaughter in their pursuit of plunder; and as the day turned to evening, the legions struggled out onto the open and solid ground.[47]

Just like at Kalkriese Hill and Fort Aliso, instead of finishing the Romans off when they had the chance, the warriors instead sought to take their share of the plunder and allowed the legionaries to escape. The Romans built a fortified camp, and against Arminius' sound advice, which warned against attacking the legions in a defensive position, his uncle Inguiomerus won the warriors over and the Germans tried to storm the Roman camp. The attack was a disaster with the Germans suffering massive losses, and Inguiomerus was seriously wounded. The Roman victory was shortlived, as a storm in the North Sea all but destroyed two Roman legions marching by the coast.[48]

In 16 AD, distinctions were awarded to Germanicus' subordinate commanders. The Romans raided Chatti lands with little success. Then came a flawed amphibious operation into the heart of Germania in which many drowned. Afterwards, the Romans all but destroyed the Angrivarians.

By this time, the Romans and Germanic rebels were separated by the Weser River. Arminius and his younger brother Flavus (who had lost one of his eyes fighting the Illyrian rebels several years earlier) stood on opposite shores and exchanged harsh words with each other concerning loyalty to Rome. The following day, a battle was to be fought. The Romans sent their cavalry and their Batavian allies across the river to soften up the rebel defences. The German rebels fell back, luring the Batavian auxiliaries into a trap, who were only spared by the arrival of the Roman cavalry, though they suffered many casualties. Afterwards, with the rebels withdrawn into the interior, Germanicus sent his infantry across the river. The two forces met each other at a plain called Idisiaviso. The battle ended in a bloody defeat for the Germans, largely due to Germanic indiscipline, and Arminius himself was severely wounded during the fighting. Despite their severe losses that day, the Germans counter-attacked soon afterwards while the Romans were on the march, much to the surprise of the Roman soldiers who probably didn't expect to see the Germans attacking them so soon after their defeat. Guessing that Arminius was planning another massacre similar to that of the Battle of Teutoburg, Germanicus organized his men and attacked the rebel positions, and the Romans were once again victorious.[49]

Once again, victory was tainted by defeat at the hands of nature, when Germanicus' fleet transporting his soldiers and supplies was devastated by a storm. After recovering from his losses, Germanicus quickly assembled a large army, knowing that the rebels would take the opportunity to strike the Romans if they were slow to recover. The Germans, seeing the fresh troops, exclaimed that the Romans couldn't be beaten for they always returned with renewed vigour regardless of the losses they bore. A second legionary eagle (it isn't stated which legion) was recovered from the Marsi after their chief Mallovendus, who had been overthrown and expelled by his people, confessed to Germanicus that it had been buried in a nearby forest. Due to his involvement in Arminius' rebellion, ex-chief Mallovendus likely gave the Romans this information in exchange for not being immediately executed. Mallovendus disappears from the historical records after this event, although he was almost certainly one of the captives brought back to Rome by Germanicus following the end of the war. Satisfied that the losses of the naval disaster had been balanced by the recovery of the lost eagle, by the end of 16 AD, the army marched back to winter quarters.[50]

Germanicus believed that the rebels were on the verge of asking for peace, and that one more campaign the following year in 17 AD would assure the Germans' defeat. But Emperor Tiberius said no, stating that the few surviving rebels should be left to their own devices. Germanicus protested, demanding one more year to finish off the rebels once and for all, but still the emperor refused. Germanicus suspected that Tiberius was jealous of his victories.[51] This might be true, but a better explanation for Tiberius suddenly cancelling military operations in Germania might have had something to do with what was happening in northern Africa at that time. Another serious rebellion against the Roman Empire had broken out, this time led by the Berber warlord Tacfarinas.

Tacfarinas was a native Numidian from what is now northern Algeria, and had once been an auxiliary in the Roman Army, but he had deserted in 15 AD, and gathered around him an ever growing band of brigands who terrorized Roman settlements in the area. For two years, Tacfarinas and his marauders had burned, pillaged, and killed, and his personal private army had reached unprecedented size. They were no longer considered a minor pack of bandits – they were now a serious threat. North Africa was one of the major breadbaskets of the Roman Empire. Tons of grain and other food supplies came from this region. If the African grain supply was suddenly cut off, Rome would literally starve. Now, Tacfarinas and his African rebel army were threatening to do just that. Protecting the African grain supply was far more important than teaching the rebellious Germanic barbarians a lesson. So, weighing his options, Emperor Tiberius told his nephew Germanicus to cancel all military operations against Arminius and his surviving rebels.

The emperor's will was the Germans' saving grace, for Tiberius had spared them from complete annihilation at the hands of Germanicus, or at least the shame of asking for mercy. On 26 May 17 AD, Germanicus was awarded a triumph over the Germans, carrying before him the spoils of war and prisoners, including Arminius' wife Thusnelda, her three-year-old son Thumelicus, and the enigmatic Sesithacus and his wife.[52] This triumph not only commemorated the defeat of Arminius, but also the defeat of the Illyrian rebels several years earlier – Tiberius was scheduled to hold this triumph, but it had been postponed. Ovid vividly describes the scenes from the celebratory parade, stating that the displays featured captured enemy leaders bound with chains (including the rebel Illyrian commander Bato), floats depicting the German landscape, and Germanicus riding in his victory chariot garbed in purple, the pathway before him carpeted with rose petals.[53]

Thusnelda and her son would be exiled to the city of Ravenna. Tacitus states that Thumelicus was forced to deal with mockery, which he states he will discuss later on but never does – that section has unfortunately disappeared.[54] Other interpretations of this fleeting passage state that Thumelicus suffered 'an ironic fate'. What exactly that means isn't certain. There's a popular belief that Arminius' son Thumelicus was enslaved, trained as a gladiator, and died in the arena. There is no evidence to support this claim. What do I think? I believe that it would be much more of an irony if Thumelicus was enrolled into the Roman Army like his father had once been, became a Roman soldier, and then fought against his fellow Germans in a future war, perhaps the campaign conducted by Emperor Claudius, and was killed by the Germans during some nameless skirmish, possibly even by members of the Cherusci tribe. Or perhaps, in keeping with the idea that he was an auxiliary in Claudius' army (Thumelicus would have been in his late 20s at that time), he accompanied the army into Germania and was instrumental in the recovery of the lost third eagle, which was found during this campaign, as well as freeing the Romans kept prisoner since that battle. I consider such a story to be filled with far more irony than dying as a gladiator.

The Deaths of Germanicus and Arminius

In 18 AD, Germanicus was made a consul along with Emperor Tiberius, and was granted supreme power over all of Rome's holdings in the eastern Mediterranean. Germanicus was sent into Asia Minor, where he led Rome's armies against the kingdom of Cappadocia, turning it into Rome's newest province.[55]

Germanicus afterwards began a grand tour of the East, and he made one of his stops in Syria. Immediately upon his arrival, he came into conflict with Syria's governor, Gnaeus Calpurnius Piso, who claimed that Germanicus was using his new powers to boss him around. After returning to Syria in late summer of 19 AD following a trip to Egypt, Germanicus discovered that Governor Piso was taking measures to undo everything that Germanicus had done while in Syria. Piso ceased to be Syria's governor (it isn't known whether he quit or was fired, but probably the latter), and retired to an island. Afterwards, Germanicus fell ill.[56]

Germanicus died on 10 October, 19 AD in the city of Antioch, Syria. Suspicions immediately arose that he had been assassinated, specifically poisoned. Accusations of the plot fell on the person and associates of Gnaeus Calpurnius Piso, and he was summoned to Rome to stand trial.[57]

Tiberius had withdrawn his nephew Germanicus from Germania so that the tribes could be left to their own affairs. If he had placed any bets that the tribes would dissolve into their prior state of factionalism and inter-tribal warfare, he would have collected. As long as the Romans had a large military presence in Germania, the Germanic tribes would be united against a common enemy, but once the Romans were gone, the tribes began to turn on each other. One tribe, the Sueves, even petitioned Rome for assistance against the Cherusci. Arminius, despite his constant setbacks during the war, 'enjoyed goodwill as a warrior for freedom'.[58] Arminius used his good standing to his advantage when he declared war on King Maroboduus.

King Maroboduus of the Marcomanni had declined Arminius' invitation to join him in his grand crusade against the Romans. He had even sent Varus' decapitated head back to Rome for decent burial. I image that the reason why Arminius raised the warcry against Maroboduus was because Arminius saw him as a collaborator. In addition to the troops that Arminius already commanded, the Semnones and the Lombards joined him in his war against the Marcomanni. But not everyone was flocking to Arminius' side. His uncle Inguiomerus – the hot-headed uncle who thirsted for glory and who cost Arminius victory during the revenge campaign – took a small band of followers and defected to Maroboduus' side; his reason was that he refused to obey orders from someone who was younger than he was. In a pitched battle, Arminius barely won victory. Maroboduus asked Rome for assistance, but he was refused. Rome's reason was that the Marcomanni hadn't helped the Romans in their war against Arminius, so why should the Romans help the Marcomanni?[59]

Although the Roman Army was no longer present in Germania, the Romans still tried to manipulate the situation among the various tribes to their advantage. Tacitus states that in the year 18 AD, while Germanicus was still alive and was making the rounds of the eastern provinces, Emperor Tiberius' son Drusus Castor was attempting to undermine the power of the Marcomanni kingdom. He found an ideal instrument for his plan in the person of Catualda, a young Marcomannic noble who was a rival of King Maroboduus. The king had banished him some time before, and was then living in exile among the Gothones, a northeastern Germanic tribe who lived on the shores of the Baltic Sea on Germania's absolute extreme edge. The reasons for Catualda's banishment are not given by Tacitus, but I suspect that it may have been because Catualda was a supporter of Arminius and his cause. Realizing that this man had a capability to undermine his power as well as bring the wrath of Rome upon his head due to his support of the rebel leader, Maroboduus expelled him from his kingdom. When Catualda learned that King Maroboduus was in a very weak position, he immediately seized the advantage.[60]

Tacitus states that Catualda entered the Marcomannic kingdom with a large force of warriors, perhaps allies that he gathered together amongst his Gothone hosts as well as from other tribes that he encountered along his march. So, Maroboduus would have been pressed on both sides, with Arminius attacking from the northwest and Catualda attacking from the northeast.[61] Although it is never stated in the historical accounts, I strongly suspect that some sort of arrangement was made between Arminius and Catualda – Catualda agreed to join forces with Arminius and place himself and his troops under Arminius' command, and in exchange, Arminius would make Catualda, not himself, the next king of the Marcomanni when Maroboduus was defeated.

The war had been going badly for King Maroboduus from the outset, but now that Catualda and his men had joined in, his doom was assured. Tacitus states that Catualda won many of Maroboduus' noble supporters over to his side by bribery. In a dramatic flair, Tacitus states that Catualda and his men seized control of both the king's palace as well as a nearby fort, and had taken hold of the large stockpiles of treasure that Maroboduus had accumulated over the years through trade and conquest. Yet, King Maroboduus was nowhere to be found. Sometime before the palace fell, he had escaped. With no one currently sitting on the throne, Catualda was made the new king of the Marcomanni.[62]

Now on the run and deserted by everyone around him, Maroboduus had no choice but to beg to Emperor Tiberius to be granted asylum within the Roman Empire. After crossing the Danube River and entering the Roman province of Noricum, he wrote a letter to Tiberius, despairing that he had once been a great king now reduced to nothing, and he had always been Rome's friend. Tiberius sent a reply, stating that he was willing to show pity to Maroboduus and grant him a home in Italy. However, in a speech that he made to the Senate, Tiberius was not so merciful, stating in very exaggerated language that Maroboduus and his Marcomannic warriors were one of the most dangerous enemies that Rome had ever faced and that he did not deserve any kindness. In the end, it was decided that Rome would take him in. Maroboduus, once King of the Marcomanni, the most powerful tribe in all of Germania, commander of a professional army of 74,000 well-trained warriors, would spend the remainder of his days as an exile in the Italian city of Ravenna. He would remain there for the next eighteen years, and died in 36 AD.[63]

As for Arminius, Tacitus records that following the withdrawal of the Romans from Germania, and his defeat of the Marcomanni and the expulsion of his adversary King Maroboduus, he felt increasingly secure in his power. He now felt confident enough to take a stab at establishing himself as more than just a war leader, and more than just a local clan chief, but as a king in his own right. It isn't stated if Arminius wished to declare himself 'King of the Cherusci' (remember, as far as we can tell, the Cherusci never had a single person commanding the whole tribe) or, even more daringly, 'King of the Germans'. Making himself the sole ruler of Germania would have been an impressive feat indeed, and Arminius certainly felt that he deserved such distinction. He had, after all, been in the saddle of his war horse for most of his adult life. He had clout and prestige. He had been instrumental in driving the Romans from his land, and had defeated the Marcomanni, the most powerful of all of the Germanic tribes. He was the hero of his people.[64]

But regardless of how expansive Arminius wished his dominion over his people to be, he wanted to establish himself as a monarch, something that the Germans, who were accustomed to showing loyalties only towards their individual tribes, refused to tolerate. Moreover, the Germans might have believed that even if they were to choose a king, Arminius might not have been the best option. Arminius was a man imbued with a strong sense of mission, and he would not tolerate anyone who opposed him or remained neutral. He was a strong believer in the old adage 'He who is not with me is against me', and those whom he felt were not with him suffered for their lack of loyalty. He coerced and threatened people into joining his side, and punished those who refused. Boiocalus, the chief of the Ampsivarians, had refused to join forces with Arminius in his war against the Romans; in response, Arminius had Boiocalus arrested and imprisoned. King Maroboduus, likewise, refused to enter into a war with Rome; in response, Arminius declared war on the Marcomanni and turned Maroboduus' kingdom into ruins.

The Germans, who were staunch lovers of their own independence and liberty, had no desire to be ruled over by a monarch, especially one as pushy as Arminius had become. They shuddered to think of what would happen if Arminius was ever given supreme power. Something needed to be done to prevent him from establishing himself as a ruler, and the only definite way to stop him was death. Adgandestrius, the new chief of the Chatti, asked Rome to send poison to assassinate Arminius, but Rome refused, saying that death by poison was an underhanded and dishonourable way of killing someone, despite the fact that the Romans used it quite frequently to dispose of each other.[65]

In the end, those who wished to dispose of Arminius decided to take matters into their own hands. It is said that he 'became the target of their arms, and, while his struggle with them was meeting with variable fortune, he fell to the cunning of his kinsmen'.[66] 'Variable fortune' means that he probably killed a few of his assailants before he himself was struck down in the end. But what of 'kinsmen'? This could mean either of two things. Firstly, it could mean his tribesmen – he was killed by fellow members of the Cherusci tribe. Secondly, it could mean his own family members, and I can think of no better candidate than his uncle Inguiomerus. In a way, Arminius' demise mirrored that of Julius Caesar. Both of them were assassinated because it was felt that they were aspiring to monarchy and stripping people of their liberties. Both were killed by their peers – in Caesar's case fellow senators, in Arminius' case fellow Cherusci. Both were military men who were seen as having stepped beyond acceptable social limits.

Arminius, at the age of 37, died sometime in 21 AD, assassinated by members of his own tribe who were possibly members of his own family.[67] In the minds of some Germans, he was a dangerous man aspiring to become a tyrant who wanted to assert his wishes on others. But in Tacitus' mind, 'He was the liberator without doubt of Germania and who challenged the Roman people not in their earliest times like other kings and leaders, but at the height of their power...and to this day, he is sung of in tribal poems.'[68] Arminius, therefore, must have been regarded by some as a national hero, as the Gallic Celts had done with Vercingetorix and as the Britonic Celts would do in the future with Queen Boudicca.

The Battle's Legacy

Many years after the battle, the shadow of Teutoburg still loomed over Rome. Only two of the three lost legionary eagles were discovered in the years immediately following the Battle of Teutoburg. More than thirty years after the battle, during the reign of Emperor Claudius, the third eagle was finally discovered in the land of the Chauci tribe. As I stated earlier, it's likely that Arminius had given this eagle to the Chauci as a show of good faith, for they had presumably been among those who joined Arminius' side at the last minute and fought with him on the fourth and last day of the Battle of Teutoburg.

> Sulpicius Galba overcame the Chatti, and Publius Gabinius conquered the Cauchi (sic) and as a crowning achievement recovered a military eagle, the only one that still remained in the hands of the enemy from Varus' disaster.[69]

Not long afterwards, a large body of Roman prisoners was released who had been taken prisoner during the battle. As much as the Romans wanted to put this unfortunate mess behind them in order to maintain their image as the ever-victorious omnipotent conquerors, things still kept popping up that were reminding them of the disaster, like the slave whispering into the ear of a triumphant general dressed like a god, saying that he was not a god but only a mortal man.

Tiberius had ordered his nephew Germanicus to leave Germania, saying that he was comfortable leaving the Germanic tribes to their own internal disputes. Knowing that the Germans spent just as much time fighting each other as they fought the Romans, he perhaps had some foresight in believing that Arminius' coalition would dissolve. By the time that Tacitus wrote his *Germania* at the end of the first century AD, one of the tribes that had aligned themselves with Arminius, the Bructeri, was already extinct, destroyed by neighbouring tribes. Tacitus did not weep at news of the Bructeri's destruction. Rather, he and all of Rome were overjoyed, commenting that he hoped that the Germanic tribes always remained hateful and distrustful of each other, because there could be no greater blessing to Rome than to have Rome's enemies fighting amongst themselves.[70]

The Battle of Teutoburg has been acknowledged by some as one of the most decisive battles in history. Personally, I never understood why. Arminius' victory during those four days in September didn't obliterate the Roman presence in Germania forever, nor did it make the Romans terrified of setting foot on that soil lest a similar disaster occur once again; the Romans would return multiple times afterwards. In fact, several emperors felt that it was their patriotic duty to invade Germania at least once during their reign and slaughter hundreds if not thousands of people, just to let the barbarians know *who* and *whom*. The first Roman war against the Germans following Arminius' victory over Varus and his legions was the revenge campaign led by Tiberius and Germanicus. In 28 AD, during the reign of Tiberius, a Roman army campaigned against the Frisians, a tribe from the Netherlands, and although initially successful, the Romans were defeated at the Battle of Baduhenna Wood. Tiberius' grand-nephew and imperial successor Gaius Caligula planned large-scale military operations against both Germania and Britain, but these were aborted before they began; he himself lamented that no great disasters such as the Romans' defeat at Teutoburg had occurred during his reign. Claudius launched the campaign that eventually discovered the lost third legionary eagle of Varus' ill-fated expedition, as well as rescuing many of the Roman prisoners who

Figure 6. The *Hermannsdenkmal*, or Arminius Monument. Located at Detmold, Germany, the heroic Wagner-esque portrayal of the German prince faces towards the River Rhine, in the direction of Germania's traditional enemy, Rome, and towards one of Germany's traditional enemies, France. (*Wikimedia Commons, public domain image*)

had been kept as slaves following that battle. Emperor Nero launched a campaign against the Germans after two tribes crossed the Rhine and began squatting on Roman territory. Emperor Domitian, who reigned thirty years later, also undertook a war against the Germans, which the historian Suetonius comments was completely unnecessary. Domitian even granted himself a triumph for this war, which Tacitus comments was a joke, in which he bought slaves in the markets, dressed them up like Germanic barbarians, and claimed that they were warriors his army had captured in battle, but the Roman people weren't fooled. Emperor Marcus Aurelius fought a long and costly war against the Marcomanni in the second century AD, and it was during this war that he wrote his *Meditations*. In 2008, a new battlefield was discovered at a place called Harzhorn Hill near Kalefeld, Germany, dating to the early to mid third century AD, possibly in relation to Emperor Max Thrax' declaration of war on the Germans.[71]

Aside from the fact that the battle didn't end the Roman presence in Germania, Arminius himself was not the best of commanders. Although highly-skilled in strategy and tactics, he failed to convey his wisdom to his subordinates who were more interested in plunder than with scoring decisive blows against their enemies. Multiple times, Arminius lost battles that he could have easily won due to the indiscipline of the men that he led. In the end, the Battle of Teutoburg was the only battle that Arminius won – all of the others he either lost or ended in a draw.

The Battle of Teutoburg has been a popular academic subject for centuries. As a testament of its popularity among scholars, from 2001 to 2012, four books were published on the subject in English alone – other books have been published in German, of course. But the battle is just as appealing to art as it is to history. The battle has been lavishly and heroically portrayed in paintings and engravings. It has been written about in many works of poetry and fiction (it has been proposed that Arminius was the blueprint for the Siegfried legend). The tale has even been turned into stage drama, being portrayed in plays and even an opera. In film, it has been the focus of a few German movies, some television documentaries, and was mentioned in the 1970s BBC series *I, Claudius*, where one of the few survivors of the battle reports directly to the emperor, and tells Augustus in a shaky voice that the 17th, 18th, and 19th Legions don't exist anymore.[72]

During the 1800s and early 1900s, when much of Europe was in the grips of nationalistic sentiment, the German people, who were in the process of uniting their various independent states into a united country, were looking for heroes from their history. One of the figures which they immediately seized hold of as a great figure from their ancient past was Arminius. Not only was he held to be a great military commander, which must have appealed to the martial Prussian morals of the Germans during that time, but he was also seen as a leader of an independent united Germany in the face of foreign aggression. During the Napoleonic Wars, when a still fragmented Germany was invaded by France, Arminius' legacy must have been apparent, and many of the German states joined forces in fighting a common enemy. In time, Arminius began to be regarded as the archetypal Germanic warrior, and possibly more importantly, the archetypal German. During the 1930s and early 1940s, when the Nazi Party was ruling Germany, Arminius was given near saint-like status.

In 1875, following Germany's victory over the French in the Franco-Prussian War, a large copper statue of Arminius was erected at Detmold, which was considered to be the location of the battle at that time. The statue still stands, eyes fixed towards the Rhine, in the direction of Germania's traditional enemy Rome, and Germany's traditional enemy France.[73] Arminius is depicted in the classic Victorian image of what a Germanic barbarian chief is supposed to look like. Reminiscent of a character from one of Wagner's operas, he stands with a winged helmet upon his head, his sword raised towards the sky. Surrounding the monument are the trees of the legendary Germanic forests, which the Romans feared just as much as they feared the people who dwelt within them. Into the stone base that the statue rests on are carved the following words from Tacitus' *Annals*, and it is with these words that this book concludes:

ARMINIUS

LIBERATOR HAUD DUBIE GERMANIAE
ET QUI NON PRIMORDIA POPULI ROMANI
SICUT ALII REGES DUCESQUE SED FLO-
RENTISSIMUM IMPERIUM LACESSIE-
RIT PROELIIS AMBIGUUS BELLO
NON VICTUS

He was the liberator without doubt of Germania, and who challenged the Roman people not in their earliest times like other kings and leaders, but at the height of their power, in battle with ambiguous results, in war unvanquished.

Notes

Chapter One

1. Online Etymology Dictionary. 'Italian', by Douglass Harper (November 2001). http://www. etymonline.com/index.php?term=Italian; Mary Boatwright, et al, *The Romans: From Village to Empire* (Oxford: Oxford University Press, 2004), 182; 'History of Calabria, Italy' (2004). http://www.kwintessential.co.uk/articles/article/Italy/History-of-Calabria-Italy/762

2. Mary Boatwright, et al, *The Romans: From Village to Empire* (Oxford: Oxford University Press, 2004).

3. *The History of Ancient Rome*, lecture 3 – 'Pre-Roman Italy and the Etruscans'; *The History of Ancient Rome*, lecture 4 – 'The Foundation of Rome'.

4. *The History of Ancient Rome*, lecture 3 – 'Pre-Roman Italy and the Etruscans'; *Rome: Power and Glory*, episode 1 – 'The Rise'.

5. *The History of Ancient Rome*, lecture 3 – 'Pre-Roman Italy and the Etruscans'; *The History of Ancient Rome*, lecture 9 – 'Roman Expansion in Italy'.

6. Mary Boatwright, et al, *The Romans: From Village to Empire* (Oxford: Oxford University Press, 2004), 180–183; *The History of Ancient Rome*, lecture 21 – 'Marius and Sulla'.

7. *The History of Ancient Rome*, lecture 3 – 'Pre-Roman Italy and the Etruscans'.

8. *The History of Ancient Rome*, lecture 3 – 'Pre-Roman Italy and the Etruscans'; *The History of Ancient Rome*, lecture 21 – 'Marius and Sulla'; Diodorus Siculus, 'Romans and Celts Battle in Umbria' in *Chronicles of the Barbarians* (New York: History Book Club, 1998), 27–31; Livy, 'The Celts Enter Rome' in *Chronicles of the Barbarians* (New York: History Book Club, 1998), 32–38.

9. Peter S Wells, *The Battle That Stopped Rome* (New York: W. W. Norton & Co., 2003), 57.

10. 'Etruscan Religion' (February 14, 2006). http://www.mysteriousetruscans.com/religion. html

11. 'Role of the Imperial Cult during the Augustan Age' (1995). http://janusquirinus.org/ essays/Cult.html

12. 'Vestales', by William Smith (1875). http://penelope.uchicago.edu/Thayer/E/Roman/ Texts/secondary/SMIGRA*/Vestales.html

13. 'Janus', by Jona Lendering. http://www.livius.org/ja-jn/janus/janus.html

14. Peter S Wells, *The Battle That Stopped Rome* (New York: W. W. Norton & Co., 2003), 57.

15. Titus Livius, *The History of Rome*, book 1, chapter 8.

16. 'Roman Social Class and Public Display', by Barbara F. McManus (January 2009). http:// www.vroma.org/~bmcmanus/socialclass.html

17. 'Roman Senate'. http://www.unrv.com/empire/the-senate.php

18. 'Roman Social Class and Public Display', by Barbara F. McManus (January 2009). http:// www.vroma.org/~bmcmanus/socialclass.html

19. 'Civitas', by William Smith (1875). http://penelope.uchicago.edu/Thayer/E/Roman/ Texts/secondary/SMIGRA*/Civitas.html

20. 'Roman Social Class and Public Display', by Barbara F. McManus (January 2009). http:// www.vroma.org/~bmcmanus/socialclass.html; 'Civitas', by Wiliam Smith (1875) http:// penelope.uchicago.edu/Thayer/E/Roman/Texts/secondary/SMIGRA*/Civitas.html

21. 'Roman Social Class and Public Display', by Barbara F. McManus (January 2009). http://www.vroma.org/~bmcmanus/socialclass.html
22. Peter S Wells, *The Battle That Stopped Rome* (New York: W. W. Norton & Co., 2003), 58; 'Roman Slavery'. http://www.unrv.com/culture/roman-slavery.php
23. Graham Webster, *The Roman Imperial Army of the First and Second Centuries A.D.*, third edition (Norman: University of Oklahoma Press, 1998), 109; Lawrence Keppie, *The Making of the Roman Army* (Norman: University of Oklahoma Press, 1998), 145; *Warrior Challenge*, episode 1 – 'Romans'.
24. Lawrence Keppie, *The Making of the Roman Army* (Norman: University of Oklahoma Press: 1998), 147–148; Mary Boatwright, et al, *The Romans: From Village to Empire* (Oxford: Oxford University Press, 2004), 304.
25. Cassius Dio, *The Roman History*, book 40, chapter 41.
26. *Rome: Power and Glory*, episode 1 – 'The Rise'
27. Jerome Carcopino, *Daily Life in Ancient Rome* (New Haven: Yale University Press, 2003), 22–26; Suetonius, *The Twelve Caesars*, book 3, chapter 40; Tacitus, *The Annals*, book 4, chapters 62–64 (Indianapolis: Hackett Publishing Company, Inc., 2004), 152–153.

Chapter Two
1. Tacitus, 'Germania', in *Chronicles of the Barbarians* (New York: History Book Club, 1998), 78. The suffix –*i* was a Roman grammatical device which was applied to a word, and which denoted a plural of something, not a singular. Tacitus comments that the Germani tribe later re-named itself, and by the time that he was alive, they were called the Tungrians.
2. Strabo, *Geography*, book 7, chapter 1; 'Free Online Translators from English to Latin'. http://www.translation-guide.com/free_online_translators.php?from=English&to=Latin; 'Genuine'. http://www.archives.nd.edu/cgi-bin/lookdown.pl?genuine.
3. 'Cartographica Neerlandica Map Text for Ortelius Map No. 200'. http://www.Orteliusmaps.com/book/ort_text200.html
4. Tacitus, 'Germania', in *Chronicles of the Barbarians* (New York: History Book Club, 1998), 78–79; Hans Delbruck, *History of the Art of War, volume 2: The Barbarian Invasions* (Lincoln: University of Nebraska Press, 1990), 15; Adrian Murdoch, *Rome's Greatest Defeat* (Sutton Publishing Limited, 2006), 110–111; Gaius Julius Caesar, *Commentaries*, book 6, chapter 22.
5. Tacitus, 'Germania', in *Chronicles of the Barbarians* (New York: History Book Club, 1998), 78–79.
6. Gaius Julius Caesar, *Commentaries*, book 6, chapters 26–28.
7. Doyne Dawson, *The First Armies* (London: Cassell & Co., 2001), 63, 66.
8. Gaius Julius Caesar, *Commentaries*, book 1, chapter 31.
9. Pliny the Elder, *The Natural History*, book 4, chapter 28; Tacitus, 'Germania', in *Chronicles of the Barbarians* (New York: History Book Club, 1998), 77–78.
10. Hans Delbruck, *History of the Art of War, volume 2: The Barbarian Invasions* (Lincoln: University of Nebraska Press, 1990), 15, 24.
11. 'Barbarian Europe: Germanic or Gaulish?', by Edward Dawson (July 2, 2011). http://www.historyfiles.co.uk/FeaturesEurope/BarbarianTribes01.htm.
12. Strabo, *Geography*, book 7, chapter 1, verse 3.
13. Gaius Velleius Paterculus, *The Roman History*, book 2, chapter 108.
14. Strabo, *Geography*, book 7, chapter 1, verse 3.
15. Cassius Dio, *The Roman History*, book 55, chapter 10a.
16. Tacitus, *The Annals*, book 13, chapter 57 (Indianapolis: Hackett Publishing Company, Inc., 2004), 273–274.
17. Strabo, *Geography*, book 7, chapter 1, verse 3. Strabo lists the tribes under Maroboduus' authority as the Marcomanni themselves, as well as the Butones, Coldui, Ligians, Mugilones,

Semnones, Sibini, and Zumi. Since Ligians (who were actually a culture group made of several tribes) and Semnones are attested to have their own domains, it seems that these two were not conquered and absorbed into the Marcomanni kingdom, but were vassals who were forced to acknowledge the Marcomanni as their masters and pay tribute to them.

18. Gaius Velleius Paterculus, *The Roman History*, book 2, chapters 108–110.
19. Gaius Julius Caesar, *Commentaries*, book 4, chapter 1; Strabo, *Geography*, book 7, chapter 1, verse 3.
20. Gaius Julius Caesar, *Commentaries*, book 4, chapters 1–2.
21. Tacitus, 'Germania', in *Chronicles of the Barbarians* (New York: History Book Club, 1998), 93–94; Strabo, *Geography*, book 7, chapter 1, verse 3.
22. Tacitus, 'Germania', in *Chronicles of the Barbarians* (New York: History Book Club, 1998), 90–91.
23. Tacitus, 'Germania', in *Chronicles of the Barbarians* (New York: History Book Club, 1998), 91; Tacitus, *The Annals*, book 2, chapter 25 (Indianapolis: Hackett Publishing Company, Inc., 2004), 51; Thomas Smith, *Arminius: A history of the German people and of their legal and constitutional customs, from the days of Julius Caesar to the time of Charlemagne* (London: James Blackwood, 1861), 12; 'Germanic Tribes – The Marsi'. http://www. kalkriese-varusschlacht.de/en/varusschlacht-varus-battle-2-14/germanic-tribes-2-57/ marsi-2-208/germanic-tribes-the-marsi.html
24. Adrian Murdoch, *Rome's Greatest Defeat* (Sutton Publishing Limited, 2006), 102; Tacitus, 'Germania', in *Chronicles of the Barbarians* (New York: History Book Club, 1998), 91.
25. Cassius Dio, *The Roman History*, book 54, chapter 32; book 56, chapter 18; Strabo, *Geography*, book 7, chapter 1; E. A. Thompson, *The Early Germans* (Oxford: Clarendon Press, 1965), 72.
26. Thomas Smith, *Arminius: A history of the German people and of their legal and constitutional customs, from the days of Julius Caesar to the time of Charlemagne* (London: James Blackwood, 1861), 100–102.
27. Tacitus, 'Germania', in *Chronicles of the Barbarians* (New York: History Book Club, 1998), 92.
28. Publius Annius Florus, *Epitome*, book 2, chapter 30.
29. Derek Williams, *Romans and Barbarians* (New York: St. Martin's Press, 1998), 92.
30. Tacitus, 'Germania', in *Chronicles of the Barbarians* (New York: History Book Club, 1998), 91.
31. Tacitus, 'Germania', in *Chronicles of the Barbarians* (New York: History Book Club, 1998), 80–81.
32. Tacitus, 'Germania', in *Chronicles of the Barbarians* (New York: History Book Club, 1998), 78.
33. Gaius Julius Caesar, *Commentaries*, book 6, chapter 21.
34. Tacitus, 'Germania', in *Chronicles of the Barbarians* (New York: History Book Club, 1998), 89; Adrian Murdoch, *Rome's Greatest Defeat* (Sutton Publishing Limited, 2006), 24.
35. Tacitus, 'Germania', in *Chronicles of the Barbarians* (New York: History Book Club, 1998), 81; *The Germanic Tribes*, episode 1 – 'Barbarians against Rome'; Malcolm Todd, *The Early Germans* (Malden: Blackwell Publishing, 1995), 107.
36. *The Germanic Tribes*, episode 1 – 'Barbarians against Rome'; Malcolm Todd, *The Early Germans* (Malden: Blackwell Publishing, 1995), 111.
37. Malcolm Todd, *The Early Germans* (Malden: Blackwell Publishing, 1995), 111; Strabo, *Geography*, book 7, chapter 2, verse 3; Tacitus, *The Annals*, book 13, chapter 57 (Indianapolis: Hackett Publishing Company, Inc., 2004), 273–274.
38. Tacitus, 'Germania', in *Chronicles of the Barbarians* (New York: History Book Club, 1998), 82.
39. Tacitus, 'Germania', in *Chronicles of the Barbarians* (New York: History Book Club, 1998), 81.

40. Gaius Julius Caesar, *Commentaries*, book 6, chapter 21.
41. Gaius Julius Caesar, *Commentaries*, book 6, chapter 22.
42. Gaius Julius Caesar, *Commentaries*, book 6, chapter 23.
43. Doyne Dawson, *The First Armies* (London: Cassell & Co., 2001), 57–63.
44. Doyne Dawson, *The First Armies* (London: Cassell & Co., 2001), 63, 66.
45. Malcolm Todd, *The Early Germans* (Malden: Blackwell Publishing, 1995), 110.
46. Tacitus, 'Germania', in *Chronicles of the Barbarians* (New York: History Book Club, 1998), 83.
47. Tacitus, 'Germania', in *Chronicles of the Barbarians* (New York: History Book Club, 1998), 80–83.
48. Guy Halsall, *Warfare and Society in the Barbarian West* (London: Routledge, 2003), 49.
49. Doyne Dawson, *The First Armies* (London: Cassell & Co., 2001), 63; Lawrence H. Keeley, *War Before Civilization* (Oxford: Oxford University Press, 1996), 26–27; Tacitus, 'Germania', in *Chronicles of the Barbarians* (New York: History Book Club, 1998), 81–82.
50. Tacitus, 'Germania', in *Chronicles of the Barbarians* (New York: History Book Club, 1998), 79.
51. Malcolm Todd, *The Early Germans* (Malden: Blackwell Publishing, 1995), 20–22, 125.
52. E A Thompson, *The Early Germans* (Oxford: Clarendon Press, 1965), 20–23.

Chapter Three

1. 'Publius Quinctilius Varus', by Jona Lendering. http://www.livius.org/q/quinctilius/varus.html; *The History of Ancient Rome*, lecture 17 – 'Governing the Roman Republic, part I'; Dionysius of Halicarnassus, *Roman Antiquities*, book 10, chapter 53; Titus Livius, *The History of Rome*, book 29, chapter 38; book 30, chapter 1; book 30, chapter 18.
2. Marcus Tullius Cicero, *Post Reditum in Senatu*, chapter 9.
3. Gaius Julius Caesar, *Commentaries*, volume 2, book 1, chapter 23; volume 2, book 2, chapter 28; Gaius Velleius Paterculus, *The Roman History*, book 2, chapters 71, 119.
4. Adrian Murdoch, *Rome's Greatest Defeat* (Sutton Publishing Limited, 2006), 52.
5. Adrian Murdoch, *Rome's Greatest Defeat* (Sutton Publishing Limited, 2006), 54.
6. Adrian Murdoch, *Rome's Greatest Defeat* (Sutton Publishing Limited, 2006), 53.
7. 'Legio XIX', by Jona Lendering. http://www.livius.org/le-lh/legio/xix.html
8. Adrian Murdoch, *Rome's Greatest Defeat* (Sutton Publishing Limited, 2006), 54–55. Varus the Younger became rich due to his parents' inheritance. Apparently, the death of his father at Teutoburg and the death of his mother (she had been exiled as part of Sejanus' treason trials) had led to a substantial sum of money being granted to him. But he too was to face misfortune. In 27 AD, he was accused by Lucius Aelius Sejanus of treason and condemned to death.
9. Although different secondary sources give different years for Varus' governorship of Africa (as examples, Murdoch says 8–7 BC, while Wells says 7–6 BC), all of them agree that he served in this post for two years; Adrian Murdoch, *Rome's Greatest Defeat* (Sutton Publishing Limited, 2006), 57; 'Publius Quinctilius Varus', by Jona Lendering. http://www.livius.org/q/quinctilius/varus.html
10. *Rome: Power and Glory*, episode 1 – 'The Rise'; Adrian Murdoch, *Rome's Greatest Defeat* (Sutton Publishing Limited, 2006), 57. The amounts are converted from metric.
11. Adrian Murdoch, *Rome's Greatest Defeat* (Sutton Publishing Limited, 2006), 56–57.
12. Adrian Murdoch, *Rome's Greatest Defeat* (Sutton Publishing Limited, 2006), 57.
13. 'Publius Quinctilius Varus', by Jona Lendering. http://www.livius.org/q/quinctilius/varus.html; Adrian Murdoch, *Rome's Greatest Defeat* (Sutton Publishing Limited, 2006), 57; Peter S Wells, *The Battle That Stopped Rome* (New York: W. W. Norton & Co., 2003), 82; 'Roman Provinces – Syria'. http://www.unrv.com/provinces/syria.php
14. Josephus, *The Jewish Wars*, book 1, chapter 14, verse 4.

15. Josephus, *The Jewish Wars*, book 1, chapter 31, verse 5.
16. Josephus, *The Jewish Wars*, book 1, chapter 32, verses 1–7.
17. Josephus, *The Jewish Wars*, book 1, chapter 33, verses 1–2.
18. Josephus, *The Jewish Wars*, book 1, chapter 33, verse 2.
19. Josephus, *The Jewish Wars*, book 1, chapter 33, verse 3.
20. Josephus, *The Jewish Wars*, book 1, chapter 33, verses 5–9.
21. Josephus, *The Jewish Wars*, book 2, chapter 1, verses 1–2.
22. Josephus, *The Jewish Wars*, book 2, chapter 2, verses 1–2.
23. Josephus, *The Jewish Wars*, book 2, chapter 3, verses 1–5.
24. Josephus, *The Jewish Wars*, book 2, chapter 3, verse 1.
25. Adrian Murdoch, *Rome's Greatest Defeat* (Sutton Publishing Limited, 2006), 58; Josephus, *The Jewish Wars*, book 2, chapter 5, verses 1–3.
26. Gaius Velleius Paterculus, *The Roman History*, book 2, chapter 117.
27. Adrian Murdoch, *Rome's Greatest Defeat* (Sutton Publishing Limited, 2006), 65.
28. 'Germania Inferior', by Jona Lendering. http://www.livius.org/ga-gh/germania/inferior03.html.
29. Gaius Velleius Paterculus, *The Roman History*, book 2, chapter 104.
30. Gaius Velleius Paterculus, *The Roman History*, book 2, chapter 117.
31. Cassius Dio, *The Roman History*, book 55, chapter 28.
32. Gaius Velleius Paterculus, *The Roman History*, book 2, chapters 105, 109.
33. 'Publius Quinctilius Varus' , by Jona Lendering. http://www.livius.org/q/quinctilius/varus.html.
34. Adrian Murdoch, *Rome's Greatest Defeat* (Sutton Publishing Limited, 2006), 41–47.

Chapter Four
1. Terry Jones and Alan Ereira. *Terry Jones' Barbarians* (London: BBC Books, 2006), 87.
2. Herwig Wolfram, *History of the Goths* (Berkley and Los Angeles: University of California Press, 1988), 442.
3. Adrian Murdoch, *Rome's Greatest Defeat* (Sutton Publishing Limited, 2006), 84.
4. 'Thusnelda and Thumelicus', by James Grout. http://penelope.uchicago.edu/~grout/encyclopaedia_romana/miscellanea/teutoburg/thusnelda.html
5. 'Arminius: Ðe Original Siegfried', by Theedrich Yeat (August 13, 2009). http://www.harbornet.com/folks/theedrich/hive/Medieval/Siegfried.htm; 'Thusnelda and Thumelicus', by James Grout. http://penelope.uchicago.edu/~grout/encyclopaedia_romana/miscellanea/teutoburg/thusnelda.html
6. Guy Halsall, *Warfare and Society in the Barbarian West, 450–900* (London: Routledge, 2003), 32.
7. Derek Williams, *Romans and Barbarians* (New York: St. Martin's Press, 1998), 66.
8. 'Cartographica Neerlandica Map Text for Ortelius Map No. 200'. http://www.Orteliusmaps.com/book/ort_text200.html
9. Melville Y Stewart, ed, *The Trinity: East/West Dialogue* (Dordrecht: Kluwer Academic Publishers, 2003), 109, 127.
10. This date is based upon Tacitus' description of Arminius' lifespan: '37 years of life and 12 in power' (Tacitus, Annals, book 2, chapter 88). If Arminius came to power in 9 AD, the year of the Battle of Teutoburg, and reigned as the leader of the Germanic rebels for twelve years, he would have died in 21 AD. Having lived for 37 years, this means he was born in the year 16 BC; 'Gothic Language Dictionary – victory'. http://www.oe.eclipse.co.uk/nom/letters.htm; 'Arminius: Ðe Original Siegfried', by Theedrich Yeat (August 13, 2009). http://www.harbornet.com/folks/theedrich/hive/Medieval/Siegfried.htm
11. Tacitus, *The Annals*, book 2, chapter 10 (Indianapolis: Hackett Publishing Company, Inc., 2004), 45–46.

12. Tacitus, *The Annals*, book 11, chapter 16 (Indianapolis: Hackett Publishing Company, Inc., 2004), 45, 203.
13. Strabo, *Geography*, book 7, chapter 1; Tacitus, *The Annals*, book 1, chapter 71 (Indianapolis: Hackett Publishing Company, Inc., 2004), 37.
14. Tacitus, *The Annals*, book 1, chapter 71 (Indianapolis: Hackett Publishing Company, Inc., 2004), 37.
15. Gaius Velleius Paterculus, *The Roman History*, book 2, chapter 118.
16. Tacitus, *The Annals*, book 2, chapter 10 (Indianapolis: Hackett Publishing Company, Inc., 2004), 46.
17. Derek Williams, *Romans and Barbarians* (New York: St. Martin's Press, 1998), 92.
18. E A Thompson, *The Early Germans* (Oxford: Clarendon Press, 1965), 4.
19. Colin Michael Wells, *The Roman Empire* (Stanford: Stanford University Press, 1984), 75.
20. Gaius Velleius Paterculus, *The Roman History*, book 2, chapter 118. I should state that it is never specifically mentioned that Arminius was made a citizen, but since one had to be a citizen to be knighted, I suppose his citizenship went without saying.

Chapter Five

1. Publius Annius Florus, *Epitome*, book 1, chapter 38.
2. Plutarch, *Parallel Lives* – 'The Life of Marius', 11.
3. Tacitus, 'Germania', in *Chronicles of the Barbarians* (New York: History Book Club, 1998), 78.
4. Theodor Mommsen, *History of Rome – The Revolution*, page 67. http://italian.classic-literature.co.uk/history-of-rome/04-the-revolution/ebook-page-67.asp
5. Publius Annius Florus, *Epitome*, book 1, chapter 38.
6. Publius Annius Florus, *Epitome*, book 1, chapter 38; Theodor Mommsen, *History of Rome – The Revolution*, page 67. http://italian.classic-literature.co.uk/history-of-rome/04-the-revolution/ebook-page-67.asp
7. Theodor Mommsen, *History of Rome – The Revolution*, page 68. http://italian.classic-literature.co.uk/history-of-rome/04-the-revolution/ebook-page-68.asp
8. Theodor Mommsen, *History of Rome – The Revolution*, page 68. http://italian.classic-literature.co.uk/history-of-rome/04-the-revolution/ebook-page-68.asp; Livy, *Periochae*, book 67.
9. Plutarch, *Parallel Lives* – 'The Life of Marius', 11.
10. Plutarch, *Parallel Lives* – 'The Life of Marius', 12.
11. Plutarch, *Parallel Lives* – 'The Life of Marius', 13.
12. Plutarch, *Parallel Lives* – 'The Life of Marius', 14–27; Livy, *Periochae*, book 68; Publius Annius Florus, *Epitome*, book 1, chapter 38.
13. Gaius Julius Caesar, *Commentaries*, book 1, chapters 31–54; book 5, chapter 29.
14. Gaius Julius Caesar, *Commentaries*, book 4, chapters 6–15.
15. Gaius Julius Caesar, *Commentaries*, book 4, chapters 16–19.
16. Adrian Murdoch, *Rome's Greatest Defeat* (Sutton Publishing Limited, 2006), 23–24.
17. Adrian Murdoch, *Rome's Greatest Defeat* (Sutton Publishing Limited, 2006), 26.
18. Adrian Murdoch, *Rome's Greatest Defeat* (Sutton Publishing Limited, 2006), 25–26.
19. *The Germanic Tribes*, episode 3 – 'Pax Romana'.
20. Adrian Murdoch, *Rome's Greatest Defeat* (Sutton Publishing Limited, 2006), 26, 28.
21. Adrian Murdoch, *Rome's Greatest Defeat* (Sutton Publishing Limited, 2006), 28.
22. Adrian Murdoch, *Rome's Greatest Defeat* (Sutton Publishing Limited, 2006), 28–29.
23. Cassius Dio, *The Roman History*, book 54, chapter 20; Gaius Velleius Paterculus, *The Roman History*, book 2, chapter 97.
24. Adrian Murdoch, *Rome's Greatest Defeat* (Sutton Publishing Limited, 2006), 22, 30; Cassius Dio, *The Roman History*, book 54, chapter 22.

25. Adrian Murdoch, *Rome's Greatest Defeat* (Sutton Publishing Limited, 2006), 31–33.
26. Cassius Dio, *The Roman History*, book 54, chapter 32.
27. Cassius Dio, *The Roman History*, book 54, chapter 33.
28. Cassius Dio, *The Roman History*, book 54, chapter 33.
29. Cassius Dio, *The Roman History*, book 54, chapters 33, 36.
30. Cassius Dio, *The Roman History*, book 55, chapter 1.
31. Ovid, *The Heroïdes, or Epistles of the Heroines; The Amours ; Art of Love; Remedy of Love; and, Minor Works of Ovid* (G. Bell, 1893), 503; *The Germanic Tribes*, episode 1 – 'Barbarians against Rome'; Livy, *Periochae*, From book 142; Cassius Dio, *The Roman History*, book 55, chapters 1–2; Suetonius, *The Twelve Caesars*, book 5, chapter 1.
32. Ovid, *The Heroïdes, or Epistles of the Heroines; The Amours ; Art of Love; Remedy of Love; and, Minor Works of Ovid* (G. Bell, 1893), 509; Cassius Dio, *The Roman History*, book 55, chapter 2.
33. Ovid, *The Heroïdes, or Epistles of the Heroines; The Amours ; Art of Love; Remedy of Love; and, Minor Works of Ovid* (G. Bell, 1893), 509.
34. Suetonius, *The Twelve Caesars*, book 5, chapter 1.
35. Suetonius, *The Twelve Caesars*, book 3, chapter 7; Cassius Dio, *The Roman History*, book 55, chapter 2.
36. Suetonius, *The Twelve Caesars*, book 5, chapter 1.
37. Suetonius, *The Twelve Caesars*, book 5, chapter 1.
38. Gaius Velleius Paterculus, *The Roman History*, book 2, chapter 97.
39. Cassius Dio, *The Roman History*, book 55, chapters 6, 9.
40. Adrian Murdoch, *Rome's Greatest Defeat* (Sutton Publishing Limited, 2006), 41–42.
41. Suetonius, *The Twelve Caesars*, book 6, chapter 4.
42. Suetonius, *The Twelve Caesars*, book 6, chapter 4.
43. Cassius Dio, *The Roman History*, book 55, chapter 10a; 'Pontes longi', by Jona Lendering. http://www.livius.org/pn-po/pontes_longi/pontes_longi.html
44. Cassius Dio, *The Roman History*, book 55, chapter 10a.
45. Tacitus, *The Annals*, book 4, chapter 44 (Indianapolis: Hackett Publishing Company, Inc., 2004), 144.
46. Cassius Dio, *The Roman History*, book 55, chapter 10a.
47. Cassius Dio, *The Roman History*, book 55, chapter 10a.
48. Cassius Dio, *The Roman History*, book 53, chapter 26; Gaius Velleius Paterculus, *The Roman History*, book 2, chapters 104–106.
49. The terms 'Upper Rhine Army' and 'Lower Rhine Army' are purely modern and were probably not used in ancient times. These terms are located in Adrian Murdoch's *Rome's Greatest Defeat* (Sutton Publishing Limited, 2006), 129.
50. Cassius Dio, *The Roman History*, book 54, chapter 11.
51. 'Legio I Germanica', by Jona Lendering. http://www.livius.org/le-lh/legio/i_germanica.html; Cassius Dio, *The Roman History*, book 54, chapter 11.
52. 'Legio V Alaudae', by Jona Lendering. http://www.livius.org/le-lh/legio/v_alaudae.html
53. 'Legio XVII', by Jona Lendering. http://www.livius.org/le-lh/legio/xvii.html; 'Legio XVIII' by Jona Lendering. http://www.livius.org/le-lh/legio/xviii.html; 'Legio XIX', by Jona Lendering. http://www.livius.org/le-lh/legio/xix.html
54. Stephen Dando-Collins, *Legions of Rome* (London: Quercus Publishing, 2012), 238.
55. M. C. Bishop, *Lorica Segmentata, Vol. 1.* (Braemar: The Armatura Press, 2002), 23.
56. Lawrence Keppie, *The Making of the Roman Army* (Norman: University of Oklahoma Press, 1998), 161; 'Legio XVII', by Jona Lendering. http://www.livius.org/le-lh/legio/xvii.html; 'Legio XVIII' by Jona Lendering. http://www.livius.org/le-lh/legio/xviii.html; 'Legio XIX', by Jona Lendering. http://www.livius.org/le-lh/legio/xix.html

57. Graham Webster, *The Imperial Roman Army of the First and Second Centuries A.D.*, third edition (Norman: University of Oklahoma, 1998), 182, 184; Duncan B. Campbell, *Roman Legionary Fortresses 27 BC–AD 378* (Oxford: Osprey Publishing, Ltd., 2006), 33.

58. Graham Webster, *The Imperial Roman Army of the First and Second Centuries A.D.*, third edition (Norman: University of Oklahoma, 1998), 197–98; Duncan B. Campbell, *Roman Legionary Fortresses 27 BC–AD 378* (Oxford: Osprey Publishing, Ltd., 2006), 51–55

59. Graham Webster, *The Imperial Roman Army of the First and Second Centuries A.D.*, third edition (Norman: University of Oklahoma, 1998), 195–197.

60. Graham Webster, *The Imperial Roman Army of the First and Second Centuries A.D.*, third edition (Norman: University of Oklahoma, 1998), 193–195.

61. Graham Webster, *The Imperial Roman Army of the First and Second Centuries A.D.*, third edition (Norman: University of Oklahoma, 1998), 179–181.

62. Graham Webster, *The Imperial Roman Army of the First and Second Centuries A.D.*, third edition (Norman: University of Oklahoma, 1998), 177, 180–181.

63. Graham Webster, *The Imperial Roman Army of the First and Second Centuries A.D.*, third edition (Norman: University of Oklahoma, 1998), 181.

64. Graham Webster, *The Imperial Roman Army of the First and Second Centuries A.D.*, third edition (Norman: University of Oklahoma, 1998), 176–179.

65. Peter S. Wells, *The Battle That Stopped Rome* (New York: W. W. Norton & Co., 2003), 90; 'Castra Vetera (Xanten-Birten)', by Jona Lendering (April 28, 2009). http://www.livius.org/x/xanten/vetera.html

66. Lawrence Keppie, *The Making of the Roman Army* (Norman: University of Oklahoma Press, 1998), 161, 195; Peter S. Wells, *The Battle That Stopped Rome* (New York: W. W. Norton & Co., 2003), 90; 'The Batavian Revolt – The Siege of Xanten', by Jona Lendering. http://www.livius.org/ba-bd/batavians/revolt05.html

67. Tacitus, *Histories*, book 4, chapters 22–23.

68. Peter S. Wells, *The Battle That Stopped Rome* (New York: W. W. Norton & Co., 2003), 90.

69. Suetonius, *The Twelve Caesars*, book 2, chapter 21; book 3, chapter 9; Pliny the Elder, *The Natural History*, book 4, chapter 31; Tacitus, *Histories*, book 4, chapter 26.

70. Carl Waldman and Catherine Mason, *Encyclopedia of European Peoples* (New York: Facts on File, Inc., 2006), 786; 'Castra Vetera (Xanten-Birten)', by Jona Lendering (April 28, 2009). http://www.livius.org/x/xanten/vetera.html; 'Cugerni', by Jona Lendering. http://www.livius.org/ct-cz/cugerni/cugerni.html

71. Anreppen', by Jona Lendering (September 16, 2008). http://www.livius.org/am-ao/anreppen/anreppen.html; Peter S. Wells, *The Battle That Stopped Rome* (New York: W. W. Norton & Co., 2003), 92.

72. 'Footnote #19, Tacitus, *Annals*, book 2, chapter 7', by Bill Thayer. http://penelope.uchicago.edu/Thayer/E/Roman/Texts/Tacitus/Annals/2A*.html#note19; Hans Delbruck, *History of the Art of War, volume 2: The Barbarian Invasions*, (Lincoln: University of Nebraska Press, 1990), 58.

73. Peter S. Wells, *The Battle That Stopped Rome* (New York: W. W. Norton & Co., 2003), 102.

74. *The Germanic Tribes*, episode 2 – 'The Battle of the Teutoburg Forest'; Peter S. Wells, *The Barbarians Speak* (Princeton: Princeton University Press, 1999), 90; 'Oberaden', by Jona Lendering. http://www.livius.org/oa-om/oberaden/oberaden.html

75. 'Dorsten-Holsterhausen', by Jona Lendering. http://www.livius.org/ho-hz/holsterhausen/holsterhausen.html; 'The Romans in Germania – A Geography Lesson', by Gabriele Campbell (January 30, 2010) http://lostfort.blogspot.com/2010/01/romans-in-germania-geography-lesson.html; 'Oberaden', by Jona Lendering. http://www.livius.org/oa-om/oberaden/oberaden.html; 'Anreppen', by Jona Lendering (September 16, 2008). http://www.livius.org/am-ao/anreppen/anreppen.html; Graham Webster, *The Roman Imperial Army of the First and Second Centuries A.D.* (Norman: University of Oklahoma, 1998), 48;

Duncan B. Campbell, *Roman Legionary Fortresses 27 BC–AD 378* (Oxford: Osprey Publishing, Ltd., 2006), 4, 9, 13; 'Marktbreit', by Jona Lendering (March 21, 2009). http://www.livius.org/man-md/marktbreit/marktbreit.html

76. *The Germanic Tribes*, episode 2 – 'The Battle of the Teutoburg Forest'.
77. Cassius Dio, *The Roman History*, book 56, chapter 18.
78. Gaius Velleius Paterculus, *The Roman History*, book 2, chapter 110.
79. Cassius Dio, *The Roman History*, book 55, chapter 29.
80. Cassius Dio, *The Roman History*, book 55, chapter 29.
81. Gaius Velleius Paterculus, *The Roman History*, book 2, chapter 110.
82. Suetonius, *The Twelve Caesars*, book 3, chapter 16; Gaius Velleius Paterculus, *The Roman History*, book 2, chapters 110–111.
83. Cassius Dio, *The Roman History*, book 55, chapters 30–31.
84. Gaius Velleius Paterculus, *The Roman History*, book 2, chapters 92, 105.
85. Cassius Dio, *The Roman History*, book 55, chapter 28.
86. Adrian Murdoch, *Rome's Greatest Defeat* (Sutton Publishing Limited, 2006), 45, 65.
87. 'Publius Quinctilius Varus', by Jona Lendering. http://www.livius.org/q/quinctilius/varus.html; Adrian Murdoch, *Rome's Greatest Defeat* (Sutton Publishing Limited, 2006), 65; Peter S. Wells, *The Battle That Stopped Rome* (New York: W. W. Norton & Co., 2003), 83.
88. Adrian Murdoch, *Rome's Greatest Defeat* (Sutton Publishing Limited, 2006), 54.
89. Gaius Velleius Paterculus, *The Roman History*, book 2, chapter 120.
90. Adrian Murdoch, Rome's Greatest Defeat (Sutton Publishing Limited, 2006), 67; Gaius Velleius Paterculus, *The Roman History*, book 2, chapter 120.
91. Adrian Murdoch, *Rome's Greatest Defeat* (Sutton Publishing Limited, 2006), 67–68.
92. Gaius Velleius Paterculus, *The Roman History*, book 2, chapter 118.
93. Cassius Dio, *The Roman History*, book 56, chapter 18.
94. Cassius Dio, *The Roman History*, book 56, chapter 19.
95. Publius Annius Florus, *Epitome*, book 2, chapter 30.
96. Cassius Dio, *The Roman History*, book 56, chapter 18.
97. Gaius Velleius Paterculus, *The Roman History*, book 2, chapters 117–118.
98. Peter S. Wells, *The Battle That Stopped Rome* (New York: W. W. Norton & Company, Inc., 2003), 77, 85.
99. Cassius Dio, *The Roman History*, book 56, chapter 19.
100. Cassius Dio, *The Roman History*, book 56, chapter 18.
101. Publius Annius Florus, *Epitome*, book 2, chapter 30.
102. Gaius Velleius Paterculus, *The Roman History*, book 2, chapter 118.
103. Tacitus, *The Annals*, book 1, chapter 60 (Indianapolis: Hackett Publishing Company, Inc., 2004), 32.
104. Tacitus, *The Annals*, book 1, chapter 58 (Indianapolis: Hackett Publishing Company, Inc., 2004), 30–31.
105. Tacitus, *The Annals*, book 1, chapters 55–57 (Indianapolis: Hackett Publishing Company, Inc., 2004), 29–30.
106. Strabo, *Geography*, book 7, chapter 1.
107. Tacitus, *The Annals*, book 13, chapter 55 (Indianapolis: Hackett Publishing Company, Inc., 2004), 272–273.
108. Tacitus, *The Annals*, book 1, chapter 60 (Indianapolis: Hackett Publishing Company, Inc., 2004), 32; book 13, chapter 55 (Indianapolis: Hackett Publishing Company, Inc., 2004), 272–273

Chapter Six
1. Cassius Dio, *The Roman History*, book 56, chapter 19.
2. Adrian Murdoch, *Rome's Greatest Defeat* (Sutton Publishing Limited, 2006), 103.

3. Tacitus, *The Annals*, book 1, chapters 55, 58 (Indianapolis: Hackett Publishing Company, Inc., 2004), 29.
4. Gaius Velleius Paterculus, *The Roman History*, book 2, chapter 118.
5. Tacitus, *The Annals*, book 1, chapter 55 (Indianapolis: Hackett Publishing Company, Inc., 2004), 29; Cassius Dio, *The Roman History*, book 56, chapter 19.
6. Publius Annius Florus, *Epitome*, book 2, chapter 30.
7. Tacitus, *The Annals*, book 1, chapter 58 (Indianapolis: Hackett Publishing Company, Inc., 2004), 30.
8. Gaius Velleius Paterculus, *The Roman History*, book 2, chapter 117.
9. Simon Anglim, et al, *Fighting Techniques of the Ancient World, 3,000 BC AD 500* (New York: Thomas Dunne Books, 2003), 64; Konstantine Nossov, *Ancient and Medieval Siege Weapons* (Guilford: The Lyons Press, 2005), 50; Peter S. Wells, *The Battle That Stopped Rome* (New York: W. W. Norton & Co., 2003), photographic plate #5.
10. Adrian Murdoch, *Rome's Greatest Defeat* (Sutton Publishing Limited, 2006), 105.
11. Tacitus, *Histories*, book 1, chapter 46.
12. Cassius Dio, *The Roman History*, book 56, chapter 19.
13. Graham Webster, *The Roman Imperial Army of the First and Second Centuries A.D.* (Norman: University of Oklahoma Press, 1998), 118–119; Peter S. Wells, *The Battle That Stopped Rome* (New York: W. W. Norton & Co., 2003), 52–53.
14. Cassius Dio, *The Roman History*, book 56, chapter 20; 'The Battle in the Teutoburg Forest (4)', by Jona Lendering (November 12, 2008). http://www.livius.org/te-tg/teutoburg/teutoburg04.html; Tacitus, 'Germania', in *Chronicles of the Barbarians* (New York: History Book Club, 1998), 80.
15. Gaius Julius Caesar, *Commentaries*, book 2, chapter 19; Josephus, *The Jewish Wars*, book 5, chapter 2, verse 1; Arrian, *Arrian's Array against the Alans*. http://s_van_dorst.tripod.com/Ancient_Warfare/Rome/Sources/ektaxis.html
16. Strabo, *Geography*, book 7, chapter 1; Gaius Velleius Paterculus, *Roman History*, book 2, chapter 118.
17. Cassius Dio, *The Roman History*, book 56, chapter 20.
18. Cassius Dio, *The Roman History*, book 56, chapter 19.
19. Cassius Dio, *The Roman History*, book 56, chapter 19.
20. Tony Clunn, *The Quest for the Lost Roman Legions* (New York: Savas Beatie, 2009), xv.
21. Tony Clunn, *The Quest for the Lost Roman Legions* (New York: Savas Beatie, 2009), 1.
22. 'Lesson 1: Principles on the Nature of Latin'. http://frcoulter.com/latin/first/lesson1.html
23. 'Cantab', by Susan Harvey-Purcell (April 15, 2009). http://virtuallinguist.typepad.com/the_virtual_linguist/2009/04/page/2/
24. 'Arminius: De Original Siegfried', by Theedrich Yeat (August 13, 2009).http://www.harbornet.com/folks/theedrich/hive/Medieval/Siegfried.htm; *We Shall Remain*, episode 4 – 'Geronimo'. PBS.
25. Peter S Wells, *The Battle That Stopped Rome* (New York: W. W. Norton & Co., 2003), 55.
26. 'Tunica & Sudarium'. Legio VI Ferrata Fidelas Constans (August 15, 2011). http://legvi.tripod.com/id92.html; 'Cold Weather Gear'. Legio VI Ferrata Fidelas Constans (August 15, 2011). http://legvi.tripod.com/id80.html
27. *Warrior Challenge*, episode 1 – 'Romans'.
28. 'Rank Structure of the Imperial Roman Army'. http://s_van_dorst.tripod.com/Ancient_Warfare/Rome/hierarchy.html
29. Adrian Murdoch, *Rome's Greatest Defeat* (Sutton Publishing Limited, 2006), 201; Peter S. Wells, *The Battle That Stopped Rome* (New York: W. W. Norton & Co., 2003), 52.
30. 'Roman Military Equipment: Helmets'. http://www.romancoins.info/Military Equipment-Helmet.html; 'Helmets'. Legio XX Online Handbook (March 14, 2011). http://www.larp.com/legioxx/helmets.html

31. Adrian Murdoch, *Rome's Greatest Defeat* (Sutton Publishing Limited, 2006), 201; 'Helmets'. Legio XX Online Handbook (March 14, 2011). http://www.larp.com/legioxx/ helmets.html; 'Roman Military Equipment: Helmets'. http://www.romancoins.info/ MilitaryEquipment-Helmet.html.
32. 'Roman Military Equipment: Helmets'. http://www.romancoins.info/Military Equipment-Helmet.html; 'Galea – Helmet'. Legio VI Ferrata Fidelas Constans (April 7, 2010). http://legvi.tripod.com/id111.html
33. Nic Fields, *The Roman Army of the Principate 27 BC–AD 117* (Oxford: Osprey Publishing, Ltd., 2009), 24–25; 'Lorica Hamata'. Legio XX Online Handbook (March 15, 2011). http://www.larp.com/legioxx/hamata.html
34. M C. Bishop, *Lorica Segmentata, Vol. 1*. (Braemar: The Armatura Press, 2002), 23.
35. 'Notes on the Kalkriese style lorica segmentata'. Legio XX Online Handbook (March 15, 2011). http://www.larp.com/legioxx/kalklor.html; M. C. Bishop, *Lorica Segmentata, Vol. 1*. (Braemar: The Armatura Press, 2002), 23.
36. 'Subarmalis'. Legio XX Online Handbook (August 8, 2004). http://www.larp.com/ legioxx/subarm.html
37. 'Balteus – Military Belt'. Legio XX Online Handbook (March 25, 2010). http://www.larp. com/legioxx/balteus.html; 'Balteus & Ventralis – Military Belt and Waistband' Legio VI Ferrata Fidelas Constans (April 8, 2010). http://legvi.tripod.com/id74.html; Nic Fields, *Roman Legionary 58 BC–AD 69* (Oxford: Osprey Publishing, Ltd., 2003), 25.
38. Ross Cowan,*Roman Legionary 68 BC–AD 69* (Oxford: Osprey Publishing, 2003), 29; 'Weapons and Catapults'. Legio XXIV (June 22, 2005). http://www.legionxxiv.org/weapons/ Default.htm
39. *Warrior Challenge*, episode 1 – 'Romans'; John Warry, *Warfare in the Classical World* (Norman: University of Oklahoma Press, 1995) 133.
40. 'Scutum – Shield'. Legio VI Ferrata Fidelas Constans (August 15, 2011). http://legvi. tripod.com/id112.html; John Warry, *Warfare in the Classical World* (Norman: University of Oklahoma Press, 1995) 148.
41. John Warry, *Warfare in the Classical World* (Norman: University of Oklahoma Press, 1995) 148.
42. Nic Fields, *The Roman Army of the Principate 27 BC–AD 117* (Oxford: Osprey Publishing, Ltd., 2009), 12, 19, 22.
43. 'Protective Equipment: Roman Helmets – Helmets with Face Masks'. http://www. romancoins.info/MilitaryEquipment-Facemasks.html
44. 'Roman Military Equipment: Helmets'. http://www.romancoins.info/Military Equipment-Helmet.html
45. Nic Fields, *The Roman Army of the Principate, 27 BC–AD 117* (Oxford: Osprey Publishing, Ltd., 2009), 28; 'Auxiliary Shield Blazons' (July 7, 2009). http://www.redrampant. com/2009/07/auxiliary-shield-blazons.html
46. Adrian Murdoch, *Rome's Greatest Defeat* (Sutton Publishing Limited, 2006), 199.
47. 'Basque Onomastics of the Eighth to Sixteenth Centuries. Appendix 4: Names Identified from Roman-Era Aquitanian Stones'. http://www.larsdatter.com/basque/appendix4.htm
48. George Leonard Cheesman, *The Auxilia of the Roman Imperial Army* (Oxford: Clarendon Press, 1914), vi.
49. Adrian Murdoch, *Rome's Greatest Defeat* (Sutton Publishing Limited, 2006), 198–199.
50. Nic Fields, *The Roman Army of the Principate 27 BC–AD 117* (Oxford: Osprey Publishing, Ltd., 2009), 15, 19.
51. 'Roman Military Equipment: Helmets'. http://www.romancoins.info/MilitaryEquipment-Helmet.html
52. Nic Fields, *The Roman Army of the Principate 27 BC–AD 117* (Oxford: Osprey Publishing, Ltd., 2009), 28, 31.

53. Graham Webster, *The Roman Imperial Army of the First and Second Centuries A.D.*, third edition (Norman: University of Oklahoma Press, 1998), 109, 265.

54. Lawrence Keppie, *The Making of the Roman Army* (Norman: University of Oklahoma, 1998), 178–180.; John Warry, *Warfare in the Classical World* (Norman: University of Oklahoma Press, 1980), 173.; Graham Webster, *The Roman Imperial Army of the First and Second Centuries A.D.*, third edition (Norman: University of Oklahoma Press, 1998), 113–115, 130–131.

55. John Warry, *Warfare in the Classical World* (Norman: University of Oklahoma Press, 1980), 173.

56. Graham Webster, *The Roman Imperial Army of the First and Second Centuries A.D.*, third edition (Norman: University of Oklahoma Press, 1998), 112.

57. Lawrence Keppie, *The Making of the Roman Army* (Norman: University of Oklahoma, 1998), 149–150.; Graham Webster, *The Roman Imperial Army of the First and Second Centuries A.D.*, third edition (Norman: University of Oklahoma Press, 1998), 112.

58. Graham Webster, *The Roman Imperial Army of the First and Second Centuries A.D.*, third edition (Norman: University of Oklahoma Press, 1998), 112–113.

59. Graham Webster, *The Roman Imperial Army of the First and Second Centuries A.D.*, third edition (Norman: University of Oklahoma Press, 1998), 113.

60. Lawrence Keppie, *The Making of the Roman Army* (Norman: University of Oklahoma Press, 1998), 67.

61. 'Signum and Vexillium'. Legio XX Online Handbook (June 18, 2007). http://www. larp.com/legioxx/signum.html; 'Imperial Aquila-Signums-Vexillium-Imago-Draco-Standards'. Legion XXIV Media Atlantica (February 22, 2010). http://www.legionxxiv. org/signum/

62. Publius Annius Florus, *Epitome*, book 1, chapter 38.

63. Polyaenus, *Stratagems*, book 8, chapter 10.

64. Gaius Julius Caesar, *Commentaries*, book 1, chapter 39.

65. Tacitus, 'Germania', in *Chronicles of the Barbarians* (New York: History Book Club, 1998), 78; Plutarch, *Parallel Lives* – 'The Life of Marius', chapter 11; Strabo, *Geography*, book 7, chapter 2; Gaius Julius Caesar, *Commentaries*, book 1, chapter 39.

66. Gaius Julius Caesar, *Commentaries*, book 6, chapter 21; Tacitus, 'Germania', in *Chronicles of the Barbarians* (New York: History Book Club, 1998), 84.

67. Tacitus, 'Germania', in *Chronicles of the Barbarians* (New York: History Book Club, 1998), 79.

68. Tacitus, *The Annals*, book 2, chapter 14. http://penelope.uchicago.edu/Thayer/E/ Roman/Texts/Tacitus/home.html

69. Peter Wilcox, *Rome's Enemies: Germanics and Dacians* (London: Osprey Publishing, 1982), 12–13, 16–17; Malcolm Todd, *The Early Germans* (Malden: Blackwell Publishing, 1995), 110; Peter S. Wells, *The Battle That Stopped Rome* (New York: W. W. Norton & Co., 2003), 119, 141.

70. Peter Wilcox, *Rome's Enemies: Germanics and Dacians* (London: Osprey Publishing, 1982), 11–17.

71. Peter Wilcox, *Rome's Enemies: Germanics and Dacians* (London: Osprey Publishing, 1982), 11–17.

72. Peter Wilcox, *Rome's Enemies: Germanics and Dacians* (London: Osprey Publishing, 1982), 11–12; Peter S. Wells, *The Battle That Stopped Rome* (New York: W. W. Norton & Co., 2003), illustration #22.

73. Peter Wilcox, *Rome's Enemies: Germanics and Dacians* (London: Osprey Publishing, 1982), 11–13.

74. Peter Wilcox, *Rome's Enemies: Germanics and Dacians* (London: Osprey Publishing, 1982), 13.

75. Peter Wilcox, *Rome's Enemies: Germanics and Dacians* (London: Osprey Publishing, 1982), 11–12.
76. Tacitus, 'Germania', in *Chronicles of the Barbarians* (New York: History Book Club, 1998), 79–80.
77. Gaius Julius Caesar, *Commentaries*, book 1, chapter 52; Hans Delbruck, *History of the Art of War, volume 2: The Barbarian Invasions* (Lincoln: University of Nebraska Press, 1990), 41–42; Tacitus, 'Germania', in *Chronicles of the Barbarians* (New York: History Book Club, 1998), 80.
78. Tacitus, 'Germania', in *Chronicles of the Barbarians* (New York: History Book Club, 1998), 79.
79. Plutarch, *Parallel Lives* – 'The Life of Marius', chapter 11.
80. Plutarch, *Parallel Lives* – 'The Life of Marius', chapter 11.
81. Sextus Julius Frontinus, *Strategems*, book 1, chapter 3.
82. Cassius Dio, *The Roman History*, book 56, chapter 20.
83. Richard M. Ketchum, *Saratoga: Turning Point of America's Revolutionary War* (New York: Henry Holt, 1997), 244.
84. Cassius Dio, *The Roman History*, book 56, chapter 19.
85. Cassius Dio, *The Roman History*, book 56, chapter 20.
86. Cassius Dio, *The Roman History*, book 56, chapter 20.
87. Cassius Dio, *The Roman History*, book 56, chapter 20.
88. Cassius Dio, *The Roman History*, book 56, chapter 20.
89. Adrian Murdoch, *Rome's Greatest Defeat* (Sutton Publishing Limited, 2006), 108.
90. Cassius Dio, *The Roman History*, book 56, chapter 21.
91. Cassius Dio, *The Roman History*, book 56, chapter 21.
92. Cassius Dio, *The Roman History*, book 56, chapter 21.
93. *A History of Britain*, episode 2 – 'Conquest'.
94. Cassius Dio, *The Roman History*, book 56, chapter 21.
95. Adrian Murdoch, *Rome's Greatest Defeat* (Sutton Publishing Limited, 2006), 110.
96. 'The Ambush that Changed History' by Fergus M. Bordewich (September 2005). Smithsonian Magazine. http://www.smithsonianmag.com/history-archaeology/ambush.html; Peter S. Wells, *The Battle That Stopped Rome* (New York: W. W. Norton & Co., 2003), 50–51.
97. Tacitus, *The Annals*, book 1, chapter 61 (Indianapolis: Hackett Publishing Company, Inc., 2004), 32.
98. Cassius Dio, *The Roman History*, book 56, chapter 21.
99. Peter S. Wells, *The Battle That Stopped Rome* (New York: W. W. Norton & Co., 2003), 55.
100. Tony Clunn, *The Quest for the Lost Roman Legions* (New York: Savas Beatie, 2009), 24.
101. Cassius Dio, *The Roman History*, book 56, chapter 21.
102. Cassius Dio, *The Roman History*, book 56, chapter 21.
103. Cassius Dio, *The Roman History*, book 56, chapter 21.
104. Derek Williams, *Romans and Barbarians* (New York: St. Martin's Press, 1998), 99.
105. Tacitus, *The Annals*, book 1, chapter 61 (Indianapolis: Hackett Publishing Company, Inc., 2004), 32.
106. Tacitus, *The Annals*, book 1, chapter 61 (Indianapolis: Hackett Publishing Company, Inc., 2004), 32.
107. Publius Annius Florus, *Epitome*, book 2, chapter 30.
108. Peter S. Wells, *The Battle That Stopped Rome* (New York: W. W. Norton & Co., 2003), 50–51.
109. Gaius Velleius Paterculus, *The Roman History*, book 2, chapter 119.
110. Adrian Murdoch, *Rome's Greatest Defeat* (Sutton Publishing Limited, 2006), 115.
111. Cassius Dio, *The Roman History*, book 56, chapter 21.
112. Gaius Velleius Paterculus, *The Roman History*, book 2, chapter 119.

113. Cassius Dio, *The Roman History*, book 56, chapter 22.
114. Publius Annius Florus, *Epitome*, book 2, chapter 30; Tacitus, *The Annals*, book 1, chapter 60 (Indianapolis: Hackett Publishing Company, Inc., 2004), 32; book 2, chapter 25 (Indianapolis: Hackett Publishing Company, Inc., 2004), 51; Cassius Dio, *The Roman History*, book 60, chapter 8.

Chapter Seven

1. Gaius Velleius Paterculus, *The Roman History*, book 2, chapter 119.
2. Seneca the Younger, *Epistulae Morales ad Lucilium*, letter 47, section 10. My translation from Latin.
3. Marcus Manlius, *Astronomicon*, book 1, section 898. My translation from Latin.
4. Publius Annius Florus, *Epitome*, book 2, chapter 30.
5. Gaius Velleius Paterculus, *The Roman History*, book 2, chapter 119.
6. Tacitus, *The Annals*, book 1, chapter 61 (Indianapolis: Hackett Publishing Company, Inc., 2004), 32.
7. Peter S. Wells, *The Battle That Stopped Rome* (New York: W. W. Norton & Co., 2003), 192–194; Adrian Murdoch, *Rome's Greatest Defeat* (Sutton Publishing Limited, 2006), 119.
8. *Secrets of the Druids*. National Geographic Channel, Tacitus, *The Annals*, book 1, chapter 60 (Indianapolis: Hackett Publishing Company, Inc., 2004), 32.
9. *Secrets of the Druids*. National Geographic Channel.
10. Gaius Velleius Paterculus, *The Roman History*, book 2, chapter 120.
11. Cassius Dio, *The Roman History*, book 56, chapter 22; Tacitus, *The Annals*, book 11, chapter 27 (Indianapolis: Hackett Publishing Company, Inc., 2004), 225.
12. Gaius Velleius Paterculus, *The Roman History*, book 2, chapter 119.
13. *The Germanic Tribes*, episode 2 – 'The Battle of the Teutoburg Forest'; Peter S Wells, *The Battle That Stopped Rome* (New York: W. W. Norton & Co., 2003), 104.
14. Tacitus, *The Annals*, book 11, chapter 16 (Indianapolis: Hackett Publishing Company, Inc., 2004), 45, 203.
15. Cassius Dio, *The Roman History*, book 56, chapter 22.
16. Sextus Julius Frontinus, *Stratagems*, book 4, chapter 7.
17. Cassius Dio, *The Roman History*, book 56, chapter 22.
18. Sextus Julius Frontinus, *Stratagems*, book 3, chapter 15.
19. Sextus Julius Frontinus, *Strategems*, book 2, chapter 9.
20. Cassius Dio, *The Roman History*, book 56, chapter 22.
21. Adrian Murdoch, *Rome's Greatest Defeat* (Sutton Publishing Limited, 2006), 123–124; Peter S. Wells, *The Battle That Stopped Rome* (New York: W. W. Norton & Co., 2003), 93, 104.
22. Cassius Dio, *The Roman History*, book 56, chapter 22.
23. Peter S Wells, *The Battle That Stopped Rome* (New York: W. W. Norton & Co., 2003), 103.
24. Adrian Murdoch, *Rome's Greatest Defeat* (Sutton Publishing Limited, 2006), 123.
25. Cassius Dio, *The Roman History*, book 56, chapter 22.
26. Gaius Velleius Paterculus, *The Roman History*, book 2, chapter 117.
27. Cassius Dio, *The Roman History*, book 56, chapter 18.
28. Suetonius, *The Twelve Caesars*, book 2, chapter 23.
29. Cassius Dio, *The Roman History*, book 56, chapter 23.
30. Cassius Dio, *The Roman History*, book 56, chapter 23.
31. Cassius Dio, *The Roman History*, book 56, chapter 23.
32. Suetonius, The Twelve Caesars, book 2, chapter 49.
33. 'Marcus Caelius', by Jona Lendering (December 8, 2011). http://www.livius.org/caa-can/caelius/marcus_caelius.html
34. Valerie A Maxfield, *The Military Decorations of the Roman Army* (Berkeley and Los Angeles: University of California Press, 1981), 86–87.

35. Valerie A Maxfield, *The Military Decorations of the Roman Army* (Berkeley and Los Angeles: University of California Press, 1981), 89–91.
36. Suetonius, *The Twelve Caesars*, book 2, chapter 24.
37. Stephen Dando-Collins, *Legions of Rome* (London: Quercus Publishing, 2012), 178–179.
38. Cassius Dio, *The Roman History*, book 56, chapter 24; Gaius Velleius Paterculus, *The Roman History*, book 2, chapters 120–123; Suetonius, *The Twelve Caesars*, book 3, chapters 9, 18–21; Tacitus, *The Annals*, book 1, chapter 34 (Indianapolis: Hackett Publishing Company, Inc., 2004), 19–20; Adrian Murdoch, *Rome's Greatest Defeat* (Sutton Publishing Limited, 2006), 129.
39. Ovid, *Tristia*, Book 3, Poem 12 'Spring in Tomis'.
40. Suetonius, *The Twelve Caesars*, book 4, chapter 3.
41. Suetonius, *The Twelve Caesars*, book 4, chapter 3.
42. Gaius Velleius Paterculus, *The Roman History*, book 2, chapter 125.; Tacitus, *The Annals*, book 1, chapters 16–49 (Indianapolis: Hackett Publishing Company, Inc., 2004), 11–26.
43. Tacitus, *The Annals*, book 1, chapter 49 (Indianapolis: Hackett Publishing Company, Inc., 2004), 26.
44. Tacitus, *The Annals*, book 1, chapters 49–51 (Indianapolis: Hackett Publishing Company, Inc., 2004), 26–27.
45. Tacitus, *The Annals*, book 1, chapters 55–61 (Indianapolis: Hackett Publishing Company, Inc., 2004), 29–32; Suetonius, *The Twelve Caesars*, book 4, chapter 3.
46. Tacitus, *The Annals*, book 1, chapters 63–65 (Indianapolis: Hackett Publishing Company, Inc., 2004), 33–34.
47. Tacitus, *The Annals*, book 1, chapter 65 (Indianapolis: Hackett Publishing Company, Inc., 2004), 34.
48. Tacitus, *The Annals*, book 1, chapters 65–70 (Indianapolis: Hackett Publishing Company, Inc., 2004), 34–37.
49. Tacitus, *The Annals*, book 1, chapter 72 (Indianapolis: Hackett Publishing Company, Inc., 2004), 37; book 2, chapters 1–21 (Indianapolis: Hackett Publishing Company, Inc., 2004), 42–50.
50. Tacitus, *The Annals*, book 2, chapters 23–25 (Indianapolis: Hackett Publishing Company, Inc., 2004), 50–51.
51. Tacitus, *The Annals*, book 2, chapter 26 (Indianapolis: Hackett Publishing Company, Inc., 2004), 51–52.
52. Tacitus, *The Annals*, book 2, chapter 41 (Indianapolis: Hackett Publishing Company, Inc., 2004), 60; Strabo, *Geography*, book 7, chapter 1.
53. Ovid, *Tristia*, book 4, poem 12 'Tiberius' triumph'; Ovid, *Ex Ponto*, book 2, poem 1 'To Germanicus: The Triumph'.
54. Tacitus, *The Annals*, book 1, chapters 58 (Indianapolis: Hackett Publishing Company, Inc., 2004), 31.
55. Tacitus, *The Annals*, book 2, chapters 42 (Indianapolis: Hackett Publishing Company, Inc., 2004), 60–61.
56. Tacitus, *The Annals*, book 2, chapters 43, 53–71 (Indianapolis: Hackett Publishing Company, Inc., 2004), 61–62, 66–76.
57. Tacitus, *The Annals*, book 2, chapters 71–79 (Indianapolis: Hackett Publishing Company, Inc., 2004), 75–78.
58. Tacitus, *The Annals*, book 2, chapter 44 (Indianapolis: Hackett Publishing Company, Inc., 2004), 62.
59. Tacitus, *The Annals*, book 2, chapters 44–46, 62–63 (Indianapolis: Hackett Publishing Company, Inc., 2004), 62–63, 71–72.
60. Tacitus, *The Annals*, book 2, chapter 88 (Indianapolis: Hackett Publishing Company, Inc., 2004), 82.

61. Tacitus, *The Annals*, book 2, chapter 62 (Indianapolis: Hackett Publishing Company, Inc., 2004), 71-72.
62. Tacitus, *The Annals*, book 2, chapter 62 (Indianapolis: Hackett Publishing Company, Inc., 2004), 71-72
63. Tacitus, *The Annals*, book 2, chapters 62–63 (Indianapolis: Hackett Publishing Company, Inc., 2004), 71-72.
64. Tacitus, *The Annals*, book 2, chapter 63 (Indianapolis: Hackett Publishing Company, Inc., 2004), 71-72; Suetonius, *The Twelve Caesars*, book 3, chapter 37.
65. Tacitus, *The Annals*, book 2, chapter 88 (Indianapolis: Hackett Publishing Company, Inc., 2004), 82.
66. Tacitus, *The Annals*, book 2, chapter 88 (Indianapolis: Hackett Publishing Company, Inc., 2004), 82.
67. Tacitus, *The Annals*, book 2, chapter 88 (Indianapolis: Hackett Publishing Company, Inc., 2004), 82.
68. Tacitus, *The Annals*, book 2, chapter 88. My own translation.
69. Cassius Dio, *The Roman History*, book 60, chapter 8.
70. Tacitus, 'Germania', in *Chronicles of the Barbarians* (New York: History Book Club, 1998), 91.
71. Tacitus, *The Annals*, book 4, chapters 72–74 (Indianapolis: Hackett Publishing Company, Inc., 2004), 158–159; book 12, chapter 27 (Indianapolis: Hackett Publishing Company, Inc., 2004), 225; book 13, chapter 55 (Indianapolis: Hackett Publishing Company, Inc., 2004), 272–273; Suetonius, *The Twelve Caesars*, book 4, chapters 31, 43–47; book 12, chapter 6; Cassius Dio, *The Roman History*, book 60, chapter 8; Tacitus, *The Life of Cnaeus Julius Agricola*, chapter 39; 'German Archaeologists Hail New Find', by Andrew Curry (December 16, 2008). Spiegel Online. http://www.spiegel.de/international/germany/0,1518,596720,00.html
72. 'Arminius: Ðe Original Siegfried', by Theedrich Yeat (August 13, 2009). http://www.harbornet.com/folks/theedrich/hive/Medieval/Siegfried.htm; Adrian Murdoch, *Rome's Greatest Defeat* (Sutton Publishing Limited, 2006), 159–174.
73. Adrian Murdoch, *Rome's Greatest Defeat* (Sutton Publishing Limited, 2006), 169–172.

Bibliography

Primary Sources

Arrian, *Arrian's Array against the Alans*. http://s_van_dorst.tripod.com/Ancient_Warfare/Rome/Sources/ektaxis.html. Accessed on 1/8/13.

Caesar, Gaius Julius. *Commentaries on the Gallic and Civil Wars*. http://etext.virginia.edu/toc/modeng/public/CaeComm.html Accessed on 12/14/09.

Cicero, Marcus Tullius. *Post Reditum in Senatu*, chapter 9. http://en.wikipedia.org/wiki/Post_Reditum_in_Senatu. Accessed on 1/8/13.

Dio, Cassius. *The Roman History*. Translated by Earnest Cary. Loeb Classical Library. Harvard University Press, 1914–1927. Lacus Curtius. http://penelope.uchicago.edu/Thayer/E/Roman/Texts/cassius_dio/home.html Accessed on 12/14/09.

Dionysius of Halicarnassus. *Roman Antiquities*, book 10, chapter 53.http://penelope.uchicago.edu/Thayer/E/Roman/Texts/Dionysius_of_Halicarnassus/10D*.html. Accessed on 1/8/13.

Florus, Publius Annius. *Epitome*. Translated by E. S. Forster. Loeb Classical Library, 1929. Lacus Curtius. http://penelope.uchicago.edu/Thayer/E/Roman/Texts/Florus/Epitome/home.html Accessed on 12/14/09.

Frontinus, Sextus Julius. *Strategems*. Translated by Charles E. Bennett. Loeb Classical Library, 1925. Lacus Curtius. http://penelope.uchicago.edu/Thayer/E/Roman/Texts/Frontinus/Strategemata/home.html Accessed on 12/14/09.

Josephus. *The Jewish Wars*. Translated by William Whiston. Christian Classics Etherial Library. http://www.ccel.org/j/josephus/works/JOSEPHUS.HTM Accessed on 12/28/09.

Livius, Titus. *The History of Rome*, book 1, chapter 8. http://www.perseus.tufts.edu/hopper/text?doc=Perseus%3Atext%3A1999.02.0151%3Abook%3D1%3Achapter%3D8. Accessed on 1/8/13.

Livius, Titus. *The History of Rome*, book 29, chapter 38. http://www.perseus.tufts.edu/hopper/text?doc=Perseus%3Atext%3A1999.02.0148%3Abook%3D29%3Achapter%3D38. Accessed on 1/8/13.

Livius, Titus. *The History of Rome*, book 30, chapter 1. http://www.perseus.tufts.edu/hopper/text?doc=Perseus%3Atext%3A1999.02.0144%3Abook%3D30%3Achapter%3D1. Accessed on 1/8/13.

Livius, Titus. *The History of Rome*, book 30, chapter 18. http://www.perseus.tufts.edu/hopper/text?doc=Perseus%3Atext%3A1999.02.0144%3Abook%3D30%3Achapter%3D18. Accessed on 1/8/13.

Livy. 'The Celts Enter Rome'. Chapter 3 in *Chronicles of the Barbarians: Firsthand Accounts of Pillage and Conquest from the Ancient World to the Fall of Constantinople* (New York: History Book Club, 1998), 32-38.

Livy, Titus. *Periochae*. Livius: Articles on Ancient History. http://www.livius.org/li-ln/livy/periochae/periochae00.html. Accessed on 1/9/13.

Manlius, Marcus. *Astronomicon*, book 1. The Latin Library. http://www.thelatinlibrary.com/manilius1.html. Accessed on 2/1/13.

Ovid. *The Heroïdes, or Epistles of the Heroines; The Amours; Art of Love; Remedy of Love; and, Minor Works of Ovid*. Translated by Henry Thomas Riley. G. Bell, 1893.

Ovid, *Tristia*, Book 3, Poem 12 'Spring in Tomis'. http://www.poetryintranslation.com/PITBR/Latin/OvidTristiaBkThree.htm#_Toc34217045. Accessed on 1/9/13.

Ovid, *Tristia*, book 4, poem 12 'Tiberius' triumph'. http://www.poetryintranslation.com/PITBR/Latin/OvidTristiaBkFour.htm#_Toc34217185. Accessed on 1/9/13.

Ovid, *Ex Ponto*, book 2, poem 1 'To Germanicus: The Triumph'. http://www.poetryintranslation.com/PITBR/Latin/OvidExPontoBkTwo.htm#_Toc34217665. Accessed on 1/9/13.

Paterculus, Gaius Velleius. *The Roman History*. Translated by Frederick W. Shipley. Loeb Classical Library, 1924. Lacus Curtius.http://penelope.uchicago.edu/thayer/e/roman/texts/velleius_paterculus/home.html Accessed on 12/14/09.

Pliny the Elder, *The Natural History*, book 4, chapter 28. http://www.perseus.tufts.edu/hopper/text?doc=Perseus%3Atext%3A1999.02.0137%3Abook%3D4%3Achapter%3D28. Accessed on 1/9/13.

Pliny the Elder, *The Natural History*, book 4, chapter 31. http://www.perseus.tufts.edu/hopper/text?doc=Perseus%3Atext%3A1999.02.0137%3Abook%3D4%3Achapter%3D31. Accessed on 1/9/13.

Plutarch, *Parallel Lives* – 'The Life of Marius'. http://penelope.uchicago.edu/Thayer/E/Roman/Texts/Plutarch/Lives/Marius*.html. Accessed on 1/9/13.

Polyaenus, *Stratagems*, book 8, chapter 10. http://www.attalus.org/translate/polyaenus8A.html#10.3. Accessed on 1/8/13.

Seneca the Younger, *Epistulae Morales ad Lucilium*, letter 47. The Latin Library. http://www.thelatinlibrary.com/sen/seneca.ep5.shtml. Accessed on 2/1/13.

Siculus, Diodorus. 'Romans and Celts Battle in Umbria'. Chapter 3 in *Chronicles of the Barbarians: Firsthand Accounts of Pillage and Conquest from the Ancient World to the Fall of Constantinople* (New York: History Book Club, 1998), 27-31.

Strabo. *Geography*. Translated by Horace Leonard Jones. Loeb Classical Library. Harvard University Press, 1917-1932. Lacus Curtius.http://penelope.uchicago.edu/Thayer/E/Roman/Texts/Strabo/home.html. Accessed on 12/14/09.

Suetonius. *The Twelve Caesars*. Translated by J. C. Rolfe. Loeb Classical Library, 1913-1914. Lacus Curtius. http://penelope.uchicago.edu/Thayer/E/Roman/Texts/Suetonius/12Caesars/home.html Accessed on 12/14/09.

Tacitus. *The Annals*. Translated by J. Jackson. Loeb Classical Library. Harvard University Press, 1925-1937. Lacus Curtius. http://penelope.uchicago.edu/Thayer/E/Roman/Texts/Tacitus/home.html Accessed on 12/14/09.

Tacitus. *The Annals*. Translated with Introduction and Notes by A. J. Woodman.Indianapolis: Hackett Publishing Company, Inc., 2004.

Tacitus. 'Germania'. Chapter 5 in *Chronicles of the Barbarians: Firsthand Accounts of Pillage and Conquest from the Ancient World to the Fall of Constantinople* (New York: History Book Club, 1998), 77-98.

Tacitus, *Histories*. Translated by C. H. Moore. Loeb Classical Library. Harvard University Press, 1925-1937. Lacus Curtius. http://penelope.uchicago.edu/Thayer/E/Roman/Texts/Tacitus/home.html. Accessed on 1/9/13.

Tacitus, *The Life of Cnaeus Julius Agricola*, chapter 39. http://elfinspell.com/ClassicalTexts/TacitusAgricola/Part3.html#refch39. Accessed on 1/9/13.

Secondary Sources
Books
Anglim, Simon. et al. *Fighting Techniques of the Ancient World, 3,000 BC–AD 500: Equipment, Combat Skills, and Tactics*. New York: Thomas Dunne Books, 2003.

Bishop, M C. *Lorica Segmentata, Vol. 1: A Handbook of Articulated Roman Plate Armor*. Braemar: The Armatura Press, 2002. http://www.mcbishop.co.uk/armatura/vol1.htm

Boatwright, Mary, et al. *The Romans: From Village to Empire – A History of Ancient Rome from Earliest Times to Constantine*. Oxford: Oxford University Press, 2004.

Campbell, Duncan B. *Roman Legionary Fortresses 27 BC–AD 378*. Oxford: Osprey Publishing, Ltd., 2006.

Carcopino, Jerome. *Daily Life in Ancient Rome: The People and the City at the Height of the Empire*, second edition. Edited and annotated by Henry T. Rowell. Translated by E O Lorimer. New Haven: Yale University Press, 2003.

Cheesman, George Leonard. *The Auxilia of the Roman Imperial Army*. Oxford: Clarendon Press, 1914.

Clunn, Tony. *The Quest for the Lost Roman Legions: Discovering the Varus Battlefield*. New York: Savas Beatie, 2009.

Cowan, Ross. *Roman Legionary 58 BC–AD 69*. Oxford: Osprey Publishing, 2003.

Dando-Collins, Stephen. *Legions of Rome: The Definitive History of every Imperial Roman Legion*. London: Quercus Publishing, 2012.

Dawson, Doyne. *The First Armies*.London: Cassell & Co., 2001.

Delbruck, Hans. *History of the Art of War, volume 2: The Barbarian Invasions*. Lincoln: University of Nebraska Press, 1990.

Fields, Nic. *Roman Legionary 58 BC–AD 69*.Oxford: Osprey Publishing, Ltd., 2003.

Fields, Nic. *The Roman Army of the Principate, 27 BC–AD 117*.Oxford: Osprey Publishing, 2009.

Halsall, Guy. *Warfare and Society in the Barbarian West, 450–900*. London: Routledge, 2003.

Jones, Terry; Ereira, Alan. *Terry Jones' Barbarians*. London: BBC Books, 2006.

Keeley, Lawrence H. *War Before Civilization: The Myth of the Peaceful Savage*. Oxford: Oxford University Press, 1996.

Keppie, Lawrence. *The Making of the Roman Army: From Republic to Empire*. Norman: University of Oklahoma Press, 1998.

Ketchum, Richard M. *Saratoga: Turning Point of America's Revolutionary War*. New York: Henry Holt, 1997.

Maxfield, Valerie A. *The Military Decorations of the Roman Army*. Berkeley and Los Angeles: University of California Press, 1981.

Murdoch, Adrian. *Rome's Greatest Defeat: Massacre in the Teutoburg Forest*. Sutton Publishing Limited, 2006.

Nossov, Konstantine. *Ancient and Medieval Siege Weapons: A Fully Illustrated Guide to Siege Weapons and Tactics*. Guilford: The Lyons Press, 2005.

Smith, Thomas. *Arminius: A history of the German people and of their legal and constitutional customs, from the days of Julius Caesar to the time of Charlemagne*. London: James Blackwood, 1861.

Stewart, Melville Y, ed. *The Trinity: East/West Dialogue*. Dordrecht: Kluwer Academic Publishers, 2003.

Thompson, E A. *The Early Germans*. Oxford: Clarendon Press, 1965.

Todd, Malcolm. *The Early Germans*.Malden: Blackwell Publishing, 1995.

Waldman, Carl, and Catherine Mason. *Encyclopedia of European Peoples*. New York: Facts on File, Inc., 2006.

Warry, John. *Warfare in the Classical World: An Illustrated Encyclopedia of Weapons, Warriors and Warfare in the Ancient Civilisations of Greece and Rome*. Norman: University of Oklahoma Press, 1995.

Webster, Graham. *The Roman Imperial Army of the First and Second Centuries A.D*, third edition. Norman: University of Oklahoma Press, 1998.

Wells, Colin Michael. *The Roman Empire*. Stanford: Stanford University Press, 1984.

Wells, Peter S. *The Barbarians Speak: How the Conquered Peoples shaped Roman Europe*. Princeton: Princeton University Press, 1999.

Wells, Peter S. *The Battle that Stopped Rome: Emperor Augustus, Arminius, and the Slaughter of the Legions in the Teutoburg Forest*. New York: W. W. Norton & Co., 2003.

Wilcox, Peter. *Rome's Enemies: Germanics and Dacians*. London: Osprey Publishing, 1982.
Williams, Derek. *Romans and Barbarians: Four Views from the Empire's Edge*. New York: St. Martin's Press, 1998.
Wolfram, Herwig. *History of the Goths*. Berkley and Los Angeles: University of California Press, 1988.

Websites
'Arminius: Ðe Original Siegfried', by Theedrich Yeat (August 13, 2009). http://www.harbornet. com/folks/theedrich/hive/Medieval/Siegfried.htm. Accessed on 12/14/09.
'Basque Onomastics of the Eighth to Sixteenth Centuries Appendix 4: Names Identified from Roman-Era Aquitanian Stones'. http://www.larsdatter.com/basque/appendix4.htm. Accessed on 1/8/13.
Cartographica Neerlandica. 'Cartographica Neerlandica Map Text for Ortelius Map No. 200'. http://www.orteliusmaps.com/book/ort_text200.html. Accessed on 12/14/09.
First Experience Latin with Fr. Reginald Foster. 'Lesson 1: Principles on the Nature of Latin'. http://frcoulter.com/latin/first/lesson1.html. Accessed on 12/14/09.
'Free Online English to Latin Translator'
http://www.translation-guide.com/free_online_translators.php?from=English&to=Latin. Accessed on 12/14/09.
'Gothic Language Dictionary – victory'. http://www.oe.eclipse.co.uk/nom/letters.htm. Accessed on 12/14/09.
The History Files. 'Barbarian Europe: Germanic or Gaulish?' by Edward Dawson (July 2, 2011). http://www.historyfiles.co.uk/FeaturesEurope/BarbarianTribes01.htm. Accessed on 2/13/15.
Janus Quirinus. 'Role of the Imperial Cult during the Augustan Age' (1995). http://janusquirinus. org/essays/Cult.html Accessed on 12/14/09.
Kwintessential. 'History of Calabria, Italy' (2004). http://www.kwintessential.co.uk/articles/ article/Italy/History-of-Calabria-Italy/762 Accessed on 5/10/10.
Lacus Curtius. 'Civitas', by William Smith (1875). http://penelope.uchicago.edu/Thayer/E/ Roman/Texts/secondary/SMIGRA*/Civitas.html. Accessed on 12/14/09.
Lacus Curtius. 'Footnote #19, Tacitus, *Annals*, book 2, chapter 7', by Bill Thayer.http:// penelope.uchicago.edu/Thayer/E/Roman/Texts/Tacitus/Annals/2A*.html#note19. Accessed on 12/14/09.
Lacus Curtius. 'Vestales', by William Smith (1875). http://penelope.uchicago.edu/Thayer/E/ Roman/Texts/secondary/SMIGRA*/Vestales.html. Accessed on 12/14/09.
Legio VI Ferrata Fidelas Constans. 'Balteus & Ventralis – Military Belt and Waistband' (April 8, 2010). http://legvi.tripod.com/id74.html. Accessed on 1/8/13.
Legio VI Ferrata Fidelas Constans. 'Cold Weather Gear'. (August 15, 2011). http://legvi.tripod. com/id80.html. Accessed on 1/8/13.
Legio VI Ferrata Fidelas Constans. 'Galea – Helmet'. (April 7, 2010). http://legvi.tripod.com/ id111.html. Accessed on 1/8/13.
Legio VI Ferrata Fidelas Constans. 'Scutum – Shield' (August 15, 2011). http://legvi.tripod. com/id112.html. Accessed on 1/8/13.
Legio VI Ferrata Fidelas Constans. 'Tunica & Sudarium' (August 15, 2011). http://legvi.tripod. com/id92.html. Accessed on 1/8/13.
Legio XX. 'Balteus – Military Belt'. Legio XX Online Handbook. (March 25, 2010). http:// www.larp.com/legioxx/balteus.html. Accessed on 1/8/13.
Legio XX. 'Lorica Hamata'. Legio XX Online Handbook (March 15, 2011). http://www.larp. com/legioxx/hamata.html. Accessed on 1/8/13.
Lego XX. 'Signum and Vexillium'. Legio XX Online Handbook (June 18, 2007). http://www. larp.com/legioxx/signum.html. Accessed on 1/8/13.

Legio XX. 'Subarmalis'. Legio XX Online Handbook (August 8, 2004). http://www.larp.com/legioxx/subarm.html. Accessed on 1/8/13.

Legio XX. 'Helmets'. Legio XX Online Handbook (March 14, 2011). http://www.larp.com/legioxx/helmets.html. Accessed on 1/8/13.

Legio XX. 'Notes on the Kalkriese style lorica segmentata'. Legio XX Online Handbook (March 15, 2011). http://www.larp.com/legioxx/kalklor.html. Accessed on 1/8/13.

Legion XXIV Media Atlantica. 'Imperial Aquila-Signums-Vexillium-Imago-Draco-Standards'. (February 22, 2010). http://www.legionxxiv.org/signum/. Accessed on 1/8/13.

Legio XXIV Media Atlantica. 'Weapons and Catapults' (June 22, 2005). http://www.legionxxiv.org/weapons/Default.htm. Accessed on 1/8/13.

Livius: Articles on Ancient History. 'Anreppen', by Jona Lendering (September 16, 2008). http://www.livius.org/am-ao/anreppen/anreppen.html. Accessed on 1/8/13.

Livius: Articles on Ancient History. 'Castra Vetera (Xanten-Birten)', by Jona Lendering (April 28, 2009). http://www.livius.org/x/xanten/vetera.html. Accessed on 1/8/13.

Livius: Articles on Ancient History. 'Cugerni', by Jona Lendering. http://www.livius.org/ct-cz/cugerni/cugerni.html. Accessed on 1/8/13.

Livius: Articles on Ancient History. 'Dorsten-Holsterhausen', by Jona Lendering. http://www.livius.org/ho-hz/holsterhausen/holsterhausen.html. Accessed on 1/8/13.

Livius: Articles on Ancient History. 'Germania Inferior', by Jona Lendering. http://www.livius.org/ga-gh/germania/inferior03.html. Accessed on 12/26/14.

Livius: Articles on Ancient History. 'Janus', by Jona Lendering. http://www.livius.org/ja-jn/janus/janus.html. Accessed on 12/14/09.

Livius: Articles on Ancient History. 'Legio I Germanica', by Jona Lendering http://www.livius.org/le-lh/legio/i_germanica.html. Accessed on 12/14/09.

Livius: Articles on Ancient History. 'Legio V Alaudae', by Jona Lendering. http://www.livius.org/le-lh/legio/v_alaudae.html. Accessed on 12/14/09.

Livius: Articles on Ancient History. 'Legio XVII', by Jona Lendering. http://www.livius.org/le-lh/legio/xvii.html. Accessed on 12/14/09.

Livius: Articles on Ancient History. 'Legio XVIII', by Jona Lendering. http://www.livius.org/le-lh/legio/xviii.html. Accessed on 12/14/09.

Livius: Articles on Ancient History. 'Legio XIX', by Jona Lendering. http://www.livius.org/le-lh/legio/xix.html. Accessed on 12/14/09.

Livius: Articles on Ancient History. 'Marcus Caelius', by Jona Lendering (December 8, 2011). http://www.livius.org/caa-can/caelius/marcus_caelius.html. Accessed on 12/14/09.

Livius: Articles on Ancient History. 'Marktbreit', by Jona Lendering (March 21, 2009).http://www.livius.org/man-md/marktbreit/marktbreit.html. Accessed on 1/8/13.

Livius: Articles on Ancient History. 'Oberaden', by Jona Lendering. http://www.livius.org/oa-om/oberaden/oberaden.html. Accessed on 12/14/09.

Livius: Articles on Ancient History. 'Pontes longi', by Jona Lendering http://www.livius.org/pn-po/pontes_longi/pontes_longi.html. Accessed on 4/8/11.

Livius: Articles on Ancient History. 'Publius Quinctilius Varus', by Jona Lendering. http://www.livius.org/q/quinctilius/varus.html Accessed on 12/14/09.

Livius: Articles on Ancient History. 'The Batavian Revolt – The Siege of Xanten', by Jona Lendering. http://www.livius.org/ba-bd/batavians/revolt05.html. Accessed on 1/8/13.

Livius: Articles on Ancient History. 'The Battle in the Teutoburg Forest (4)', by Jona Lendering (November 12, 2008). http://www.livius.org/te-tg/teutoburg/teutoburg04.html. Accessed on 1/8/13.

Mommsen, Theodor. *History of Rome – The Revolution*, page 67. http://italian.classic-literature.co.uk/history-of-rome/04-the-revolution/ebook-page-67.asp. Accessed on 1/8/13.

Mommsen, Theodor. *History of Rome – The Revolution*, page 68. http://italian.classic-literature.co.uk/history-of-rome/04-the-revolution/ebook-page-68.asp. Accessed on 1/8/13.

Mysterious Etruscans. 'Etruscan Religion' (February 14, 2006). http://www.mysterious etruscans.com/religion.html. Accessed on 12/14/09.

'Online Etymology Dictionary – Italian', by Douglass Harper (November 2001). http://www. etymonline.com/index.php?term=Italian. Accessed on 12/14/09.

'Protective Equipment: Roman Helmets – Helmets with Face Masks'. http://www.romancoins. info/MilitaryEquipment-Facemasks.html. Accessed on 1/8/13.

'Rank Structure of the Imperial Roman Army', by Sander van Dorst (2001). http://s_van_dorst. tripod.com/Ancient_Warfare/Rome/hierarchy.html. Accessed on 1/8/13.

Red Rampant. 'Auxiliary Shield Blazons' (July 7, 2009). http://www.redrampant.com/2009/07/ auxiliary-shield-blazons.html. Accessed on 1/8/13.

'Roman Military Equipment: Helmets'. http://www.romancoins.info/MilitaryEquipment-Helmet.html. Accessed on 1/8/13.

Smithsonian Magazine. 'The Ambush that Changed History' by Fergus M. Bordewich (September 2005). http://www.smithsonianmag.com/history-archaeology/ambush.html. Accessed on 4/23/10.

Spiegel Online. 'German Archaeologists Hail New Find: Discovery of Roman Battlefield Poses Historical Riddle', by Andrew Curry (December 16, 2008). http://www.spiegel.de/ international/germany/0,1518,596720,00.html. Accessed on 5/1/10.

The Lost Fort. 'The Romans in Germania – A Geography Lesson', by Gabriele Campbell (January 30, 2010). http://lostfort.blogspot.com/2010/01/romans-in-germania-geography-lesson.html. Accessed on 1/8/13.

'Thusnelda and Thumelicus', by James Grout. http://penelope.uchicago.edu/~grout/ encyclopaedia_romana/miscellanea/teutoburg/thusnelda.html. Accessed on 12/14/09.

University of Notre Dame. 'Genuine'. English to Latin. http://www.archives.nd.edu/cgi-bin/ lookdown.pl?genuine. Accessed on 12/14/09.

UNRV History: Roman Empire. 'Roman Provinces – Syria' http://www.unrv.com/provinces/ syria.php. Accessed on 12/14/09

UNRV History: Roman Empire. 'Roman Senate' http://www.unrv.com/empire/the-senate. php. Accessed on 12/14/09.

UNRV History: Roman Empire. 'Roman Slavery' http://www.unrv.com/culture/roman-slavery.php. Accessed on 12/14/09.

Varusschlact Museum und Park Kalkriese. 'Germanic Tribes – the Marsi'. http://www.kalkriese-varusschlacht.de/en/varusschlacht-varus-battle-2-14/germanic-tribes-2-57/marsi-2-208/ germanic-tribes-the-marsi.html. Accessed on 12/14/09.

The Virtual Linguist. 'Cantab' by Susan Harvey-Purcell (April 15, 2009). http://virtuallinguist. typepad.com/the_virtual_linguist/2009/04/page/2/. Accessed on 12/14/09.

VROMA. 'Roman Social Class and Public Display', by Barbara F. McManus (January 2009). http://www.vroma.org/~bmcmanus/socialclass.html. Accessed on 12/14/09.

Videos

A History of Britain, episode 2 – 'Conquest'. Hosted by Simon Schama. BBC, 2000. VHS.

The Germanic Tribes, episode 1 – 'Barbarians against Rome'. Directed by Alexander Hogh. Kultur International Films, Ltd., 2007. DVD.

The Germanic Tribes, episode 2 – 'The Battle of the Teutoburg Forest'. Directed by Alexander Hogh. Kultur International Films, Ltd., 2007. DVD.

The Germanic Tribes, episode 3 – 'Pax Romana'. Directed by Alexander Hogh. Kultur International Films, Ltd., 2007. DVD.

Fagan, Garrett G. 'Lecture 3 – Pre-Roman Italy and the Etruscans'. *The History of Ancient Rome*. DVD. Chantilly, VA: The Teaching Company, 1999.

Fagan, Garrett G. 'Lecture 4 – The Foundation of Rome'. *The History of Ancient Rome*. DVD. Chantilly, VA: The Teaching Company, 1999.

Fagan, Garrett G. 'Lecture 9 – Roman Expansion in Italy'. *The History of Ancient Rome*. DVD. Chantilly, VA: The Teaching Company, 1999.

Fagan, Garrett G 'Lecture 17 – 'Governing the Roman Republic, part I'. *The History of Ancient Rome*. DVD. Chantilly, VA: The Teaching Company, 1999.

Fagan, Garrett G. 'Lecture 21 – Marius and Sulla'. *The History of Ancient Rome*. DVD. Chantilly, VA: The Teaching Company, 1999.

Rome: Power and Glory, episode 1 – 'The Rise'. Narrated by Peter Coyote. Questar, 1998. VHS.

Secrets of the Druids. Narrated by John Benjamin Hickey. National Geographic Channel. Aired 11/15/2009.

Warrior Challenge, episode 1 – 'Romans'. Narrated by Henry Strozier. PBS, 2003.

We Shall Remain, episode 4 – 'Geronimo'. Narrated by Benjamin Bratt. PBS, 2009. DVD.

Index